THE LATINO GENERATION

THE LATINO GENERATION

GENERATION

Voices of the New America

MARIO T. GARCÍA

The University of North Carolina Press *Chapel Hill*

*This book was published with the assistance of the
Thornton H. Brooks Fund of the University of North Carolina Press.*

Library of Congress Cataloging-in-Publication Data
García, Mario T.
The Latino generation : voices of the new America / Mario T. García.
pages cm
Includes bibliographical references and index.
ISBN 978-1-4696-1411-3 (hardback) — ISBN 978-1-4696-1412-0 (ebook)
1. Hispanic American college students. 2. Hispanic Americans. I. Title.
LC2670.6.G37 2014
378.1'98268073—dc23   2013041625

18 17 16 15 14   5 4 3 2 1

To my daughter, Giuliana, and to my son, Carlo,

part of the Latino Generation,

AND

in memory of Sal Castro

CONTENTS

ACKNOWLEDGMENTS

I would like to first thank my former students whose stories serve as the basis of this book for their support for this project and their patience. I am proud of them and equally proud to present their inspiring narratives.

I want to thank my research assistants, Taylor Rentería and Amber Workman, for transcribing some of the interviews, helping to edit the manuscript, and assisting me in various other ways.

At the University of North Carolina Press, I want to thank my long-time editor, Charles Grench, for his support for this project. Thanks also to the staff of the press who worked with me on the review process and in the publication of the book.

I am grateful to the two anonymous readers who provided me with very thoughtful and important suggestions for revisions, especially concerning the introduction.

I was aided in my work by grants and support from the Chicano Studies Institute at the University of California, Santa Barbara; UC MEXUS; and the Academic Senate at UCSB.

I am indebted to Eddie Peralta in instructional development at UCSB, who expertly processed all of the photos for publication.

Finally and as always, my love and admiration go to Professor Ellen McCracken, who helped inspire this project and provided her moral support. Of course, I also want to acknowledge my children, Giuliana and Carlo, who are part of the Latino Generation.

THE LATINO GENERATION

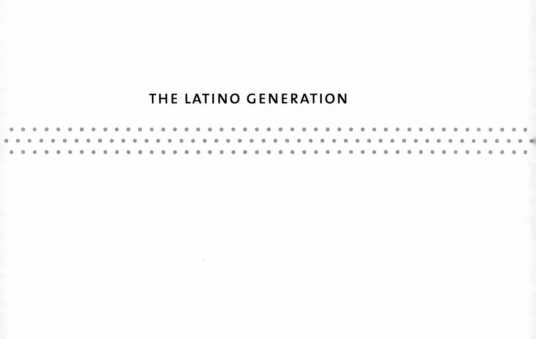

INTRODUCTION

The reciprocal process of interaction between the historian and his facts,
what I have called the dialogue between present and past, is a dialogue not
between abstract and isolated individuals, but between the society of today and
the society of yesterday. —EDWARD HALLETT CARR, *What Is History?* (1961)

Latinos in American Society

Latinos are now the largest minority in the United States, but they also
are the least understood. Stereotypes and gross generalizations abound
concerning this significant and growing ethnic group. This study about
the life stories or the "truths" of what I call the Latino Generation is an
attempt to challenge these distortions that are fueled by anti-immigrant
or nativist views toward Latinos, as more recently witnessed in a number of states such as Arizona, Alabama, and Georgia that have passed
anti-immigrants laws aimed at Latinos.[1] In this study, I try to go beyond
the superficial views about Latinos, including Chicanos (Mexican Americans), Central Americans, and other Latino groups, held by a number
of non-Latinos and to present contemporary young Latinos—in their
own voices—as whole and complex Americans. Defying the charges of
being "illegal aliens," foreigners, strangers, and un-American or anti-
American, the oral histories or *testimonios* of these representatives of
the Latino Generation in this volume belie all of these indictments and
instead reveal aspiring and committed young Americans—the voices of
the new America.

I tell students in my courses on Chicano studies that there are three
main reasons why it is important for all of us, whatever ethnic background we are from, to have a deeper understanding of Latinos. First,
just the demographics alone should force us to learn more. Latinos, as

the largest U.S. minority, represent some 53 million people and 16 percent of the total U.S. population. It is estimated that by 2050, Latinos will make up close to one-third of all Americans. This means that all Americans will be directly and indirectly affected by these demographic changes and will surely be in some form of contact with Latinos. For this practical reason alone, it is important we know about them. Who will fill the openings for our skilled workers and professionals in the future if not Latinos? Economic self-interest would dictate that we know about Latinos, since the economic fortunes of the country will be based on our abilities to integrate them into the key sectors of the economy if the United States is to remain competitive in world markets. Yet to do so, we need to overcome common stereotypes that Latinos are not capable of achieving quality and demanding education. This pragmatic equation should almost mandate our increased awareness of the Latino population.

The second reason that I mention to my students is that we cannot fully appreciate the history of the United States and its culture without including the stories of many ethnic groups, such as Latinos, that we have tended in the past to ignore or marginalize. Latinos, especially Mexican Americans, have a long and important history in the United States. Despite the stereotype that portrays Latinos as "just off the boat" (although for most Latinos, no boat is needed to cross a mostly land border), the fact is that people of Latino background have been a part of this country for generations—and in some cases, for centuries. For example, Mexican Americans (or Hispanos, as some call themselves) have been living in the area of present-day New Mexico since the first Spanish settlements appeared in 1598. Others were living in the Southwest at the time of the U.S. conquest and annexation of this area (referred to as "El Norte" by Mexico) as the result of the U.S.-Mexican War (1846–48). During the early twentieth century, over a million Mexican immigrants crossed into the United States to work on the railroads, farms, mines, and growing urban areas in the Southwest and Midwest at the same time that millions of new immigrants from eastern and southern Europe also arrived as the so-called New Immigrants. Throughout most of that century, still other Mexican immigrants—also joined by Puerto Ricans, Cubans, Dominicans, and Central Americans—entered and added to the growing but heterogeneous Latino population. As newcomers from Mexico and other Latin American areas settled permanently, new generations of U.S.-born Latinos added to this population. This history plus continued emigration from Mexico and Latin America has contributed to the current and sizable Latino communities in the United States. This long and varied history of Latinos underscores the importance of integrating their stories into our understanding of the "American experience." Too often, I further tell my students, when we say "American," what is important is not whom we include but whom we exclude. From an intellectual and academic perspective, it is important to know and study the Latino experience if we are to fully understand American history and American studies. We need a more inclusive history, and the inclusion of Latinos into that history is one way of achieving this.

The third reason has to do with citizenship. By this I mean that in order for us to become good citizens in a democratic society, we have to be aware of the totality of experiences in the United States. This awareness, at the same time, has to be achieved by an understanding and appreciation of the complexity of all American ethnic experiences, including the Latino one. Only in this way can we go beyond stereotypes and fears of the "other" and relate to diverse people in a rational and less emotional way. Only a citizenry that has a historical and reasonable understanding of the issues can accomplish sensible social policy. This begins by knowing those we have tended to marginalize as non-Americans, such as Latinos.

But in order to get to a better and more comprehensive acknowledgment and understanding of the Latino experience, we must, as noted, overcome common stereotypes. What stereotypes? "Latinos are the last of the immigrants." No, they have been here, historically speaking, for generations and centuries. As such, some, like those native Hispanos of New Mexico, have little to do with immigration. At the same time, one of the interesting and unique characteristics of Latinos is that they are both old and new citizens. There are those, such as the Hispanos of New Mexico, who have been here for centuries, and then just today, new Latino immigrants have arrived. Hence, Latinos are both old and new Americans. Still other stereotypes: "Unlike European immigrants, Latino immigrants don't want to fully become Americans." Yet Latinos for years have worked and contributed to this country. Latinos, for example, have served in all of this country's wars, even the American Revolution—New Spain (Mexico) aided the revolutionaries by sending troops into the South. In World War II alone, it is estimated that anywhere between 250,000 and 500,000 Latinos fought in the Good War, and many never returned. Latinos, per capita, received more Medals of

Honor for extraordinary bravery than any other American ethnic group. There is nothing more American than putting one's life on the line for the sake of the nation. They are part of the "Greatest Generation." And yet many still consider Latinos "illegal aliens." Other stereotypes: "They don't want to be like the rest of Americans; they want to live only among themselves and speak their own language and practice their own culture." The problem here is that since we have had almost continuous immigration since the early twentieth century, this constant infusion of immigrants makes it appear that there is no change or acculturation. Immigrants, especially adults, are always going to appear different in their language and culture, and this is a fact for all immigrants, whether from Europe, Latin America, or Asia. Consequently, if we focus only on first-generation immigrants, they are going to suggest no change, even though as immigrants they are subtly changing. Just being an immigrant is already a change.

What I further tell my students is that we have to look at the children of immigrants, including Latino immigrants, to see the more fundamental changes and acculturation. The children of immigrants will speak more English and incorporate more mass American cultural influences. They are becoming Americans. They are Americans. Indeed, an examination of the second-generation experience is key to debunking these common stereotypes concerning Latinos. This is one of the major reasons, if not the most important one, for my study. I want to show through the life stories of contemporary young Latinos, the children of immigrants, how they are in fact acculturating and working to become very much a part of this country that unfortunately still does not embrace them as full Americans. But this lack of embrace or exclusion tells us more about other Americans than it does about Latinos.[2]

As a historian, I have concentrated some of my studies in Chicano history on the emergence of second-generation Mexican Americans. After my initial foray into Chicano history with my book *Desert Immigrants: The Mexicans of El Paso, 1880–1920*, a study of what I refer to as the Immigrant Generation, I became interested in what happened to the U.S.-born children of these immigrants or to those children who immigrated with their parents but whose full lives were on this side of the border. I was curious about the relationship of the second generation to American society. In a sense, this was partly autobiographical because I was the product of a Mexican immigrant father, although my mother was a U.S.-born Mexican American. So I grew up in part as a second-generation ethnic, which led to my interest in what I term the Mexican American Generation, which came of age between the 1930s and the 1960s. Latinos of this generation in the Southwest and partly in the Midwest attended segregated and inferior public schools called "Mexican schools." They grew up during the Great Depression, and some witnessed the shameful mass deportations of Mexicans. Many served in World War II and in the Korean War. Those of the Mexican American Generation became bilingual and bicultural, although not without tensions between their Mexican cultural roots and the pull of Americanization. At the same time, they had to contend with racial discrimination not only in the schools but also at such public facilities as movie theaters, swimming pools, parks, and beaches. The impact of their acculturation plus their reaction to discrimination resulted in a particular Mexican American identity that brought together dual cultural worlds, if not multiple cultural ones, including African American influences. This was also the generation that engaged in the first significant Mexican American civil rights struggle aimed at desegregating the Mexican schools as well as other public arenas and fought discrimination in jobs and wages. My research challenged the stereotypes of Mexican Americans and other Latinos as a passive, lazy, unambitious, and un-American group.[3]

More recently, I have further examined the second-generation phenomenon through my studies of the Chicano Movement and the Chicano Generation of the 1960s and 1970s. The Chicano Movement was the largest and most widespread Mexican American civil rights and empowerment movement in U.S. history up to that time. It involved a new search for historical and cultural roots that would empower Chicanos in their struggles for self-determination and liberation from racism and cultural and economic discrimination. They discovered the older working-class and barrio term "Chicano" and resurrected it with pride and defiance as they exercised their right to name themselves. Many of the Chicano activists were also second generation (and some third generation), and my studies of the Chicano Movement have added to my understanding and appreciation of what it means to be second generation. These studies further revise common stereotypes about Latinos, who some consider to be ahistorical subjects.[4]

Yet while I and other colleagues in Chicano history have researched and produced various studies that touch on this second-generation experience, more contemporary Chicanos and other Latinos still are faced with mistaken views by others about their place in American society.

Hence, I decided to extend my second-generation studies to include the contemporary Latino Generation, which includes the children of the most recent waves of Latino immigrants into the United States since the 1970s and 1980s. They are the products of the "New Immigrants," which include not only the continuation of Mexican and other Latino economic refugees or those motivated to cross the border by largely economic hardships in their own societies, but also political refugees, in particular those from Central America, such as El Salvador and Guatemala, where civil wars and political repression drove thousands out of those countries in the 1980s. Their children, like earlier Latino second-generation children, have also undergone similar acculturating and transculturating changes as they struggle to find their place in a new and changing America, just as their predecessors did.

Let me say here a word about the term "Latino." At one level, it, like the term "Hispanic," is used by both people of Latin American descent and non-Latinos as a broad umbrella term to cover such various groups as Mexican Americans (Chicanos), Puerto Ricans, Cuban Americans, Central Americans, Dominicans, and those from other parts of Latin America. Hence, in part it is a pragmatic term. But, as I will argue, it is also a living term for a new generation of Latinos who in their particular experiences are attempting to relate to a more pan-Latino identity. The term Latino for them is not just a strategic one but one relating to a new social, cultural, and political experience.

I also want to make it clear that these oral history narratives—thirteen in all—do not represent a social scientific study. My concept of the Latino Generation is uniquely mine, but I do not attempt to quantify it. It is an oral history of thirteen young Latinos who I suggest are representative of what I am interpreting and proposing as the Latino Generation. This is my interpretation based not only on the life stories of these narrators but on my analysis of the historical context of their lives, as I will further explain in this introduction. My interpretation of the Latino Generation is my attempt to make some historical sense of the more contemporary changes affecting Latinos coming of age at the end of the twentieth century and the beginning of the new millennium. In a way, this is no different than what I did in my 1989 book, *Mexican Americans: Leadership, Ideology and Identity, 1930–1960*. In that work, based on ten case study chapters, I proposed and analyzed what I called the "Mexican American Generation" that emerged in this time period. My chapters focused on the leadership of this generation and served as my evidence. This was also not a social scientific study, but it was my interpretation as a historian analyzing the factual evidence. Since this book was published, my concept of the Mexican American Generation has been adopted in one form or another by most other historians of Chicano history. What I am doing here regarding the Latino Generation is similar and, as in the previous case, attempts to contextualize the periodization of Chicano/Latino history. I have championed a generational approach to Chicano history, and my putting forth the concept of the Latino Generation is consistent with my previous efforts to periodize and contextualize history—to give meaning to history.

History and the Latino Generation

As a historian of the Chicano experience, and since the majority of the stories in this book concern Mexican Americans, I want to further attempt to put these *testimonios* into a broader historical perspective. From a long view of history, the current Latino Generation bears the legacy of previous generations of Latinos. This legacy is composed of three major experiences: (1) the immigrant story, (2) the evolving ethnic and race identity of Chicanos/Latinos, and (3) what I call historical agency, that is, Latinos making history. There is no question that immigration is the connecting link of these three experiences. As mentioned, mass Mexican immigration to the United States is not new. It has deep roots beginning in the late nineteenth and early twentieth centuries. Between 1900 and 1930, thousands of Mexican immigrants entered the country, significantly adding to the already existing Mexican American population, some of whom could trace their ancestries to the early Spanish *entradas* or entries into New Mexico and other later southwestern states beginning in the late sixteenth century. With the exception of areas such as New Mexico, the new immigrants overwhelmed these earlier Mexican settlements and came to represent the majority experience. Many came as economic refugees fleeing dislocation caused by the new economic policies set forth by dictator Porfirio Díaz during his long reign that came to be referred to as the Porfiriato (1877–1910). Others came as political refugees fleeing the Mexican Revolution of 1910 that overthrew Díaz but also resulted in a decade of civil war in Mexico. As economic and political refugees, these Mexicans became the foundation for a new and expansive Mexican-origin population in the United States. This helped to establish a pattern of Mexican immigration that, with the exception of the depression years of the 1930s, would be continuous to the very present, bolstered by additional Latino migrants from other parts of Latin America such as Cuba, Puerto Rico, and Central America. In this sense, the Latino Generation is the inheritor of this great migration legacy, since the parents of this generation and some of their children represent immigrants or the children of immigrants. They include the undocumented. Tania Picasso, for example, whose story is part of this text, notes that her Mexican-born mother entered the United States without documents: "When my mom was seventeen, she and her older siblings crossed the border and joined their dad working the cotton fields in Corcoran [California]. By this time, my grandfather was no longer a bracero [contract worker] but didn't have legal documents, either. That was also true of my mother and her siblings."

Although not all Mexicans and Latinos can trace their origins to mass immigration, most of them can. This applies to those whose *antepasados* came in the early twentieth century; to those who came as braceros beginning in the 1940s; to those who entered without documents since the 1950s; to those who came from Puerto Rico in large numbers after World War II, not as immigrants but as U.S. citizen migrants; to those who fled in large numbers from the Cuban Revolution of 1959; and to those who left political upheavals in Central America in the 1980s, as well as other variations of these movements. Oscar Handlin, a pioneer historian of immigration to the United States, famously said that when he started to study the history of this country, he quickly discovered that it was the history of immigrants. This is not completely correct, since groups such as Native Americans, African Americans, and conquered Mexican Americans after the U.S.-Mexican War did not represent immigrants. Still, Handlin's assertion is mostly correct. The same could be said of Chicano/Latino history, that much of this history is the history of immigrants and of their children.[5]

These immigrant antecedents provide context for the Latino Generation. For example, historically Mexican and Latino immigrants have been affected by what some students of immigration call "push and pull" factors. In other words, to understand why some people become immigrants, one has to understand that immigration is the result of dual forces: conditions in the homeland and conditions in the receiving country. At the same time, I agree with Gilbert González and Raul Fernández, who have critiqued the push and pull theory by arguing that it can be ahistorical and by suggesting that immigrants often choose whether they will become immigrants or not. They stress that one also has to understand that such push and pull forces result from even larger forces that affect conditions in both the sending and receiving societies. In the case of the beginning of mass Mexican immigration to the United States, González and Fernández specifically cite the role of American imperialism: it helped to dislocate Mexicans, especially in the rural areas of Mexico, aided and abetted by Díaz's policies of favoring American investments (hence financial imperialism) to promote Mexican agribusiness, but in the process it dislocated thousands upon thousands of peasants, many of whom became immigrants. The other side of American imperialism was in the United States, where the extension of Yankee dollars in Mexico and other parts of the Caribbean and Central America resulted in new mining and agricultural supplies to help further the advancement of industrial capitalism in the United States, or the domestic side of imperialism. González and Fernández are right in their critique, and I employ the concept of push and pull within this larger context.[6] And so whether in the early twentieth century or into the new millennium, many of the same broad forces are at work that continue to affect Mexican and Latino immigration to the United States. This might be called "globalization" or "neo-liberalism" now rather than imperialism, but in many respects the results are the same: American needs in other countries, whether economic, political, or strategic, help to dislocate people in their homelands, and in turn, these policies and actions set off changes within the United States that lead to many of these people migrating to this country. The Latino Generation is a continuation of this history.

This continuity is seen in the case of Álvaro Sánchez, one of the narrators in this study. His parents decided to go to the United States in 1991 due to the peso devaluation in Mexico as the result of international debt in the pre-NAFTA era. Álvaro's parents had invested in a company operated by relatives that failed: "This was the peso devaluation of the early 1990s, in conjunction with bad accounting and some bad business deals on the part of our cousins. They ended up owing millions of dollars. The company fell apart. We couldn't even afford our apartment anymore, and so we were forced to move into my maternal grandmother's house. These hard times are what made my dad decide that we should return to LA."

Let me expand further on the process of the pull side of this equation that has historically influenced the conditions of Mexicans and other Latinos in the United States. Most Latinos have been affected over time by changes in the U.S. economy that have necessitated new sources of cheap labor. This was the case in the early twentieth century, when most Mexican immigrants, poor, uneducated, and unskilled, were largely tracked into dead-end, cheap labor jobs in the developing and booming expansion of the railroads in the Southwest and elsewhere; in mining of key industrial ores, such as copper, especially in southern Arizona; in agribusiness; in urban construction; and in sundry other industries and services that also desired access to cheap Mexican labor. These became the "Mexican jobs" of the southwestern economy. Hence, a tradition of various industries institutionalizing Mexican immigrant labor as part of their labor practices was laid and later expanded into other economic sectors.[7] This relationship between Mexican immigration and cheap labor was further augmented with the Bracero Program (1942–64) that brought in some 5 million contract laborers. What started as a World War II emergency program primarily for agribusiness in states such as California continued for two more decades. The braceros represented another source of cheap labor for American employers.[8] The bracero experience forms part of the narrative of this study; Susana Gallegos notes that both her grandfather and father first entered the United States as braceros: "Migrating to the U.S. to work was a common pattern in my parents' town. My paternal grandfather had come as a bracero in 1942. The first time my father came was as a bracero in 1961. Both worked in Arizona and California. So my dad was already familiar with others from his town who lived in California, and so he knew where to go and find work. It wasn't unusual for young men like my dad to come to the U.S. and work some growing seasons here and then return and work their lands in Mexico."

Globalization and the deindustrialization of the U.S. economy since at least the 1970s has brought in its wake, despite periodic recessions including the recent Great Recession, additional waves of Mexican and Latino immigrants who have also been tracked into new sources of cheap labor. This labor supports some lingering American manufacturing industries, such as garment production in the Los Angeles area, that, unlike other competitors who have outsourced to the Third World, have brought the Third World to Los Angeles in the form of Latino immigrants, especially female labor, to do dirty work for meager wages. Deindustrialization, more significantly, has led to the loss of many traditional industries, which have fled abroad to take advantage of cheap labor in China, other parts of Asia, Mexico, and Central America. They have been replaced by high-tech industries such as in Silicon Valley. The expansion of high-tech workers with college degrees and advanced degrees who receive high wages, in turn, has increased the demand for a variety of services for this new professional and highly educated class in the form of bigger and better housing, expensive restaurants, gardening services, nannies, car washers, and so on. All of these kinds of services are based largely on the employment of cheap Latino immigrant workers.[9] Hence, for over a century this linkage between Latino immigrants and the need and greed for cheap labor on this side of the border has affected the Latino condition and is part of the legacy of the Latino Generation to the extent that most if not all of this generation's parents, as noted in these *testimonios*, entered the United States and found employment in the low-skilled and low-paying labor market.

This connection between immigration and cheap labor is illustrated in Alma Cortez-Lara's story, in which she observes that her father worked in the grape fields of Napa Valley doing farm labor. In addition to being "hard and hot work," the job also ran other risks: "The immigration officials sometimes would raid the fields. In fact, according to my dad, it would be the employer who would call in *la migra* so that he wouldn't have to pay the workers. My dad was caught two or three times after we were all living in Napa. My mother, before she went to work herself, would always worry about him. She knew that if he didn't get home at the usual hour, something was wrong. Sure enough, she would later get a phone call from Tijuana."

In the case of Gabriela Fernández, her father, after migrating to LA, worked at several blue-collar jobs. In this passage, she describes one of them: "My father after about six months finally got another job working in the *yarda* or the yard of a company where he did a lot of the heavy lifting of material. It was a company that filled up gas tanks for hospitals and clinics. He had done that kind of hard manual labor for years and is still doing it. He's changed companies but still does the same kind of work."

The children of such immigrants—the Latino Generation—have had to deal with this experience and to struggle to overcome it. Some have succeeded, as is the case of those represented in this volume, but many more have not.

Ethnicity and the Latino Generation

But if immigration is a defining part of being Chicano/Latino, including for the Latino Generation, so also is the role that ethnicity and ethnic identity plays in the immigrant experience. Historians such as George Sánchez, David Gutiérrez, Gloria Arredondo, and Vicki Ruiz, among others, all suggest in one way or another that ethnic identity among Mexican immigrants and their offspring is fluid and emerging.[10] That is, ethnic culture and ethnic identity, as also proposed by other students of immigration and ethnicity, are always, to borrow from Sánchez, in the process of becoming.[11] It is never static, even though some nativists might allege that it is. For example, Mexican immigrants in the early twentieth century, as the historians above have studied, changed just from the process of being immigrants. The fact that they chose to leave Mexico already marked them as different. Their immigrant passage added to their new sense of being transformed. Even more important, their new life, such as it became in the United States, changed them and their perception of themselves even more. They may have crossed the border with a localized or regionalized Mexican culture and identity, but many, especially in urban areas such as El Paso, San Antonio, Los Angeles, and Chicago, began to encounter Mexicans from other parts of Mexico with their own particular regional cultures and identities. This mixing or new form of ethnic *mestizaje* assisted in developing a Mexican immigrant nationalism, as Arredondo, for example, discovered in her study of Mexican immigrants in Chicago.[12] They become *mexicanos* in the United States or *México de afuera*, as the Mexican Spanish-language newspapers on this side of the border referred to them, as opposed to primarily identifying them with their home regions in Mexico.[13]

Some might believe that immigrants brought and now continue to bring with them an "authentic" national Mexican culture, but in fact they bring with them many subcultures and ethnic identities that become more amalgamated in the United States to form not an "authentic" culture but a hybrid and evolving one that is quite complex and innovative.[14] There is no such thing as an "authentic" culture or cultures, since that would imply a culture and an identity that never change, and that is impossible unless one lives in a totally isolated environment. What is instead at work is an internal Mexican transculturation or cultural fusion within the Mexican immigrant communities that, in turn, is also affected by a seeping Anglo-Americanizing that takes place, for instance, at the worksite or just by being in the United States and being exposed to many mass American and English-speaking influences. These Mexican and other Latino immigrant ethnic cultures and identities serve as a foundation and catalyst for succeeding generations that will undergo their own particular transculturations, although still influenced by the parental immigrant culture. Since those of the Latino Generation as revealed in the stories in this volume are all children of immigrants, their own evolving ethnic culture and identity will be framed in part by that of their immigrant parents.

This includes not only customs at home but also cyclical visits to the home country. In one of the stories, for example, Sandy Escobedo observes that this involved trips to Mexico, where her father was born, as well as trips to El Salvador, where her mother was born. Although she grew to resent these trips, still they reminded her of her ethnic backgrounds: "Family visits to Mexico and El Salvador were also a part of my growing up. Prior to my starting high school, we went three times to Mexico and once to El Salvador. I was much younger for the first two visits, but for the one in 1992, I didn't want to go. I hated going to Mexico, and I also didn't want to go to El Salvador that year. I had felt out of place in Mexico because it didn't seem very Americanized. However, the trip to El Salvador in 1993 wasn't too bad because my cousins there, who were my age, were very much into the same kind of U.S. music I was into. They went out of their way to make me feel comfortable. They took me to Pizza Hut and things like that. But since then, I haven't gone back with my parents to either country."

While Sandy expressed disfavor about these trips, Gabriela Fernández in her story relates just the opposite: "In the summer after I completed the second grade, my parents made the decision to return to Purépero [in Mexico]. We had never lost contact with family back there, and even though I was a child we went there each summer. I came to enjoy these trips and getting to play with my cousins. I came to love Purépero, my *pueblito* or village."

Moreover, Gabriela was also influenced by family Mexican cultural traditions at home that certainly affected her own sense of herself: "On this side of the border, we try to maintain ... traditions. My mother and aunts are the key to all of this. They are the ones who arrange for the *posadas* and cook the tamales for Noche Buena [Christmas Eve]. The difference between here and Purépero is that in my Mexican village the whole community participates, while here it's only the family. There isn't that community participation."

Food, of course, is one such family tradition passed on to second-generation Latinos. Of this, Amílcar Ramírez narrates: "We ... eat mostly Honduran food at home, especially *arroz con frijoles* [rice and beans] and chicken and corn tortillas. My mother has never gotten into 'American' cooking." At the same time, Amílcar adds: "As for me, I love McDonald's. I always tell people you can never go wrong with burgers, fries, and a Coke."

Ethnicity and ethnic identity continue to play a major role beyond the immigrant generations. Here, my own work on historical generational change is suggestive of this process that is also at play among the Latino Generation. In my discussion of Chicano history of the twentieth century, for example, I interpret those masses of Mexican immigrants and refugees who entered the United States in the early 1900s as the Immigrant Generation in Chicano history.[15] I do so understanding that there will be other succeeding waves of Mexican immigrants into the rest of the century; however, what distinguished the immigrants of the early years was that not only was the immigration process at the center of their experience and of their new identity, but at no other later time in Chicano history would immigrants so totally dominate the Mexican-origin experience in the United States. Demographically, economically, politically, and culturally, the immigrants—the Immigrant Generation—became the prevailing force.

While I have studied the Immigrant Generation, I have also been interested in what happened to the children who either were born in the United States or grew up in this country (an early "Dream Act Generation"). Hence, in several studies, I have focused on what I term the Mexican American Generation. This is a generation that came of age in its own particular historical era characterized by the Great Depression, World War II, and the commencement of the Cold War. It is a generation that can be seen at three levels: demographic, cultural, and political. Demographically, this generation represented a new generational cohort that came of age between the 1930s and the 1950s. By 1940, according to the U.S. Census, the majority of Mexicans in the country were no longer immigrants but U.S.-born.[16]

As a new ethnic generation, or what some scholars refer to as ethnic Mexicans, the Mexican American Generation displayed its own version of ethnicity and identity that reflected the duality and even multiplicity of its experiences. As children of immigrants, they were born into a mostly Spanish-speaking parental culture and were initially shaped by it. However, as they began to attend English-language public or even religious schools, they became bilingual and bicultural. They were the new "mestizos." They would invent themselves as Mexican Americans and create a new Mexican American ethnic culture. They were not betraying their parents' culture or becoming less "authentic"; they were extending their own parents' process of themselves becoming, again to quote from Sánchez, "Mexican Americans" and establishing their own form of "authenticity."[17] But Mexican American culture and identity is just as fluid as that of the immigrants. Mexican immigrants influenced Mexican American culture and identity then in the same way that they still do today, as Tomás Jiménez in his study of this contemporary relationship reveals, but they do not dominate it.[18] U.S.-born Mexican Americans and other Latinos as part of the Latino Generation, as observed in this volume, are shaped and influenced by their immigrant parents, but they go beyond them due to their own social context and forge their own generational culture and identity that reflect their own reality. They are who they are. But, at the same time, they are not reinventing the wheel because previous generations of other U.S.-born Latinos, such as those of the Mexican American Generation and the later Chicano Generation of the 1960s and 1970s, also underwent the same process of ethnic cultural and identity changes. This further reflects the legacy passed on to the Latino Generation.

Race and the Latino Generation

While immigration and ethnicity have played major roles in defining the Chicano/Latino experience, including that of the Latino Generation, so too has the issue of race. This is a complicated subject historically for Chicanos and other Latinos. Do they make up a race or an ethnic group or both? Of course, the larger matter of whether there are specific races is itself a debatable issue. Is there a white race? A black race? A yellow race? A Mexican/Latino race? Clearly, different groups have different phenotypes, but most scientists would not necessarily consider them races since all have the same gene pool. They would consider all as members of one race—the human race. I agree with this, but at the same time, I am aware that politically and socially there are differentiations based on "race." Much of this goes back to efforts to "scientifically" classify races in the nineteenth century with the implication that there were superior "races" (white) and inferior ones (black). But these classifications, as Michael Omi and Howard Winant have shown, have nothing to do with biology and everything to do with political and economic domination by one race (white) over others (non-white). Omi and Winant, as well as other scholars, refer to this classification process as racialization.[19] This process has also historically affected Chicanos and other Latinos in the United States.

People of Mexican descent as well as most other Latinos are ethnically mixed, having gone through a process of *mestizaje* as the result of the Spanish conquest of indigenous peoples in Mexico and elsewhere in what came to be the Spanish American empire during the colonial era. In their conquest, Spaniards raped and mated with Indian women and produced a new mixed offspring referred to as mestizos. Such hybridization continued throughout three hundred years of Spanish colonial rule. As a result, most people of Mexican descent were and are mestizos, although some are more white or European and some are darker and more Indian and even African.

Most Mexicans immigrants who entered the United States at the turn of the twentieth century were mestizos and Mexican nationals. However, whites saw them as a different and inferior race, which helped to justify their exploitation and discrimination against Mexicans of all backgrounds. For whites, being "Mexican" was to belong to an inferior race. They transformed a term of nationality and ethnicity (Mexican) into a racialized term implying racial inferiority. As a result, racialization intersected with ethnicity and class as Mexican immigrants were hired to do "Mexican jobs," paid "Mexican wages," and forced to live in "Mexican barrios." To add insult to injury, their children, many of them U.S. citizens, were forced to attend "Mexican schools."[20] This is how racialization played itself out with respect to Mexican immigrants and their children. In turn, this racialization had an impact on the ambivalent identity of many Mexicans in the United States, as Laura Gómez stresses in her work on what she calls the "making of the Mexican American race."[21] Were they part of a Mexican race (La Raza) or part of the "white race"?

This ambivalence was further complicated by the fact that legally, people of Mexican descent were considered to be white. The origins of this whiteness is in the conclusion of the U.S.-Mexican War of the 1840s, when in order to annex Mexico's northern territory from Texas to California, the prize of the American victory, the resident Mexican population (some 100,000) had to also be annexed.[22] As part of this process, the Treaty of Guadalupe Hidalgo (1848) at the end of the war allowed for this relatively small Mexican population in what became the American Southwest to legally become U.S. citizens. But this had to conform to a 1790 naturalization law that permitted only people of white racial descent to legally become naturalized American citizens.[23] While U.S. officials at the time of the treaty understood that most Mexicans in the conquered region were of mixed ethnic descent and not "white" in a Euro-American sense, they looked the other way and determined that they could become naturalized citizens, implying that Mexicans were "white" without categorically saying so. Hence, the Mexicans who remained in the territory after the war were automatically conferred citizenship as "white Americans." Later legal efforts well into the 1930s to deny Mexicans their whiteness, as Natalia Molina notes, were rejected by U.S. courts and federal officials.[24]

Legally, Mexicans were white, but they were not treated as such in the post–Mexican War period, when many lost their lands and were subjected to American racism and considered second-class citizens. As noted, those of the Immigrant Generation of Mexicans were treated no better and probably worse and were exposed to various forms of discrimination and segregation. Moreover, continued efforts to reclassify Mexicans as non-white or "colored" extended into the 1930s, for example, when the 1930 census for the first time included a category for Mexicans, defined as those not appearing to be "white." In the mid-1930s in some Texas communities such as El Paso, San Antonio, and Houston, additional efforts were made by local officials to reclassify Mexicans as colored. These efforts failed due to the strenuous objections by Mexican American leaders as part of the new Mexican American Generation.[25]

Nevertheless, racial ambivalence continued to affect many Mexicans in the United States. Civil rights leaders of the Mexican American Generation, for example, embraced the issue of whiteness as a way of claiming that no racial basis existed for forced discrimination and segregation against people of Mexican descent. They argued that if Mexicans were legally considered white, then they needed to be treated as white, and this meant no forms of racial discrimination should apply to them.[26] Historian Neil Foley alleges that the embrace of whiteness by these leaders is evidence that they were in denial of their true mestizo "racial" identity, all for the sake of inclusion into the American mainstream. The issue, as I see it, is much more complex. I do not believe that these Mexican Americans were ashamed of their mestizo backgrounds, although I grant that they may also have harbored racial ambivalences, but I also believe that for political and strategic purposes, they saw a civil rights opening by using the concept of whiteness, in a sense, against itself. They understood what the implications of publicly denying their whiteness might mean for Mexicans in Texas and elsewhere. That is, for Mexicans in the 1930s, for example, to assert that they were a "people of color" would have instead exposed them not only to de facto segregation but to de jure segregation.[27] No responsible Mexican American leader of that generation was going to do this. Instead, they chose to fight the system using its own ideology of whiteness. They may have been wrong in the long run, but given their context, they probably felt they had no other choice.

This generation's whiteness strategy, of course, was premised on racialization spilling over to those of the Mexican American Generation. Despite their transculturation and the fact that most were U.S. citizens, they, like their immigrant parents, were subjected to racial discrimination and segregation. This began almost from day one, since it was the children of this generation who attended the "Mexican schools" that segregated them throughout the Southwest. While some consider this to be de facto segregation in that no state laws in the region mandated such segregation, I agree with Gilbert González that it was still a form of de jure segregation in that it involved local school boards officially adopting such separation.[28] The Mexican schools were not only segregated but inferior. Both in rural and urban areas, they provided a limited number of school years, were overcrowded, lacked financial and material resources, possessed no ethnic and cultural sensitivity, had high dropout rates, and had too many teachers who had low expectations of their students. In addition, school officials and teachers looked at the low performance by Mexican American students not as the result of cultural and language differences but as proof of their mental inferiority and hence their racial inferiority.[29]

Besides racism in the schools, those of the Mexican American Generation also faced discrimination and segregation at such public facilities as restaurants, theaters, swimming pools, parks, and beaches. Moreover, despite their access to more education by the 1930s and 1940s, including high school, many still faced limited economic opportunities as Mexican jobs and Mexican wages still prevailed. Part of the racism that they experienced was how they were often lumped in with immigrants, as many whites considered all Mexicans to be immigrants, even "illegal" immigrants. They witnessed this in the early 1930s when perhaps as many as half a million people of Mexican descent were deported or faced forced repatriation to Mexico during the Great Depression on the basis that not only were they allegedly "illegal," but they were taking jobs from "real

Americans" and, as Natalia Molina documents, represented a health threat to other Americans (dirty Mexicans).[30] Such racialization helped in part to create the racial and ethnic ambivalence of many Mexican Americans as they had to wrestle with why they were not being treated as "real Americans" and why they were being considered as racial inferiors. Racism, like immigration and ethnicity, therefore helped to influence the identity of the Mexican American Generation, as it would continue to do so for the later Chicano Generation and today's Latino Generation. Taking the long view of history, each generational experience has been affected in one way or another by these larger forces.

Race, for example, also affected the issue of identity for the Chicano Generation of the late 1960s and 1970s. The Chicano Movement expanded on the civil rights efforts of the Mexican American Generation but in a more militant and radical direction, in keeping with the heightened oppositional political culture of the 1960s. Those of the Chicano Generation in some cases were children of immigrants themselves or second-generation U.S.-born. Irrespective of their backgrounds, members of this new demographic, cultural, and political generation also faced similar forms of discrimination and segregation. For example, the Mexican schools (although no longer called as such) were still alive and well, and while segregation in public facilities was not as widely practiced, still Mexican Americans faced prejudice and exclusion in many settings, including housing, lack of economic opportunities, and ineffective political representation. Chicanos and other Latinos, such as Puerto Ricans, were still perceived as second-class citizens and as racially inferior to white Americans. However, the response by the Chicano Generation on the race issue was dramatically different from the whiteness strategy of the previous generation. Influenced by the Black Power movement and the emphasis on blackness ("Black is beautiful!") as well as by the rediscovery of the importance of ethnicity in American history, Chicanos rejected the whiteness strategy and instead proclaimed that they were a "people of color" ("Brown is beautiful!") by rediscovering and asserting not only their mestizo heritage but their indigenous racial profile. They now traced their history to Aztlán, the mythical historic homeland of the Aztecs that the Chicano Generation asserted was in the Southwest, where most of them lived.[31] Hence, they were not immigrants or strangers to this region; this was their ancestral, indigenous homeland. It also was the lost homeland, due to the Yankee conquest of the 1840s. The Chicano Movement's task was to somehow regain this homeland, if not physically at least spiritually and culturally. Hence, race was just as significant for this generation, and individuals responded by inventing a new Chicano race identity. This transformation would continue to influence subsequent cohorts of Chicanos and other Latinos to the extent that most of the representatives of the Latino Generation in this study speak of themselves as being distinct racially from whites. This is illustrated in Tania Picasso's story. She remembers that one of the first things that struck her about going to the University of California, Santa Barbara, after coming from a high school that was almost 100 percent Latino, was how many white students attended the university; this made her initially question her decision to go there: "I didn't think that UCSB was for me. It was too white and too relaxed."

This is clearly part of the Latino Gereration's legacy, not only because of the long history of racialization toward people of Mexican and Latino descent in this country but also due to the oppositional racial response by the Chicano Movement that influenced Chicanos and Latinos to see themselves no longer as whites but as people of color.

Historical Agency and the Latino Generation

Finally, the Latino Generation of today is also the recipient of a Chicano/Latino legacy of historical agency if it chooses to learn from it and be inspired by it and, more important, continues *la lucha*—the struggle. By historical agency, I mean that Chicanos/Latinos have struggled over the years for their civil and human rights in this country. Although victims of history, they have also made history by their labor, their community building, and their political movements. Immigrants, beginning with the Immigrant Generation, although they were more vulnerable if they engaged in overt political acts because of their immigrant status, have displayed historical agency in a number of ways. Some participated in labor struggles such as strikes and unionization in the early twentieth century. Others, to protect themselves, formed *mutualistas* or mutual benefit societies that served as both self-help groups and organizing centers for immigrant workers and also created community leadership. Immigrants and refugees also engaged in other forms of community building through organizing in Catholic and additional religious groups, led in many cases by women. Still others, especially the political exiles, rallied around various political forces in support of the different factions involved in the Mexican Revolution. Although stereotyped as being lazy, passive Mexicans, those of the Immigrant Generation were anything but that.[32]

Their children—the Mexican American Generation—displayed even more historical agency in that they did not have to concern themselves as much about their vulnerable immigrant status since they were mostly U.S.-born. As noted, this generation launched the first significant civil rights movement among Mexican Americans in the United States. Members of this generation, more than the immigrants, understood that they had rights protected by the U.S. Constitution; they had learned this in the schools. Moreover, because they were bilingual, they could address their grievances in the language of the system and confront it more directly than could their immigrant parents. Their acculturation empowered them. They formed numerous organizations that expressed their interests as U.S.-born Mexican Americans (although in their struggles, many did not neglect immigrants). Exercising their leadership, members of this generation confronted the system on a number of fronts and in different areas. In education, they campaigned to do away with segregation and inferior education in the Mexican schools. Besides challenging local school boards, they mounted legal campaigns highlighted by the historic Méndez case in 1946 in Orange County, California, in which a federal court ruled for the first time that such segregation of Mexican American children was unconstitutional based on the 14th Amendment, especially the equal protection clause. Other successful legal battles followed in its wake, such as the 1948 Delgado case in Texas.[33]

In addition to educational issues, the Mexican American Generation struggled to end discrimination in a number of other areas such as public facilities, jobs, wages, and housing. In many cases, through the threat of economic boycotts, these efforts succeeded. One other significant area of discrimination taken on was the issue of discrimination against Mexican Americans in the jury system. In Texas, Mexican Americans led by the League of United Latin American Citizens (LULAC) and the G.I. Forum took the Hernández case all the way to the U.S. Supreme Court in 1954, the first case involving Mexican Americans to reach the nation's highest court. In a unanimous decision, the Court ruled that exclusion of Mexican Americans on a jury was unconstitutional, also based on the 14th Amendment.[34] Politically, the Mexican American Generation, especially after World War II, initiated important and groundbreaking efforts to achieve effective representation in city councils, school boards, and state legislatures. Organizing major voter registration drives throughout the

Southwest, Mexican American leaders secured the election of more Mexican Americans to public offices. The most significant breakthrough occurred in 1949 with the election of Edward Roybal to the Los Angeles City Council, the first Mexican American elected to that body since the late nineteenth century. A few years later, in 1957, Raymond Telles became the first Mexican American mayor of El Paso, Texas, and the first Mexican American elected as mayor of an important southwestern city. These and many more struggles by those of the Mexican American Generation exemplified their historical agency.[35]

Members of the Chicano Generation furthered these struggles. They took on the system in a more forceful and militant fashion because even though the previous political generation had made important gains against racism and discrimination, they did not wipe out all vestiges of such treatment. By every educational and economic indicator, Mexican Americans still lagged behind other ethnic Americans, including Blacks. Moreover, inspired by the general political upheaval of this period, those of the Chicano Generation challenged the system as never before. The litany of their struggles is long and impressive and includes the farm workers' struggle led by César Chávez and Dolores Huerta; the land grant movement in New Mexico led by Reies López Tijerina; the 1968 East Los Angeles school blowouts; the organization of the Chicano student movement through MEChA (Movimiento Estudiantil Chicano de Aztlán); the organization of La Raza Unida Party; the unprecedented Chicano antiwar movement; and the Chicana feminist movement.[36] All of these engaged thousands of young Chicanos and Chicanas and not only changed their perceptions of themselves but also forced the system to address more directly Chicano and Latino issues. There is no question that the increased national political importance of Latinos today has a direct connection to the Chicano Movement, as was manifested in the 2012 presidential election. In this sense, those who have come later, including the Latino Generation, not only are the recipients of this legacy but, I believe, have a responsibility to it.

Some of those students whose stories appear here seem to have embraced this responsibility. For example, David Guerra, who studied dramatic arts, notes that he hopes that in his future theatrical endeavors, he will be able to draw from his Chicano identity and make Chicanos proud of his achievements: "But whatever my future is, I also know that I will never lose my Chicanismo; my ethnic identity is embedded within me. If I do a role in a Chekov play with an Anglo ensemble, I don't want my

Chicano community saying that I sold out. But I want my community to be proud of me that I can perform Chekov. I haven't had the time to be involved in Chicano issues on campus. . . . But this doesn't mean I don't support Chicano issues. I do."

Defining the Latino Generation

What defines the Latino Generation? How can we say that this is a particular historical generation as well as a new biological and cultural one? It is perhaps a bit more difficult to distinguish this generation from the previous ones, mainly because of greater Latino ethnic diversity today and less visible historical markers, such as the beginning of mass immigration as in the early twentieth century, the Great Depression and World War II, or the social upheavals of the 1960s. Nevertheless, I believe that certain characteristics together define the Latino Generation. These characteristics are both internal and external to this generation.

The first is based on demographics and has been earlier noted. That is, the Latino Generation is composed of the children of the so-called New Immigrants from Mexico, Central America, the Caribbean, and to a lesser extent other parts of Latin America. The New Immigrants are those who came in the wake of new immigration laws, such as the 1965 Immigration Act that opened up immigration to the families of legal immigrants already in the United States. This provision of the law led many Mexican immigrants to legally bring to the United States their families left behind in Mexico. These new immigrants who entered beginning in the 1970s were then augmented by thousands of Central Americans, especially from El Salvador and Guatemala, who entered as political refugees due to civil wars in those countries. Although at first not accepted as legal political refugees by the U.S. government under the administration of Ronald Reagan, many by the 1990s were granted such status. Finally, due to the increasing numbers of undocumented immigrants, especially from Mexico, who crossed the border in the 1970s and 1980s, the federal government, again under the Reagan administration, sponsored the 1986 Immigration and Control Act (IRCA) that made it possible for 3 million undocumented immigrants and their families to legalize their status; many later achieved citizenship. Their children, who grew up in the 1980s and over the next two decades, constitute what I refer to as the Latino Generation.

But this demographic characterization of the Latino Generation is not just linked to the New Immigrants; it also results from this generation's "coming of age" at a time when Latinos have become the largest minority group in the country, exceeding African Americans. Most Latinos realize the enormity of their numbers and see that in many communities, such as Los Angeles, they represent the majority or close to the majority. This is an unprecedented demographic transformation, and, it seems to me, it has allowed those of the Latino Generation to come of age with the recognition (to quote from Che Guevara) "We are not a minority!" Being cognizant of this has empowered members of this generation, in my estimation, to be even more assertive of their Latino identity and of their sense of entitlement to equal opportunity with other Americans. Those of the Latino Generation recognize the contributions that Latinos by their large numbers make to this country (they can see it in their parents' work), and they will not be denied the fruits of their parents' labor or of their rights in the United States.

The Latino Generation, as noted earlier, is also the product of vast new international economic changes, commonly referred to as globalization. The immigrant parents of those of the Latino Generation were influenced by such economic transformations. As U.S. corporations beginning in the 1970s became even more transnational and exported industries and related jobs to Third World countries, including Mexico and Central America, this expansion led to, on the one hand, a dislocation of many Mexican and Central American peasants from their own lands. They were uprooted by U.S.-influenced new agribusiness concerns, resulting in their eventual diaspora to the United States in search of a livelihood. Likewise, urban workers who could not find employment in new transnational factories such as the maquiladoras in Mexico, which tended to hire primarily female labor as opposed to male workers, also began to cross the border in search of jobs. On the other hand, globalization further led to the deindustrialization of the U.S. economy and its replacement, on one level, by high-tech industries with a highly educated workforce and jobs beyond the reach of poor immigrants and, at another level, by new service industries to complement the high-tech sector with jobs more easily accessible to new immigrants. This globalization created both the New Immigrants and the succeeding Latino Generation.[37]

At the same time, globalization also impacts Latino Generation identity through new technologies of communication such as the Internet, Facebook, twitter, e-mail, and the like, which help put Latinos in touch with the rest of the world, unlike their earlier generational antecedents.

Latinos of today's generation not only know more about what is trans-piring in other countries and cultures but can communicate with their peers in these locations. It also means that internally, Latinos, more so than in the past, are in touch with themselves throughout the country. This globalized means of communication tempers any sense of isola-tion and provincialism. It makes Latinos broader in their identity, feed-ing not only into a pan-Latino one but also into what literary theorist Ellie Hernández calls a postnationalist identity that embraces multiple Latino identities, including those based on gender and sexuality and a more transnational identity, especially with Latin America and with other Third World cultures.[38]

The Latino Generation from a larger historical perspective has also been affected by an almost permanent neo-nativism during the last two or three decades. Neo-nativism represents a surge of anti-immigrant sentiment in this country in response to increased undocumented im-migration, especially from Mexico. This has led to such anti-immigrant actions as the passage of Proposition 187 in California in 1994 that de-nied most state services to the undocumented, including hospital care and education for their undocumented children. Although the proposi-tion was declared unconstitutional by a federal court, it still revealed a growing neo-nativist movement that would only continue to escalate for the next several years and that made efforts in the U.S. Congress to accomplish comprehensive immigration reforms almost impossible. Various states such as Arizona and Alabama more recently have passed harsh anti-immigrant legislation that, while in large part struck down by federal courts, including the Supreme Court, has revealed the persis-tence of neo-nativism. Members of the Latino Generation mostly born in the 1980s and coming of age in the following two decades, such as the subjects of this study, have had to live with this anti–Latino immigrant sentiment that has directly and indirectly affected their lives. Since many of their parents entered the country without papers, the mobil-ity and living conditions of these families and their children have been affected. Those children, including some in this study, who crossed the border as babies or as very young children became Dream Act Latinos who have had to live, if not in the shadows, at least with the burden of their personal limitations, such as in education, due to their status. For example, Alma Cortez-Lara came with her mother to the United States, without documents, when she was only one year old: "My mother joined my father about a year after I was born. I was born on August 6, 1984, and around September of 1985 my mom and I crossed the border. My dad was still in St. Helena, so my paternal grandfather took my mom and me by plane to Tijuana. There he hired a coyote who got us across without papers. Somehow we got all the way up to Napa."

But even those born in the United States have had to define themselves in part in reaction to neo-nativism. That is, their conception of themselves as Americans is tempered by the hostility expressed by some Americans toward Latinos. All this is not to say that the previous generations of Chicanos/Latinos did not face such nativism. They did, but not to the extent and permanency as has been the case in the more recent past. In the early twentieth century, Mexican immigrants in many locations were welcomed for their labor contributions. While the Mexican American Generation was certainly affected by the mass deportations of the early 1930s, this nativism was tempered by the New Deal of the Roosevelt administration and even more so by World War II and Mexican American and Puerto Rican contributions in that war. Later postwar nativism, especially against so-called wetbacks in the early 1950s, did not result in a sustained anti-immigrant movement against Latinos. By contrast, the Latino Generation has been exposed to a consistent and even growing neo-nativism since at least the 1990s.

Because he and his parents did not have their documents, narrator Álvaro Sánchez especially recalls the impact of Proposition 187, the anti-immigrant measure, approved by voters in California in 1994:

In 1994, when I was in junior high, Proposition 187 became a big political issue. If passed, it would deny public social services, such as in hospitals, to undocumented immigrants. It would also deny public education to the undocumented children of undocumented immigrants. This was all very threatening and frightening to me and to my parents. We lived in fear of being reported to the immigration people. I was taking the bus to school, but we heard rumors that the *migra*—immigration officers—were rounding up kids at bus stops or were going into the schools looking for undocumented students. I was terrified. I worried about taking the bus and having someone come up to me and say, "Let me see your papers." I didn't have any. I didn't want to go to school. But my mother calmed me down.

"You know what?" she said, "You can't live afraid. You just have to go out there. Just go to school and act normal. Don't be afraid."

But it was hard not to be afraid.

Fortunately, nothing happened to me or to my parents.

Neo-nativism, moreover, has affected the Latino Generation by the movement against affirmative action, especially in higher education. In 1996, California voters approved Proposition 209, which did away with affirmative action based on race in state institutions. This had an immediate effect on the recruitment and admission of Latinos in the University of California system and, to a lesser extent, in the state university system. While these systems and other state systems also affected by anti–affirmative action movements have created new ways to still diversify their student university bodies by utilizing class-based criteria or personal hardship evidence as well as, in the case of California, by adopting new policies prioritizing the admission of the top 10 percent of graduates in all of the state's public schools, still the stigma of affirmative action has marked the Latino Generation and its efforts to achieve quality education. Anti–affirmative action policies have limited the number of Latinos and African Americans, for example, who can attend the most prestigious UC campuses, such as Berkeley and UCLA. Up to 1995, the percentage of underrepresented minorities, including Latinos, admitted to Berkeley stood at 27 percent of the total. Following the UC system in outlawing affirmative action based on race and bolstered by the passage of Proposition 209, the percentage of underrepresented minorities admitted to Berkeley had declined by 1998 to 13 percent. A similar drop occurred at UCLA. That decline has still not been overcome, even though the percentage of underrepresented minorities admitted to those two campuses have increased so that by 2010 the percentage at Berkeley was 17 percent and at UCLA 21 percent, but both are still below the 1995 figures.[39] Several of the narrators, for example, applied to either Berkeley or UCLA, or both, but were not admitted. Of course, for the Dream Act members of the Latino Generation, their immigration status has only compounded their problems in achieving educational mobility by hindering their access to programs such as student aid.

At the same time, despite these neo-nativist hurdles, it is remarkable, as attested to by this study, how much educational mobility some of the Latino Generation has achieved. While my study, of course, is selective and showcases Latino students who entered college, many others of the Latino Generation have also made this great leap from being children of working-class immigrants to becoming college-educated Latinos. This educational aspiration and mobility frames Tania Picasso's story when she recalls: "It was in my junior year that I started to think about attending college in a serious way. No one in my immediate family, of course, had attended college, so there was no prior experience to fall back on. At the same time, my parents supported the idea of further education. They would tell me, 'Siga adelante'—keep going forward."

This attitude is found more and more throughout Latino communities. The increase in Latino children of recent immigrants attending college is a totally new historical experience among Latinos in the United States. In no other period in Chicano history have so many children or grandchildren of immigrants gone on to college. In part, this change can be traced to the Chicano Movement that forced institutions of higher education to begin to recruit Chicanos and other Latinos. But this change may also be the result of the global economy that has left little room for good employment in this country for those only with a high school education. There are no longer good industrial jobs, for example, that one can get only with a high school education, as has been the case in the past. Hence, those of the Latino Generation, or at least a noticeable number, have had no choice but to realize the importance of a college education in order to obtain some of the better jobs in a postindustrial economy that in many cases necessitates even advanced degrees to secure more lucrative employment. About four in ten Latino high school graduates today are enrolled either in a community college or a four-year university. As a result, one of the distinguishing features characterizing the Latino Generation is its impressive educational mobility relative to past generations.

The Latino Generation has also been affected by the era of multiculturalism. The impact of earlier more ethnic and cultural nationalist movements, exemplified by the Chicano Movement and the Black Power Movement, in time led to the development of an ideology of multiculturalism in order to contain the more oppositional threats of the nationalist struggles. By the 1990s, multiculturalism became a new buzzword for a revised pluralist ideology that suggested that the country could live with and accept different ethnic cultures without any major structural changes to the American capitalist system. While it is a policy of containment, multiculturalism nevertheless has provided a certain safe space for the promotion of ethnic and cultural identities of people of color, such as Latinos. Unlike earlier periods, such as in the 1960s and 1970s, when such movements were seen as threatening, this new era has embraced a safer multiculturalism as long as it does not in fact threaten the dominant class structure. The effect of this more "tolerant" multicultural period has allowed members of the Latino Generation to be less guarded about expressing their Latino identity. It is more acceptable both within the communities and without to be Latino. The Latino subjects of this study, for example, seem to have grown up with little shame or embarrassment about being Latino since their schools and the mass culture (both mainstream and Latino) promoted or at least tolerated their identity and culture. Of this condition, Sandy Escobedo observes:

> UCSB also exposed me to Chicano studies classes. I first took Introduction to Chicano Studies and then a few upper-division courses. Taking these classes has affected me tremendously. If anything, they've made me definitely become more critical. I've learned a lot more critical thinking skills in my Chicano studies classes than in other ones. Chicano studies classes have also made me question my own identity. I didn't do that before. My parents told me that I was both Mexican and Salvadoran but born in the U.S., so I was an American. But now I was thinking about what all that meant. In addition, I was now exposed to the term "Chicano." I really believe that the term Chicano is like a process. You don't become Chicano overnight, especially someone of my background. This is especially true if you don't grow up with that term, as I didn't. I understand now through my Chicano studies classes the meaning of Chicano; although I'll use it for myself at times, I don't use it most of the time. It can be confusing because sometime it's used to refer to someone's Mexican background, but then also to someone's politics. If someone calls me a Chicana, I don't have a problem with it. However, I prefer the term "Latina." If someone were to call me Hispanic, I would have a problem, but I would explain why I had a problem.

This is a far cry from earlier periods when expressions of being Mexican or Chicano could be met with racist antagonism and, in the case of the Chicano Generation, with hostility from more conservative Mexican Americans. Such attitudes seem less visible today, especially toward generic ethnic labels such as Latino or Hispanic. One could thus argue that members of the Latino Generation have had more security in resolving and asserting their identity issues.

Because of the diversity of the Latino population since the 1980s as well as a greater national acceptance of the concept of being Latino due to multiculturalism, the Latino Generation is further distinguished by its pan-Latino identity. That is, Latinos of this new generation are more and more identifying themselves as Latinos in the public sphere. By public sphere, I mean where Latinos of different backgrounds (such as Mexicans, Salvadorans, and Puerto Ricans) engage with each other and necessitate a common marker—in this case, Latino—in public places, such as schools, campuses, political settings, cultural events, and myriad other public settings. Many reject or are ambivalent about the term "Chicano," including some of the Mexican Americans in this study. Those of Central American background find the term completely foreign to their experiences. For example, Adriana Valdez from Los Angeles observes this about her ethnic identity:

Until I came to UCSB, I didn't think about ethnic identity. I didn't consider myself anything. I was never asked, "What are you?" I guess everyone just assumed I was Mexican. However, when I came to UCSB, everyone, or at least many of the Latinos, were identifying as Chicanos. I didn't relate to the term and, in fact, don't recall hearing it very much if at all before UCSB. I didn't like the term "Chicano," and I still don't. Slowly, I started learning that it's OK for those who want to use the term to use it. But it's not for me. Forced to state my ethnic identity, I'll say Mexican and of course Latina. I also don't like the term "Mexican American." Why add the American?

In this pan-Latino process, Latinos, especially in locations such as Los Angeles where there is now a significant diversity of Latino groups, are undergoing a new form of *mestizaje* where different Latino groups influence each other culturally. This is another version of transculturation where people are becoming Latinos. This is not to say that they do not still fall back on their specific ethnic identities as Mexicans and Salvadorans, for example. They do, but this is also nuanced and negotiated with an accompanying pan-Latino identity. At no other period in Chicano/Latino history has such significant pan-Latinismo taken place.

This pan-Latino manifestation, moreover, is also due to other influencing factors, three in particular: (1) greater Latino geographic mobility, (2) greater Latino mass media institutions, and (3) greater Latino political influence in the country. The significant growth of the Latino population has brought in its wake greater Latino geographic diversity. For example, Mexican immigrants and U.S.-born Mexican Americans can be found in sizable numbers throughout the United States. In the past, most Mexican Americans lived mostly in the Southwest with important pockets in the Midwest. Today, however, such enclaves have expanded to every state, including eastern ones such as New York. This Mexican expansion means that Mexicans are in closer connection with other Latino groups, whether Central Americans, Puerto Ricans, Cubans, or Dominicans. The same is true for these other Latino groups who also have experienced a similar geographic diversity. The effect of this has been to further the creation of a pan-Latino identity as these different groups interact with one another, including intermarrying.

The impressive growth of a Latino mass media apparatus in the United States, in my opinion, has facilitated a pan-Latino identity. This is especially the case in television, as exemplified by the two major Spanish-language networks, Univision and Telemundo, which focus on reaching a pan-Latino audience especially through their news programs, as well as with their entertainment ones. This has aided in instilling a sense of being Latino, especially among the new generation. As noted in several of the narratives of this study, these Latinos growing up often watched Spanish-language TV with one or more of their parents or grandparents. Rafaela Espinoza, for example, recalls, "Spanish at first did influence my television watching. When I was younger, all I watched was Spanish-language television. I watched telenovelas with my mother all the way through high school. When I go home now, I will sit and watch a telenovela with my mom. My favorite telenovela was *Rebelde*. It was intense."

Young Latinos' bilingualism and biculturalism have facilitated their involvement with this Spanish-language media. Moreover, increasing numbers of programs on English-language TV are attempting to attract a Latino audience. The influence of the Latino mass media can also be seen in Spanish-language radio as well as in English-language programming aimed at a Latino audience. Expanding Internet services also targeting Latinos further develop the notion of being Latino. Such Latino mass media influence is unprecedented in history, and the Latino Generation has been in part shaped by it.

Finally, the Latino Generation has also been influenced by the equally unprecedented growth in Latino political power. Since the 1970s but especially during the last two decades of the twentieth century and the first one of the new millennium, more Latinos than ever before have been elected to political offices at the local and state levels, including to the U.S. Congress, or have been appointed to important administrative positions in the public sphere, including serving in the cabinets of both Democratic and Republican administrations. In addition, Latinos are voting in larger numbers than before, including in national presidential elections, as demonstrated in 2012 when over 10 million Latinos voted. The mass media have noticed this growth of Latino political involvement and in numerous stories in both visual and print media have called attention to it. In the past, even in the 1960s, some still referred to Latinos as the "sleeping giant" in American politics; that is no longer the case. Latino political power is now recognized and respected. Such recognition and respect has helped forge this new pan-Latino identity.

All of these factors and undoubtedly others can be said to characterize the Latino Generation. Members of this generation are the products of history, but they are also products of their own generational era and environment. They are a composite of both past and present, and as such they are forging their own unique identity and culture.

Characteristics of the *Testimonios*

The thirteen stories of the Latino Generation in this volume share many second-generation characteristics. These include the following:

> The parents of my subjects are of poor backgrounds, many from the rural areas of Mexico or Central America where they worked the land as *campesinos* or small farmers.
> These parents who became immigrants possess limited education, although perhaps relative to their home countries they have more schooling. Nevertheless, most have no more than an elementary or middle school education.
> The parents represent economic refugees, although those from Central America have connections to the civil wars there of the late 1970s and 1980s.
> Almost all of the immigrant parents entered the United States as a result of chain migration. This means that they followed usually another relative who first crossed the border.
> Most of these parents entered the United States without documents, although almost all legalized their status over time.

In the United States, the immigrant parents became blue-collar unskilled or at best semi-skilled workers.

The parents as immigrants settled among other Latino immigrants
in cities such as Los Angeles.

As for their children, almost all in my study were U.S.-born, but some
came as young children born in either Mexico or Central America.

Almost all of my subjects were born in the 1980s.

Some of the second generation represent transnationals in that
during their coming-of-age years, they traveled back to Mexico or
Central America with their parents for visits.

Most belong to strong nuclear and extended families.

Almost all of them attended public schools, and most of these were
Latino ones or predominantly mixed minority schools.

Of significant importance, almost all of their parents promoted education for their children.

The second generation became bilingual and bicultural. As such,
they became literally interpreters/translators for their families,
although some of their parents learned some English.

Religion played a role in the socialization of the second generation,
but much diversity of religious experiences is noted.

Almost all of the immigrant children faced strong parental discipline, especially the young women.

Almost all of my subjects are more comfortable with the term "Latino" than with "Chicano."

Some female subjects identified themselves as feminists although
all exhibited feminist tendencies.

Most (both men and women) expressed a preference to marry other
Latinos, although some revealed some flexibility in this.

All exhibited strong ambitions to attend college.

Most became more ethnically aware when they went to college or
participated in Latino/Chicano groups.

Almost all of them performed well in their schools or overcame
some adversities to eventually succeed in their education.

Oral History Methodology

As mentioned, I interviewed thirteen Latino college students, all second-
generation children of immigrants. Almost all were students of mine in
various classes. Some were upper-division students, while some were

freshmen in my lower-division Introduction to Chicano/Latino Studies class. The first interviews commenced in 2002 and concluded in 2010. The interviews feature both men and women, although without any intention the majority are of women. I used an open-ended methodology approach, asking general questions in order to allow the students to develop their stories. I followed a chronological format, first asking questions about their parents' histories, how they came to the United States, and their work and settlement on this side of the border, and then questions about the students' early life and their progression in their education, including the decision to go to college. But I also asked questions about home life and home culture and about their cultural preferences in order to get an idea about their acculturation/transculturation. Most interviews involved several meetings and averaged six to eight hours each, although some were longer. After transcribing the interviews, I then wrote the narratives as first-person autobiographical stories. After I had revised the drafts, I sent them to all of the former students for fact checking and for any additions or deletions that they preferred. After their revisions, I then finished the final draft for publication. This project was ongoing while I was working on other ones and, as a result, lasted several years. This length of time allowed me to select from different cohorts of Latino students.

Conclusion

These oral history narratives or *testimonios* are intended to put a human face on the children of Latino immigrants (and on those immigrants, their parents, as well). This is important in a society that seems to focus on Latinos only as abstract statistics centered on illegal immigration or gang-bangers. But Latinos are more than statistics, and they are more than "illegal aliens" or gangsters. They are above all human beings no different from you or me. If we are to more fully understand this growing group that in many ways will determine the future of the United States, then it is imperative that we first acknowledge the humanity of Latinos. I would even go so far as to suggest that this recognition is a moral necessity. We have a moral responsibility to relate to each other as human beings—all children of the same God whom we profess guides our country. If these portraits of the Latino Generation can advance this goal, then I will have considered my project to be successful.

NOTES

1. Yen Le Espiritu, "The Intersection of Race, Ethnicity, and Class: The Multiple Identities of Second-Generation Filipinos," in *The Second Generation: Ethnic Identity among Asian Americans*, ed. Pyong Gap Min (Walnut Creek, Calif.: Altamira Press, 2002), 25.

2. For some of these historical issues, see Mario T. García, *Desert Immigrants: The Mexicans of El Paso, 1880–1920* (New Haven: Yale University Press, 1981); and Mario T. García, *Mexican Americans: Leadership, Ideology and Identity, 1930–1960* (New Haven: Yale University Press, 1989).

3. See, for example, M. García, *Desert Immigrants*; M. García, *Mexican Americans*; Mario T. García, *Memories of Chicano History: The Life and Narrative of Bert Corona* (Berkeley: University of California Press, 1994); and Mario T. García, *Migrant Daughter: Coming of Age as a Mexican American Woman* (Berkeley: University of California Press, 2000).

4. See Mario T. García and Sal Castro, *Blowout! Sal Castro and the Chicano Struggle for Educational Justice* (Chapel Hill: University of North Carolina Press, 2011).

5. See Oscar Handlin, *The Uprooted: The Epic Story of the Great Migration That Made the American People* (New York: Grosset and Dunlap, 1951).

6. See Gilbert G. González and Raul A. Fernández, *A Century of Chicano History: Empire, Nations, and Migration* (New York: Routledge, 2003).

7. See, among others, M. García, *Desert Immigrants*; Albert Camarillo, *Chicanos in a Changing Society: From Mexican Pueblos to American Barrios in Santa Barbara and Southern California, 1848–1930* (Cambridge, Mass.: Harvard University Press, 1979); Ricardo Romo, *East Los Angeles: History of a Barrio* (Austin: University of Texas Press, 1983); Neil Foley, *The White Scourge: Mexicans, Blacks, and Poor Whites in Texas Cotton Culture* (Berkeley: University of California Press, 1997); Vicki L. Ruiz, *Cannery Women/Cannery Lives: Mexican Women, Unionization, and the California Food Processing Industry, 1930–1950* (Albuquerque: University of New Mexico Press, 1987); George J. Sánchez, *Becoming Mexican American: Ethnicity, Culture, and Identity in Chicano Los Angeles, 1900–1943* (New York: Oxford University Press, 1993); Emilio Zamora, *The World of the Mexican Workers in Texas* (College Station: Texas A&M University Press, 1993); Douglas Monroy, *Rebirth: Mexican Los Angeles from the Great Migration to the Great Depression* (Berkeley: University of California Press, 1999); Devra Weber, *Dark Sweat, White Gold: California Farm Workers, Cotton, and the New Deal* (Berkeley: University of California Press, 1994); Gilbert G. González, *Labor and Community: Mexican Citrus Worker Villages in a Southern California County, 1900–1950* (Urbana: University of Illinois Press, 1994); Zaragoza Vargas, *Labor Rights Are Civil Rights: Mexican American Workers in Twentieth-Century America* (Princeton: Princeton University Press, 2005); and Matt García, *A World of Its Own: Race, Labor, and Citrus in the Making of Greater Los Angeles, 1900–1970* (Chapel Hill: University of North Carolina Press, 2001).

8. See Ernesto Galarza, *Merchants of Labor: The Mexican Bracero Story* (Charlotte: McNally and Loftin, 1964); Erasmo Gamboa, *Mexican Labor and World War II: Braceros in the Pacific Northwest, 1942–1947* (Austin: University of Texas Press, 1990); and Deborah Cohen, *Braceros: Migrant Citizens and Transnational Subjects in the Postwar United States and Mexico* (Chapel Hill: University of North Carolina Press, 2011).

9. See Wayne Cornelius, ed., *Mexican Migration and the U.S. Economic Crisis: A Transnational Crisis* (La Jolla, Calif.: Center for Comparative Immigration Studies, 2011).

10. See Sánchez, *Becoming Mexican American*; David G. Gutiérrez, *Walls and Mirrors: Mexican Americans, Mexican Immigrants, and the Politics of Ethnicity* (Berkeley: University of California Press, 1995); Gloria F. Arredondo, *Mexican Chicago: Race, Identity, and Nation, 1916–39* (Urbana: University of Illinois Press, 2008); Ruiz, *Cannery Women*; and M. García, *Mexican Americans*.

11. See Sánchez, *Becoming Mexican American*. For social science literature on this process, see, among others, Espiritu, "Intersection of Race, Ethnicity, and Class"; Cynthia Feliciano, *Unequal Origins: Immigrant Selection and the Education of the Second Generation* (New York: LFB Scholarly Publishing, 2006); Alejandro Portes and Rubén Rumbaut, *Legacies: The Story of the Immigrant Second Generation* (Berkeley: University of California Press, 2001); Min, *Second Generation*; Tamar Jacoby, ed., *Reinventing the Melting Pot: The New Immigration and What It Means to Be American* (New York: Basic Books, 2004); Carola Suárez-Orozco and Marcelo M. Suárez-Orozco, *Children of Immigration* (Cambridge, Mass.: Harvard University Press, 2001); Nazli Kibria, *Becoming Asian American: Second Generation Chinese and Korean American Identities* (Baltimore: Johns Hopkins University Press, 2002); and Joel Perlmann and Roger Waldinger, "Second Generation Decline? Children of Immigrants, Past and Present—A Reconsideration," *International Migration Review* 31, no. 4 (Winter 1997): 893–922.

12. See Arrendondo, *Mexican Chicago*.

13. Mario T. García, "La Frontera: The Border as Symbol and Reality in Mexican American Thought," *Mexican Studies/Estudios Mexicanos*, Summer 1985, 195–225.

14. See Gutiérrez, *Walls and Mirrors*.

15. See M. García, *Desert Immigrants*.

16. See M. García, *Mexican Americans*.

17. Gutiérrez, *Walls and Mirrors*; David G. Gutiérrez, "Migration, Emergent Ethnicity, and the 'Third Space': The Shifting Politics of Nationalism in Greater Mexico," *Journal of American History* 86, no. 2 (Sept. 1999): 481–517.

18. See Tomás Jimenez, *Replenished Ethnicity: Mexican Americans, Immigrants, and Identity* (Berkeley: University of California Press, 2010).

19. See Michael Omi and Howard Winant, *Racial Formation in the United States: From the 1960s to the 1980s* (New York: Routledge, 1986).

20. M. García, *Desert Immigrants*, 110–26. Also see Gilbert G. González, *Chicano Education in the Era of Segregation* (Philadelphia: Balch Institute Press, 1990); and Guadalupe San Miguel Jr., *"Let All of Them Take Heed": Mexican Americans and the Campaign for Educational Equality in Texas, 1910–1981* (Austin: University of Texas Press, 1987).

21. See Laura E. Gómez, *Manifest Destinies: The Making of the Mexican American Race* (New York: New York University Press, 2007).

22. Oscar Martínez, "On the Size of the Chicano Population: New Estimates, 1850–1900," *Aztlán*, Spring 1975, 43–67; Richard Griswold del Castillo, *The Treaty of Guadalupe Hidalgo: A Legacy of Conflict* (Norman: University of Oklahoma Press, 1990).

23. See Ronald Takaki, *Iron Cages: Race and Culture in 19th Century America* (1979; New York: Oxford University Press, 2000).

24. See Ian F. Haney López, *White by Law: The Legal Construction of Race* (New York: New York University Press, 1996); Ignacio M. García, *White but Not Equal: Mexican Americans, Jury Discrimination, and the Supreme Court* (Tucson: University of Arizona Press, 2009); and Neil Foley, "Being Hispanic: Mexican Americans and the Faustian Pact with Whiteness," in *Reflexiones: New Directions in Mexican American Studies* (Austin: Center for Mexican American Studies, 1997), 53–70. Also see Natalia Molina, "In a Race All Their Own: The Quest to Make Mexicans Ineligible for U.S. Citizenship," *Pacific Historical Review* 79, no. 2 (May 2010): 167–201.

25. Mario T. García, "Mexican Americans and the Politics of Citizenship, 1936," *New Mexico Historical Review* 59, no. 2 (April 1984): 187–204.

26. See Foley, "Being Hispanic"; Neil Foley, *Quest for Equality: The Failed Promise of Black-Brown Solidarity* (Cambridge, Mass.: Harvard University Press, 2010); M. García, "Mexican Americans;" and M. García, *Mexican Americans*.

27. See Foley, "Being Hispanic"; and Foley, *Quest for Equality*.

28. See González, *Chicano Education*.

29. Ibid.; San Miguel, *"Let All of Them Take Heed."*

30. See Natalia Molina, *Fit to Be Citizens: Public Health and Race in Los Angeles, 1879–1939* (Berkeley: University of California Press, 2006). Also see Francisco Balderrama and Raymond Rodríguez, *Decade of Betrayal: Mexican Repatriation in the 1930s* (Albuquerque: University of New Mexico Press, 1995); and Abraham Hoffman, *Unwanted Mexican Americans in the Great Depression: Repatriation Pressures, 1929–1939* (Tucson: University of Arizona Press, 1974).

31. See Rudolfo A. Anaya and Francisco L. Lomeli, *Aztlán: Essays on the Chicano Homeland* (Albuquerque: University of New Mexico Press, 1989).

32. See M. García, *Desert Immigrants*; and Sánchez, *Becoming Mexican American*.

33. See Philippa Strum, *Mendez v. Westminster: School Desegregation and Mexican-American Civil Rights* (Lawerence: University Press of Kansas, 2010); and Carlos K. Blanton, "George I. Sánchez, Ideology, and Whiteness in the Making of the Mexican American Civil Rights Movement, 1930–1960," *Journal of Southern History* 72 (Aug. 2006): 569–604.

34. See I. García, *White but Not Equal*; Michael A. Olivares, ed., *Colored Men and Hombres Aquí: Hernández v. Texas and the Emergence of Mexican American Lawyering* (Houston: Arte Public Press, 2006). Also see the PBS *American Experience* documentary *A Class Apart: A Mexican American Civil Rights Story* (2006).

35. See Mario T. García, *The Making of a Mexican American Mayor: Raymond L. Telles of El Paso* (El Paso: Texas Western Press, 1998).

36. See Richard Griswold del Castillo and Richard A. García, *César Chávez: A Triumph of Spirit* (Norman: University of Oklahoma Press, 1995); Jacques Levy, *Cesar Chavez: Autobiography of La Causa* (New York: W. W. Norton, 1975); Randy Shaw, *Beyond the Fields: Cesar Chavez, the UFW, and the Struggle for Justice in the 21st Century* (Berkeley: University of California Press, 2008); Miriam Powell, *The Union of Their Dreams: Power, Hope, and Struggle in Cesar Chavez's Farm Worker Movement* (New York: Bloomsbury Press, 2009); Frank Bardacke, *Trampling Out the Vintage: Cesar Chavez and the Two Souls of the United Farm Workers* (New York: Verso, 2011); Matt García, *From the Jaws of Victory: The Triumph and Tragedy of César Chávez and the Farm Workers Movement* (Berkeley: University of California Press, 2012); Mario T. García, *A Dolores Huerta Reader* (Albuquerque:

University of New Mexico Press, 2008); Jorge Mariscal, *Brown-Eyed Children of the Sun: Lessons from the Chicano Movement, 1965–1975* (Albuquerque: University of New Mexico Press, 2005); Carlos Muñoz Jr., *Youth, Identity, Power: The Chicano Movement* (New York: Verso, 1989); Armando Navarro, *Mexican American Youth Organization: Avant-Garde of the Chicano Movement in Texas* (Austin: University of Texas Press, 1995); Ernesto Chávez, *"Mi Raza Primero!": Nationalism, Identity, and Insurgency in the Chicano Movement in Los Angeles, 1966–1978* (Berkeley: University of California Press, 2002); David Montejano, *Quixote's Soldiers: A Local History of the Chicano Movement, 1966–1981* (Austin: University of Texas Press, 2010); Marc Simon Rodríguez, *The Tejano Diaspora: Mexican Americanism and Ethnic Politics in Texas and Wisconsin* (Chapel Hill: University of North Carolina Press, 2011); Lorena Oropeza, *Raza Si, Guerra No! Chicano Protest and Patriotism during the Vietnam War Era* (Berkeley: University of California Press, 2005); and García and Castro, *Blowout!*

37. On Mexican and Central American immigration to the United States, the civil wars in Central America, and U.S. foreign policy and globalization, see the following recent literature: Jóse Luis Falconi, Jóse Antonio Mazzotti, and Michael Jones-Correa, *The Other Latinos: Central and South Americans in the United States* (Cambridge, Mass.: Harvard University Press, 2007); Maria Cristina García, *Seeking Refuge: Central American Migration to Mexico, the United States, and Canada* (Berkeley: University of California Press, 2006); Timothy J. Henderson, *Beyond Borders: A History of Mexican Migration to the United States* (Malden, Mass.: Wiley-Blackwell, 2011); Stephen Kinzer and Marilee S. Grindle, *Blood of Brothers: Life and War in Nicaragua* (Cambridge, Mass.: Harvard University Press, 2007); Saul Landau, *The Guerrilla Wars of Central America, Nicaragua, El Salvador, and Guatemala* (London: Weidenfeld and Nicolson, 1993); Ren de la Pedraja, *Wars of Latin America. 1948–1982: The Rise of the Guerrillas* (Jefferson, N.C.: McFarland, 2013); Stephen E. Ambrose and Douglas G. Brinkley, *Rise to Globalism: American Foreign Policy since 1938* (New York: Penguin, 2010); and David P. Forsythe, Patrice C. MacMahon, and Andrew Wedeman, *American Foreign Policy in a Globalized World* (Hoboken, N.J.: Taylor and Francis, 2013).

38. See Ellie D. Hernández, *Postnationalism in Chicano/a Literature and Culture* (Austin: University of Texas Press, 2009).

39. See Erica Pérez, "Despite Diversity Efforts, UC Minority Enrollment Down since Prop. 209," *California Watch* (online), Feb. 24, 2012.

ALMA CORTEZ–LARA

The interesting thing about my family background is that both my mom's and dad's families are from the same small rancho in Michoacán called El Llano. That means "The Plains." It used to be a hacienda with peasants. It's changed over the years, but it's still a small community. Some members of my dad's family, such as my aunts and uncles, at some point moved to Mexico City. In fact, my grandparents met in El Llano but also later relocated to Mexico City.

I don't know much about my mother's side of the family except I have the perception that they've been in El Llano for a very long time. They never moved out.

My mother's side is much more light-skinned than my dad's. They're also blue-eyed. I don't know how that came to be, and my mom doesn't know either. I have nobody to ask because most of that side of the family has passed away.

Both families worked their plots of land in El Llano. My dad's father had his little *terrenos* or plots. He grew corn. I remember visiting as a teenager, and he was still growing maize.

On my mother's side, my grandpa had cows, and he sold milk to the townspeople. He also would sell his milk in other nearby towns. He actually had a very large dairy farm.

Both sets of my grandparents are still alive, but it's my mother's family we see more often because they visit us at least once a year.

My family and I also visit El Llano. It's still a pretty poor town, but it's improving. The streets used to be unpaved and filled with rocks but are now being paved. It's being improved by the money sent back by immigrants from the town who have come to the United States. They come here to make money, but they send a portion back to their families and to the community to improve it.

My mom was born in 1962 and my dad in 1959. They met because they attended the one and only school in El Llano, even though they were three years apart. This was the *primaria*, the elementary school, which was literally a one-room school. That's how my parents came to know each other, since all the students were in the same classroom.

If you wanted to go and get more than an elementary education, you went to *secundaria*, or the equivalent of junior high. There was no *secundaria* in El Llano. The closest one was in the nearby town of Ario de Rayón. My mom didn't go because she was the oldest daughter; she had to stay home and help take care of the house. So my mom only has an elementary school education. My dad, on the other hand, did go to the *secundaria* in Zamora. He walked every day to get there. It was at least five miles from El Llano. He tells me that he wore out many shoes. If he was late, he ran all the way.

All the time that he was at that school, they were constructing a new school building. He and the other students had to help in the construction. In fact, this was part of their education. It was a form of vocational education. But they also learned a few other things. They learned some math because the teacher, who also helped in the construction, would illustrate math problems in relationship to the construction. My dad remembers his teacher saying something like, "If you can cut this piece of wood in five pieces, how many more would you need to construct this side of the building?" or something like that. It was hands-on learning.

My dad finished *secundaria*, which went up to the ninth grade. He still has his class ring. But that was the extent of his education. He felt that he needed to help his family, so he worked in the fields.

As both of my parents grew up, they got to know each other more, and eventually my dad proposed marriage. They married in 1982. My dad was twenty-three and my mom was twenty. They moved into my father's family's house, and that actually was only down the long block from my mom's house.

Before they got married, my dad had already gone to the United States to work without documents. I think he first came in either 1979 or 1980. He was able to work and save some money to go back to marry my mother. After their marriage, he returned to California to work. He would live alongside *solteros*, other single men. My mother didn't care to be left alone. She remembers telling him, "The only way you're going back next time is by taking me also."

My dad had found work in the Napa Valley of California, working in the wine vineyards. His brother and others from El Llano had earlier found work there, and that's how my dad found his way to Napa Valley.

He would always cross from Tijuana by hiring a coyote. He first worked in St. Helena.

My mother joined my father about a year after I was born. I was born on August 6, 1984, and around September of 1985 my mom and I crossed the border. My dad was still in St. Helena, so my paternal grandfather took my mom and me by plane to Tijuana. There he hired a coyote who got us across without papers. Somehow we got all the way up to Napa.

Eventually we all got our papers as a result of the 1986 Immigration and Control Act supported by President Reagan. I remember getting mine when I was seven years old. It takes a long time to get your papers, so my dad had started the process many years earlier. I still have my *mica*, my green card, which has my picture at age seven.

My dad arranged housing for us. We first shared an apartment with another family. However, when this family started to have other male relatives come up and move in, my dad didn't like this, and so he got us our own apartment in Napa. Above in another apartment, a cousin of my mother's also lived with her family. They had a girl, my cousin, whom I played with. In that same complex, another couple lived who were also from El Llano. They ended up being my *padrinos* or godparents for my confirmation.

In fact, everywhere we went we kept meeting people from our hometown. Most of the Mexican people in that area were from El Llano. This made it all seem more like home for us than a strange new country.

I think my dad first worked, like the other workers, picking the wine grapes during the summer harvest. He then was promoted to being what the Mexicans called a *tractorista*. He drove one of the tractors up and down the rows of the grape vines, and the workers would dump the grapes into the cart that my dad pulled along. But he also continued to do some picking himself.

My mom at first didn't work, but after my sister was born in 1988, she started working in the fields a year later. I remember her coming home and joking about having grape-picking races with my dad. They competed to see who could pick the most grapes in a certain amount of time. My mom always won. My dad would make out that he was ashamed at this, but it was all in fun. My mom now works as a custodian.

But it wasn't always fun in the vineyards. Not only was it hard and hot work, but the immigration officials sometimes would raid the fields. In fact, according to my dad, it would be the employer who would call in *la migra* so that he wouldn't have to pay the workers. My dad was caught two or three times after we were all living in Napa. My mother, before she went to work herself, would always worry about him. She knew that if he didn't get home at the usual hour, something was wrong. Sure enough, she would later get a phone call from Tijuana.

"They caught us and I'm back in Tijuana, but I'll cross back tonight and I'll see you in a couple of days," he would tell my mom. And sure enough, in a couple of days he would be back and start work all over again.

Other times when the *migra* showed up, my dad and the other workers sometimes had enough time to run up into the hills and hide. My dad tells a funny story about once getting caught by the *migra*. They rounded him up along with the other workers, but because the bus or van they were putting the workers in was already full by the time my dad was ready, he was made to walk in front of the vehicle until they came to the next vineyard, where they were conducting similar raids and where there was more room in the van. However, because the officers were joking around and not paying attention to my dad when their van turned into the next vineyard, my dad just kept walking, and they never noticed that he was missing. He came back home. He lucked out.

Despite these interruptions in his work, my dad did well and was able to save money. He used part of his savings eventually to buy a car. It was a white Chevy Nova. It was his pride and joy. He loved that car and would take me for rides in it.

I first went to school at Westwood Elementary School in Napa. It was a bilingual school. Half of the school day was in Spanish and the other half in English. I knew no English when I started school. I was there through the second grade but didn't learn that much English; Spanish was used so much because all of the other kids, with the exception of two white ones, were all Mexicans who spoke Spanish. But I enjoyed school and looked forward to going each day.

When I was in second grade, we moved from Napa to a small but new community called American Canyon. My dad had saved enough to buy a house, and so we moved there. It was a predominantly white community and so too was the school that I attended. I was one of two Latinos in the school. I still didn't speak much English. This was in 1991.

Because of the language issue, it was a bit traumatic at first at my new school. I had to take a test to determine how much English I knew. It was an oral test where this lady asked me to identify various items in English. I surprised myself because I passed the test. I knew English, but I hesitated to speak it. The result was that I wasn't tracked as an

English learner. Pretty soon I became more comfortable with English, even though I still didn't speak too much in class. Even now in college, I tend not to speak much in smaller classes. Part of it is shyness, but part of it is because I think I have an accent. People tell me I don't, but I'm still reluctant to speak too much.

Learning English affected my family in different ways. My dad at work picked up some English, and he understands a lot of English. But he doesn't like to speak it. My mother knows some English. When we lived in Napa, she enrolled in English classes offered at night. Yet, like my dad, she's shy about talking in English. At home we speak Spanish.

Because my parents struggled with English, I often had to serve as a translator for them. This actually helped my English because I had to translate Spanish to English. I translated for them at stores. And when my dad bought our house, I translated some of the real estate transactions for him. This wasn't complicated material but simple things, such as the descriptions of different houses and a few other things.

At school I would translate material sent to my parents. If my mother needed to meet with one of my teachers, I accompanied her and translated. Fortunately, I was a good student so that my teacher had only good things to say about me.

I remember, when I was in elementary school, seeing a commercial on Spanish-language TV where the teacher speaks only English and the man doesn't speak English. The teacher tells the parent, "It's wonderful that you've come to see me even though you don't speak English. But it's also wonderful that your child can translate for you." When I saw the commercial, I said to myself, "Hey, that's me. I translate for my parents." The commercial, obviously, was intended to encourage Spanish-speaking parents to engage with the schools for their kids' sake.

As I learned more English, I acquired more friends. I had white friends, but by sixth grade I hung around especially with a Filipino girl and an Egyptian girl. We were all good students and kind of nerds. We all got As and were teachers' pets.

My dad always believed we should own our own home. His father owned his own home in Mexico, and my dad was insistent that we become homeowners in the United States. He was so proud when we finally accomplished that. We also needed this because our family was growing. Eventually, there were two girls and two boys.

Our home in American Canyon was in a mostly white community. Some of our neighbors were Mexican, but they weren't too friendly.

Actually, they were second-generation Mexican Americans who spoke mostly English, so they didn't have much in common with my parents.

But within a couple of years, my neighborhood began to change. Because housing was expensive in Napa, other Mexicans could more easily buy or rent houses in American Canyon. The result was that more and more started moving in. Pretty soon our neighborhood was mostly Mexican.

My middle school was back in Napa, since at that time there was no such school yet in American Canyon. We were bused the short distance to Napa. There was more than one middle school in Napa, and I was assigned to the Silverado Middle School. This was predominantly Mexican, although some whites did attend. What was really interesting was that many of the Mexican kids at that school were from families who also had migrated from El Llano. It seemed the whole El Llano community had been transplanted to Napa Valley. This was because some arrived and would get jobs in the vineyards, and they would arrange for family members to join them. Still others came because they knew of others in El Llano who had gotten jobs in Napa.

I didn't know personally the other Mexican kids my age, but I knew of their families because my parents knew them. I knew who was who from my hometown. I had a few white friends from my elementary school who were with me in middle school, but because there were so many more Mexican kids whose families we knew, I started hanging around more with the Mexicans.

What I noticed, however, was that most of the Mexican kids didn't have the academic skills that I had, having gone to a predominantly white elementary school where I had been in the more advanced classes. By contrast, most of the Mexicans had gone to bilingual schools in Napa like Westwood, where I went my first two years. But because the classes there were still mainly taught in Spanish, the Mexican kids hadn't learned sufficient English to do well in middle school. The content in their bilingual classes was also not the same as in the mostly white classes, and so this left the Mexican kids even more unprepared academically.

To help these kids, my English teacher assigned me and a couple of other more advanced Mexican American students to tutor some of the Mexican students. There was tracking at my school, and most of the Mexican students were in the remedial classes and the non-advanced ones.

In the middle school and the elementary school, my teachers were all white. The only exception was a Mexican American who was a counselor at the middle school.

Because there were so many Mexicans at my middle school, there were a number of Latino clubs. There was a La Raza Club and a Latino and Latina Crew Club. I joined the Latina Crew in both seventh and eighth grade. We mostly talked about school issues or would raise money for our T-shirts and sweaters. It wasn't a big club, but it was intended to develop leadership and to get us acquainted with the idea of joining clubs once we got to high school.

It was in middle school that I became more ethnically conscious of myself as being Mexican. I knew, of course, that my family was Mexican, but because I had gone to a mostly white elementary school, I had developed a view of myself as white. The only place I spoke Spanish was at home. I didn't know how to act among other Mexicans.

But in middle school, my perceptions of myself began to change. I began to realize that there were differences between white and Mexican students. This involved the way they dressed, the way they spoke, and even the lunches they brought to school. I began to realize that I was more like the Mexicans than the whites, among other things because I was bilingual. I was a good bilingual speaker. In middle school, I learned what it was to be a Mexican from other Mexican students.

I became even more involved with the Mexican kids because I tutored some of them. This tutoring actually became an elective class for me. Students could take a certain number of electives, and I was allowed to count my tutoring in English as one of these classes. My first period, I would tutor about twenty students. There were students who were still struggling with English. I could see this very well, especially since my very first boyfriend was in this class. He spoke and read English but not yet well enough to be put into regular classes.

One thing I became more conscious of in middle school was the Mexican gangs that began to spring up in Napa around some of the middle school–age kids. Some, of course, were also high school age. They were mostly guys. They were a visible presence with well-pressed khakis. They were gangsters. There were two principal gangs in Napa. One was called Norteños. They wore red bandannas across their forehead, and for some reason, the Roman number XIV was associated with them. The Norteños were further differentiated by the fact that they were second-generation U.S.-born Mexicans. Then there were the Sureños, who were kids raised in Mexico and who had come with their families to the United States. Their color was blue, and their number that they tagged on themselves and in graffiti was XIII. The gangs never bothered me, but I certainly was aware of them.

There are two high schools in the Napa area. There's Napa High School, which is the older school, and then there's Vintage High School, which is the newer one. Napa High School is predominantly Mexican, while Vintage is mostly white. I wound up going to Vintage because that's where the school district assigned students who lived in American Canyon to attend. My parents also didn't like the reputation of Napa. It wasn't because it was Mexican but because they believed it wasn't strong academically. It had tracking. It had more gang-related problems. Going to Vintage also was easier because my parents didn't have to drive me there, and I didn't yet drive myself.

So I went to Vintage. I switched again from a Mexican school to a white school. But because in elementary and middle school, I had been in white advanced classes, this switch didn't really affect me. Where it did affect me was at lunch or break times when my Mexican friends from middle school weren't around. Most of my friends went to Napa High. They felt it was an easier school and one with less discipline. This included my boyfriend, whom I soon didn't see anymore.

There was, of course, some Mexicans at Vintage. I would say that when I entered as a freshman, about 10 percent were Mexican, but in four years this rose to about 30 percent. Some of the Mexican kids—not all, but some—weren't interested in their education. In fact, there was a continuation of the gangs into high school. Gang members at Vintage were Norteños, while those at Napa High were Sureños.

But I soon met other Mexican American girls like myself who were interested in doing well. They knew the gang members, including girls who belonged to the gangs, but they themselves were not gang members.

I continued to do well in my classes. I was again in the advanced and honors classes with mostly white students. I didn't have particular favorite classes, but I got As in all of them.

In high school I participated in some extracurricular activities. My greatest involvement was with MEChA [Movimiento Estudiantil Chicano de Aztlán], which some of the Mexican students had organized. I didn't attend their meetings during my freshman year, but in my sophomore year one of my new friends asked me to go with her to one of the meetings. I did, and I liked what I saw. I liked the fact that they discussed civil rights and student rights. I had already become interested in such issues because of my uncle, who was living with us at the time. He was my dad's cousin and had been involved in union activities in Mexico City. When he came here, he worked as a gardener for a big hotel in St. Helena. However, he hurt his back and was compensated by getting help to go to school. He enrolled at Napa Valley City College and helped organize and became president of the Hispano Club on that campus. This was around the controversy of Proposition 187 in 1994, and he would talk to me about these issues and of the importance of Latinos organizing. He also became involved with the United Farm Workers. He encouraged me to get involved with MEChA.

It was through my uncle that MEChA helped to bring Dolores Huerta to speak at Napa Valley City College. The high school wouldn't let us have her speak on our campus because they thought it was too political, but through my uncle we helped to organize a lecture for her at the college. Our club advisor, who was a Spanish teacher of Mexican descent, got in trouble for all of this. He actually was also from El Llano. He was put on probation, even though we protested against this. He was on probation, however, for only a short period.

But the visit by Dolores Huerta was a huge success. We got a chance to meet and talk with her. I have a picture with her, and she signed my MEChA T-shirt. It was incredible. I had heard about her especially from my uncle, but I had no idea what a powerful speaker she was. She is a tiny woman but has a very strong voice. At that time. MEChA was made up of all girls, and she was happy that it was all women because it would help us develop our leadership.

In my junior year, I was elected vice president of MEChA, but because one of our co-presidents couldn't be too active, I stepped in and basically functioned as one of our co-presidents. In my senior year, I was elected co-president of MEChA.

My parents had no trouble with my involvement with MEChA. They're not very politically aware. They know the things that will affect them, but that's all. They supported what I did and had confidence in my decisions. I've always been responsible for my own actions. When they used to have to go to work early in the mornings, even at a very early age I took care of myself. In the second grade, for example, I would walk to school by myself. I know that's not good, but I did it. So my parents knew I was responsible and assumed that I would do the right thing.

As part of our involvement with MEChA, we organized a Cinco de Mayo celebration where we had music, *ballet folklórico* dancing, and food. We educated students about the historical meaning of the Cinco de Mayo, which was not Mexican Independence Day but celebrated the Mexican victory over the invading French army in 1862. As part of this activity, we also had a jalapeño eating contest. It was funny. Our Cinco de Mayo grew to a weeklong series of events.

Our goal was to promote appreciation for cultural diversity, and I think we succeeded. Our administration, despite the tension over the Dolores Huerta visit, appreciated our work. We were one of the most active clubs on campus.

At home, our family culture is very Mexican, although some things are changing. We celebrate all of the Mexican holidays. We also like to have family gatherings with our uncles, aunts, and cousins who now also live in the Napa area. When I graduated from high school, our home was filled with relatives.

We celebrate Christmas by going back to El Llano. We also go back because December 20 is the day of the fiestas in our town. It's a big holiday to honor the immigrants who have gone to the United States. A lot of the immigrants return for the fiestas and for Christmas. So everyone who now lives in Napa Valley returns. This meant that I had to leave school for two weeks right before the Christmas holidays. The school gave me permission as long as I did independent study and did the work assigned to me. Because I was a good student, I did the work, but other Mexican students who left for this time didn't, so many fell further behind.

We started going back regularly when I was in elementary school. By then, we not only had our *micas*—our green cards—but my parents and I were now also U.S. citizens. My little sister and brother were born in the U.S., so they were already citizens. My parents became citizens because they didn't want to be harassed at the border when they went back to Mexico and returned. They also wanted to be able to vote. Under the law, when they became U.S. citizens, I automatically also became a citizen. But my parents wanted me to have my official citizenship papers, so I, along with them, took the citizenship test. I helped them study for it, especially the history part of it. We all passed. I became a citizen my junior year in high school.

When we went back to El Llano for Christmas, we used to drive all of the way. However, this changed when there started to be more drug-related incidents. Since then, we fly back. We have a house there that my dad built over the years on a *terreno* that his father gave him. So we actually have two homes that we own on both sides of the border.

At home, our dishes are still very Mexican. We always have beans and tortillas because those are my dad's favorite foods. At Thanksgiving, instead of a regular turkey, my mother makes turkey *carnitas*. They're delicious. But our Mexican diet has had some adjustments. One of my dad's friends from work married a white woman, and she became friends with my mom. This woman taught my mom how to cook lasagna and spaghetti and to make Taco Bell tacos with the hard shells that we never had before. Mexican tacos are always soft tacos.

We as a family also started going out once a week for dinner. It was a big treat to go to Pizza Hut or McDonald's. In this way, gradually our dietary habits have changed, even though our basic meals are still Mexican.

We're Catholic but not hard-core Catholics. We go to Mass about every other week. My siblings and I have all been baptized and confirmed and have received our First Communion. At the same time, we've been affected by other spiritual influences.

For example, a few years ago my little brother started having some medical problems. He would cry all of the time. He wouldn't eat. He was nonresponsive. My parents became very desperate. They took him to doctors and he went to the hospital for a period of time, but nothing cured him. So my parents decided to take him to a *curandero* in Nayarit, Mexico. A *curandero* is a folk healer who uses herbs and other potions along with certain rituals to heal people of all sorts of physical and emotional problems.

I remember that the ritual performed by the *curandero* on my brother was very strange. He blew smoke on my brother as a way of getting the bad spirit out of him. Whatever the *curandero* did, it worked. My brother was healed, and he's perfectly normal now.

It was also at this time when my brother was ill that my mother appealed to our Catholic priest, also a Mexican, to help my brother. But he didn't do much. When my mother asked him to say some prayers over my brother, he said he didn't know what prayer to say. My mother became disillusioned with the priest. It was also at this time that one of her friends introduced her to a Latino Christian, a Protestant minister. He was Salvadoran but was raised in Mexico. He may have been a Pentecostal. He came to our home and prayed over my brother. He gave my parents hope. As a result, we started going to his Christian church. We didn't stop going to our Catholic church, but we alternated Sundays. I found it interesting to attend the Bible readings at each service. The Christian one would have more extensive Bible readings, while the Catholic one would have shorter ones.

At home, we have an *altarcito*—a home altar. It's actually quite elaborate, and it's dedicated to Our Lady of Guadalupe. It features a picture of her with Juan Diego kneeling in front of her. My dad had me make a backdrop out of wood for the picture, and so I made it out of board and painted it with golden rays that come out of La Virgen. We have artificial roses around the image. It's very nice. We also have a very large crucifix on one of our walls. It's as big as a door.

With my parents, I speak Spanish, and they speak Spanish to us. But with my sister and brother, I speak both languages. My sister, however, is less bilingual than I am. When I speak to her in Spanish and we can't figure out some words, we then go to English. With my little brother, we're trying to teach him to speak in both English and Spanish. If he learns a new word in English, we tell him how to say it in Spanish.

I would say that I've had a strict traditional Mexican upbringing with respect to things like discipline. At the same time, at a very early age, I've had to take certain responsibilities so that my parents trust me. They know that I'm a good girl and that I won't get into any trouble.

Actually, I'm also what might be called a "radical daughter." By this I mean that I've never accepted the traditional Mexican role for women. I've always been very independent, and while I help around the house, I don't accept a subordinate role for women. I'm always on my dad's case about him not helping around the house. I always tell my dad, "Why don't you get up and put your plate in the sink?" I think I get my "radical" views on gender in general just by having observed how my dad acts around the house. He's a good father and husband, but he does have this view that it's the women who have to do all of the domestic chores. I refuse to accept this.

But my dad's views don't extend to dating and boyfriends. He's never been particularly strict on this because he trusts me. The only thing he insists is that if I go out on a date, I have to be back by 10 P.M. So I do have a curfew. But he doesn't insist on meeting and approving my boyfriends.

I've dated Mexican boys, but one of my boyfriends in high school was white. My parents had no problem with me dating the white boy. One of my last boyfriends was Mexican and an ESL student. He disliked school. I knew that we had different values, and I eventually broke up with him because I knew that this relationship wasn't going to work. I wanted more; he wanted less. He never graduated from high school and is now working construction.

I didn't work until my senior year in high school. I was taking a computer graphic art class, and my teacher owned his own business called Napa Fermentation Supplies. He and his wife sold home beer- and wine-making supplies. He hired me to be their helper. I answered phones and did billing and other office duties. I even learned a little about making wine.

I started very early thinking about going to college. In high school, I knew I was going to college. That was my goal. I knew that education was the way I was going to succeed. I didn't consider what my parents did to be bad, but I didn't want to come home tired all of the time. I wanted a profession. That's why I always thought of college.

My dream of going to college started even before high school. In eighth grade, I was in the Upward Bound program at my school. The counselors talked to us about college and told us to begin to think about it. They took us on a field trip to visit some colleges. Then when I was a junior in high school, I was in a program called Summer Search. It provided scholarships to allow juniors to attend different universities and enroll in college courses for the summer. I went to Cornell University on such a scholarship during the summer before my senior year. It was a six-week program, and I took statistics and a writing class plus a biology seminar. I got a B+ in both classes, and the seminar was not graded. It was a wonderful experience. It was my first time on an airplane. My parents supported my going because it had to do with education. The trip was made easier because another Mexican girl from Napa High was also part of the program, and so we went together. There were many white rich kids there, but there were also some minority students, including several Mexicans. Most of the kids from California were Mexican, which really blew people's minds because they thought everyone from California was a blond surfer.

In my senior year, I began to prepare my applications to several colleges. The deadlines were in November, but this was also the time when my uncle, who had first come to Napa, died. He also lived in Napa Valley. He got a brain tumor and died. It was a hectic time with the funeral and all this. The result was that I hastily did my applications and probably didn't write as strong a personal statement as I would have wanted. I think because of this I didn't get into my top choices, such as UCLA and

Berkeley. Fortunately, I did get accepted into UCSB, and it has turned out to be a great choice.

My parents were happy about my acceptance, although they really didn't understand what going to a university was all about. But, as usual, they supported me. What they did know was that I had been spared the fate of too many other Mexican girls who had either dropped out of school or gotten pregnant or both.

They were very excited about my high school graduation. I was the first in my immediate family to get a high school education.

That summer I attended the UCSB orientation. My dad drove me down. I didn't know anyone at first, but I soon made a couple of friends at the orientations. These became my close friends during my freshman year.

I lived in a university apartment off campus my first year. I roomed with four other girls, and we shared a living room and a kitchen. My roommate was white and we got along, but we didn't do things together. She liked to party a lot and often came back drunk. I enjoy partying, but I'm not into drinking.

I found college to be everything I wanted and more. I haven't been disappointed. I'm enjoying it and doing well. I think going to Cornell the previous year really helped me adjust to college-level work. I'm majoring in Chicano studies because I want to be a high school teacher and to be able to teach about Mexico and the Chicano experience. I want students to know what it means to be a Chicano. I was acquainted with the term "Chicano" in high school. In MEChA, we referred to ourselves as Chicanas and Chicanos. Even though I was born in Mexico, I consider myself to be a Chicana.

I get homesick sometimes, but it's too far and expensive to go back home regularly. I know my parents really miss me. But I've adjusted now into my sophomore and junior year. I look forward to the rest of my career at UCSB.

Alma Cortez-Lara graduated from the University of California, Santa Barbara, in 2006. She obtained an M.A.—the first in her family to do so—and teaching credential from Pepperdine University Graduate School of Education and Psychology. She teaches social studies and Spanish at Justin-Siena High School in Napa, California, and is active with Latinos Unidos del Vale de Napa y Solano. She married Raul Gallegos in 2011.

ÁLVARO SÁNCHEZ

My father, Apolinar Sánchez, was born around 1954 in the small town of San Cosme in the state of Tlaxcala in Mexico. Tlaxcala is in the center of Mexico, just north of Mexico City. I actually don't know much about his side of the family. Both of my paternal grandparents died when I was still very young. I don't even remember them.

My dad's parents were peasants. They farmed a little land where they had their house and farm. They raised and sold maize.

My dad went to elementary school in San Cosme. He has only a sixth grade education since that's all that was available in the local elementary school. To go to secondary school, you had to go to the next largest town. My dad wanted to keep going to school because he liked it, but conditions wouldn't allow it. His parents didn't have the money to pay for his going further in his education.

My dad has always told me that going to school represented the fondest years of his life. When I started school, he told me (and still does), "Take advantage of this time when you're free from the stress of having to work and earn a living." He still remembers some of his teachers who helped him. It's unfortunate that he couldn't continue in his education.

Being the youngest in a family of four brothers and four sisters, my dad was also needed to stay home and help his parents on the farm since all of his older siblings had left home and gone to Mexico City.

My mother, Victoria Sánchez, also grew up in San Cosme. Her family has a weird connection with mine. Her mother, my maternal grandmother, had my mother and her sister from another marriage. My grandmother then later met and married one of my father's older brothers. So my maternal grandpa is also my uncle. This is a bit confusing, but this is the history of my family.

My parents met because of these family connections and because they were both growing up in San Cosme. However, my mother's family at some point left to live in Mexico City.

My mother has slightly more education than my dad. She has an eighth grade education because she attended schools in Mexico City. However, unlike my dad, she didn't enjoy being in school.

I'm not sure when and how my dad started courting my mother. It's possible that when my mother's family paid visits to relatives in San Cosme and because of the ties with my father's family that both my mother and father got to know each other more.

I do know that when my dad was about twenty-five, he decided to also go to Mexico City and marry my mother. I'm not sure of the year of their marriage.

After my parents married, my dad started a career as a singer. Music apparently was always very important for his family. He and his brother along with some cousins started a *conjunto*, La Sonora Dinamar, a musical group, playing *cumbias* and salsa. My dad was the lead singer. He still has a beautiful voice. They actually did quite well and toured throughout Mexico. Their big success came when they were invited to perform in New York in the early 1980s with some famous Latino bands. My mother went along. I was too young to travel, so my brothers and I stayed with one of my aunts.

I was born February 17, 1981. My two older brothers were born some years earlier. My brother closest to me is ten years older, so there is a big gap between me and them.

Shortly after I was born, my dad stopped doing his music. I don't know why. It's possible he found it hard to make a living this way. He found a job as a laborer with the Firestone Tire Company in Mexico City. At the same time, my mom and one of my aunts and an uncle started a little restaurant.

However, after a couple of years my dad got laid off. By then one of his sisters had already come to Los Angeles, so my dad decided also to cross the border. I was three years old then.

My dad didn't have any trouble crossing because he still had his passport from when he went to New York. However, later when his visa expired, he became undocumented.

Living with his sister and her family in South Central LA, my father started working at an auto body shop. He's continued doing this kind of work until now.

My mother didn't like being left behind, so she soon demanded that my father send for us. In a year's time, she and I also crossed the border.

Because my two older brothers were in school, they stayed and lived with one of our aunts. Two years later, they also crossed.

My mother, like my dad, had a passport since she had also gone to New York a couple of years before. The problem was that I didn't have any papers. When we got to Tijuana, my parents arranged for some friends of ours already living in LA who had their papers to meet us on the Mexican side. My mother crossed first and had no problem because of her passport. I stayed behind with the friends. They had a son my age who had been born in the U.S. The deal was for us to switch. I assumed his identity and would drive across with their family. Their son would stay in Tijuana with some other friends until his parents went back for him.

"Don't say anything if they talk to you," they told me before driving across. "If they ask you something, just nod your head."

We drove up to the U.S. Immigration port where they asked our identity. I don't remember if I responded "American," but I do remember that the officer asked me, "Where are you going?" Somehow, despite the fact that I had been told to remain silent, I uttered, "Disneyland." That seemed to satisfy the officer and, of course, relieved the apprehensions of our friends driving me across. We proceeded on and picked up my mother, and the friend's son was retrieved from Tijuana; we were on our way to Los Angeles.

We moved in with my aunt in South Central. Actually, because my aunt had five kids although no husband, she and my dad agreed to rent a house nearby that would accommodate both families. It was in a predominantly African American neighborhood near Martin Luther King Boulevard, very close to the LA Coliseum. We lived there for a while until my aunt moved and we couldn't afford the rent by ourselves. There was a refurbished garage next door that had been converted into an apartment. The rent was lower, and we moved into it.

One of the first memories I have of living in South Central is of this little black kid. His name was Thomas. He lived on our block. He started coming over to play with me. However, we couldn't understand each other. I couldn't understand his English, and he couldn't understand my Spanish. But we could still play together, and we did. My parents met Thomas's parents, and despite their language differences, they started to socialize. They would invite us for barbecues. Soon I had other African American friends from my neighborhood.

I started school almost as soon as we arrived in LA. My parents put me in preschool. Most of the other kids were African American with a few other Latinos. It wasn't a bilingual school, so I struggled at first, but after about three months I was speaking English pretty well.

From preschool I then went to elementary school at the 60th Street School. I'm not sure this is the correct name of the school, but it's close. I went there for kindergarten through second grade. I remember that when I graduated from kindergarten, there was a little celebration at the school. I was excited about graduating. My mom bought me this little new outfit. My parents went with me to the little graduation ceremony.

I also have memories of one of my first elementary teachers. She was this very large African American lady. She was awesome and a lot of fun. She just had this way of making me feel comfortable in class. She wasn't intimidating at all.

There were some Latino students at my school, but because I already had my core of African American friends, I didn't interact with the Latinos.

I think I was an average student during these early years in elementary school. I wasn't excelling in anything, but I wasn't doing badly either. But I remember my mom saying that she was amazed that I was even average since I was just learning English and had no help at home with my homework since neither of my parents spoke English.

My parents had this idea that I was having difficulty with English. This was because I was shy to use it around them or when we would go out. We would go to McDonald's, and my dad would say in Spanish, "Álvaro, you order for all of us because you know English." I didn't want to because I was shy. "But we thought you knew English," they would say.

After about three years, my dad decided it was time to return to Mexico. He had saved enough money to try and start a business in Mexico City. Some of my cousins who had also come to the U.S. had already returned and started up a clothing manufacturing business. This encouraged my dad about returning. For him, success would be back in Mexico, not in the U.S. My mother, on the other hand, was more hesitant. She wasn't sure how we would fare in Mexico. She also had heard about the amnesty for undocumented immigrants that was being discussed in the late 1980s, and she felt that we might qualify since by then the entire family was undocumented. She was worried if we went back to Mexico and then decided to return to the U.S. that we wouldn't be eligible for amnesty. Despite my mother's concerns, my dad prevailed, and we went back around 1988.

We took most of our stuff and drove in a used van my dad had bought to the border at El Paso. There, before we crossed back into Mexico, the U.S. Immigration officials wanted to inspect our van. My dad didn't understand what they wanted and so my older brother translated for him. I was scared.

"If we don't let them inspect, they say we'll be put in jail," my brother told my dad.

They inspected, found nothing suspicious, and let us cross. I just remember the long, hot trip and being cramped in that van with all of our possessions.

They first thing I remember when we finally arrived in Mexico City was being frightened by the huge head statue on one of the avenues. I later learned it was a statue of Benito Juárez, one of Mexico's greatest presidents. "Where are we?" I asked my mom, shaking with fear. "This is Mexico," my mother said, trying to calm me down. I was crying. Los Angeles was clean and orderly, and here was this huge Mexican city with chaos all around me.

"We're probably going to get pulled over with our California plates," my dad said. And sure enough, we were. But my dad was already prepared. He knew this would happen, and he had a *mordida* [bribe] all ready. After a discussion with the police officer, my dad gave him a few dollars and we were allowed to go on. We moved into an apartment close to the airport. We could have purchased the place, but my dad thought he had better hold on to our savings. He later regretted that decision when having some property would have helped us financially.

My parents ended up joining our cousins in their garment business. The business really took off. It became a family-run business. My dad worked at different jobs while my mom supervised the seamstresses. We were all making money. My cousins were buying houses and new cars. We were vacationing in Oaxaca and Cuernavaca.

But then, by the end of 1992, things began to go sour. First, my cousins were now expanding the business to include non-family partners. As they brought in new people, they began laying off family members. This was cruel because they were family. My dad and mom kept their jobs but resented what was happening. The second problem nearly did the business in. This was the peso devaluation of the early 1990s, in conjunction with bad accounting and some bad business deals on the part of our cousins. They ended up owing millions of dollars. The company fell apart. We couldn't even afford our apartment anymore, and so we were forced to move into my maternal grandmother's house.

These hard times are what made my dad decide that we should return to LA. Before we left Mexico again, I, of course, spent a few years in Mexican schools. I should have started in third grade there, but after they gave me some proficiency tests, they concluded that I couldn't do the same work as the other third graders. I wasn't able to do multiplication and division. I didn't know about those things. I was put back a year and had to take second grade all over again.

I didn't find the change from an English-language school to a Spanish-language school to be all that different. I spoke only Spanish at home, so I knew the language. I could speak and read Spanish. The only problem I had at first was writing in Spanish, because I had no experience in it.

In my four and a half years in a Mexican school, I did well. As in LA, I think I was an average student. But being an average student in Mexico, I think, was harder than being one in LA. The classes were harder, and even though my parents obviously knew Spanish, they still couldn't help me because they were working all the time.

I found that I didn't miss LA. At first, I was fearful of Mexico City. But once I became adjusted, I came to like the city.

One thing that surprised me was how fast I began to lose my English, since I rarely used it now. Words here and there were familiar, but I couldn't put together a sentence anymore.

I did not react positively to my parents' decision to return to LA. I had really taken to Mexico City. My memories today are tremendous of those years. I came up with the excuse that I should be allowed to finish primary school in Mexico, and that would mean staying one more year. I would continue living with my grandmother. My parents at first objected to this, but they finally agreed. I think they saw the advantage of being able to go back and find a place to live and jobs without having to worry about me and my schooling in LA. My brothers by now were old enough to be on their own. One of my older brothers on his own had already returned to LA. He had married a girl from Mexico City, and they were living in LA. My other older brother had also gotten married in Mexico City and decided to stay there.

I really enjoyed the additional year in Mexico City. I really fell in love with the city. I also had more freedom to go out with people who took me all around and to places I had never been before. It was a really good experience.

Somehow my parents were able to renew their visas to cross this second time. Instead of returning to South Central, they went to East LA where my older brother and his wife were living. They moved in with them. My dad found a job with Guess, the clothing company, where my brother also worked. He started cutting denim. My mom got a job as a seamstress in a downtown garment factory.

In a year's time, in 1992, I joined them. My parents were able to get for me a temporary visa. My brother who had remained in Mexico brought me over with his tourist visa. My visa was also a tourist one and was good for only three days. But I never returned.

When I returned to LA, I was twelve years old and ready to start junior high. I attended Robert Louis Stevenson Junior High in East LA. My biggest adjustment this time was a cultural one. In Mexico, I went to school dressed more traditionally. Young boys were expected to tuck in their shirts, wear tighter pants, and look proper. But in school here, that's not how the boys dressed. This, in the early 1990s, was the cholo fashion days, with the big, oversized jeans and untucked gray and white shirts. Boy, did I get the looks when I showed up at school dressed differently. I also in Mexico always had a briefcase, but here all the kids had backpacks. It took me a little while to adjust to these cultural differences.

In school, because I had forgotten most of my English, I was put in ESL classes. But it didn't take me long to once again learn English. Toward the end of my first year back, I was once again conversant in English. At the same time I was picking up English, I was still forced to be in ESL classes. I became very frustrated because I wasn't learning in those classes. They were teaching me to say "house" when I already knew how to say "house." In fact, after a few months I knew how to say a lot of words in English, but the ESL teacher still taught like I didn't know much English at all. I kept asking my counselor to put me in regular English classes, but she wouldn't. In ESL they teach you English, but the rest of your academic classes are in Spanish. That was OK, except in these classes, like in math, I had already learned the material in Mexico. For a number of months, I didn't do any studying because I already knew the material. My parents began to wonder why I wasn't doing my homework. I got straight As in these classes. It took me a year and a half to get out of ESL. It wasn't until the middle of the eighth grade that I moved into the regular English-language classes.

In 1994, when I was in junior high, Proposition 187 became a big political issue. If passed, it would deny public social services, such as in hospitals, to undocumented immigrants. It would also deny public education to the undocumented children of undocumented immigrants. This was all very threatening and frightening to me and to my parents. We lived in fear of being reported to the immigration people. I was taking the bus to school, but we heard rumors that the *migra*—immigration officers—were rounding up kids at bus stops or were going into the schools looking for undocumented students. I was terrified. I worried about taking the bus and having someone come up to me and say, "Let me see your papers." I didn't have any. I didn't want to go to school. But my mother calmed me down.

"You know what?" she said, "You can't live afraid. You just have to go out there. Just go to school and act normal. Don't be afraid."

But it was hard not to be afraid.

Fortunately, nothing happened to me or to my parents.

Our anxieties increased when Proposition 187 passed. I knew it was hard on my parents. They felt really helpless because it was like they couldn't do anything. Even if they wanted to fix their papers, they couldn't do it then under that political climate. They also couldn't protect me by taking me to school because they had to work. I remember my dad saying, "I can't even feel the strength of going out there and voting against it because I can't vote!"

To this day they still haven't been able to regularize their papers. I still haven't been able to, either. We had this huge hope for our amnesty after both President George W. Bush and President Vicente Fox of Mexico early in their administrations seemed to be leaning toward an agreement, but then the opposition of conservatives plus 9/11 ended all of our hope.

I attended Garfield High School in East LA. After junior high, we moved closer to the border between East LA and Montebello. That's very close to Garfield. We needed more room. At the previous house closer to my junior high school, it was very congested. Besides my family, there was my brother and his wife, my uncle and his wife, and then four single male cousins in another room. In our new house that we rented, we no longer lived with all these cousins. I didn't have a room of my own until I was in the tenth grade, when my uncle and his wife left. Before I graduated from high school, we moved again to another house in the same area that instead of renting we could now buy. That's where my parents still live.

My memories of Garfield High are good ones. For the most part, it was a typical high school. A lot of people I meet today express shock that I went there. They have this horrible vision of it with all of these images of gang warfare.

"I don't know what movie you watched," I tell them, "because I didn't experience any of that."

Sure, there were cholos, but we never had straight-out violence.

Academically, I was doing above-average work. My parents continued to be supportive. "Just keep doing what you're doing," they said. "We know you can succeed." They were always encouraging me. "Just keep going to school," they'd say. "That's why we're working, so you can have a better future."

Because of my parents' support, both morally and financially, I didn't have to get a part-time job until the end of my senior year and that's only because I wanted to.

I did pretty well in all of my classes. Perhaps the science classes were more challenging; they were also very interesting to me. That's been a pattern for me. Classes that are not as interesting to me are the ones I struggle with the most. The classes I liked the most were the social sciences and history.

I didn't participate in too many extracurricular activities my first couple of years. Then, as a junior and senior, I became more active. I joined the French club and MEChA, and I was on the swimming team. I also joined the volleyball team for a short while.

I enjoyed swimming, even though we had a very small team. In my senior year, we had only four male swimmers. I realized that Garfield wasn't going to win any competitions. Part of our problem was that we didn't even have a swimming pool at our school. To practice, we had to be bused to the community pool.

It was through swimming that I got my first job. My coach recommended that I take a water safety instructor course. I took it at nearby Cerritos College and passed it. I received a teaching certificate so I could teach swimming that summer. As it turned out, they hired me at Cerritos. My job started on my graduation day.

I don't remember why I joined MEChA. I only went to some meetings. I didn't care for the heavy rhetoric of the student leaders. I understand criticizing the government, but this wasn't constructive criticism. I saw it as just being a whole bashing session. The leader would just get up and rant and rave about the government. It was just listening to this guy letting out his frustration. There were about forty members, but the meetings put me off so I attended less and less.

I had no idea attending Garfield that it had been one of the schools that had participated in the historic blowouts or walkouts by Chicano students in 1968. We never learned that at Garfield. It wasn't until I went to college that I learned this. However, I did know that Garfield was the school where Jaime Escalante had taught. He was a brilliant teacher who in the 1980s was able to help a sizable number of Chicano students get perfect or near perfect scores on the AP calculus test. His story was later made into the film *Stand and Deliver*. I also knew that Garfield was the school that Oscar De La Hoya, the boxing champ, had attended. But I didn't know about the blowouts.

When I graduated from high school, my undocumented status came back to haunt me. I wanted to go to a four-year institution. I had a 3.4 GPA, and although I didn't do as well as I wanted to on the SATs, I felt that I would be admitted to at least a Cal State campus. Up to this point, my undocumented status hadn't really affected me. It posed an inconvenience here and there. For example, in order to play sports, you had to get school insurance, which meant you had to provide a social security card. I didn't have one and neither did my parents because we didn't have permanent legal status. I got around this by making up a fake social security number.

But to apply to a four-year college and to request financial aid would mean a more involved check of my background. I could have applied as an international student, but the fees for such a student are ridiculously high. I talked with my high school counselor and was frank with her about my status. She sympathized but confirmed that it would be very difficult if not impossible for me to get into a four-year school being an undocumented immigrant.

"The only other possibility for you," she said, "is to go to a community college while you try to get permanent residency. The community colleges don't check as thoroughly."

I was devastated. My dream of college seemed shattered. But what she said made sense. I reluctantly ended up enrolling that fall at Cerritos College in Norwalk.

It still wasn't easy getting into Cerritos. I sought further counseling from my swim coach. It turned out that he had gone through a similar experience.

"Look," he instructed me, "what you do is that you state you're a U.S. citizen, and if they ask for ID, you tell them that you forgot it. Chances are they won't ask you to produce it."

"But how will I pay for my fees?" I asked.

"Just go to the financial aid office," he replied, "and ask for a fee waiver. Don't ask for financial assistance, because that's more complicated."

I did what he said and it worked. I was asked for my social security number and again I just made it up. I still don't have a real social security number; that has posed a problem.

I spent two years at Cerritos College. I didn't care too much at first for the classes and was still concerned about not getting into a four-year college. I lost focus. I just concentrated more on my job. Again, my swim coach was helpful to me. Besides helping me get the summer job as a swim instructor at Cerritos, he arranged for me to have an interview at the local YMCA. I first started there as a volunteer lifeguard, but within two months, they hired me as a paid lifeguard. At the Y, I didn't put down that I was a U.S. citizen, only that I had my green card and permanent residency. I just presented a fake green card purchased in East LA. Such cards are readily available.

Even though now I had a salary, what helped also was that I continued to live at home. By now my other older brother and his wife had moved in with us as well. Between my parents, who were working, and my two older brothers, who had pretty good jobs, we had more to meet our needs. As a result, even though I contributed here and there to the family income, I was able to keep more of my pay for my own expenses. Of course, this also helped my parents.

I began to think again about going to a four-year school in 2000. It had to do with my girlfriend. I had met her my senior year, and we had become a couple before I graduated. I thought that after I graduated, our relationship would just dwindle away, but we actually became more serious. She was an excellent student, and I knew she would have her pick of colleges. Unlike me, she was a U.S. citizen of Mexican background. She was accepted to all of the schools she applied to, including Berkeley and UCLA. She chose Berkeley.

Her going to Berkeley made me reassess where I was. If we were going to stay together, I knew that I would have to continue my own education and get into a four-year school. She was very interested in education, and it was important for her to be with someone who also valued education. After she left for Berkeley, I was really now motivated to continue with college.

I began to take my classes at Cerritos more seriously. I had started off by taking only one class and focusing on my job. Now, I enrolled in more classes and those that would help me transfer to a UC campus. I took some sociology classes and found that I really enjoyed the subject and began to consider it for an eventual major.

For my second year at Cerritos, I was apart that whole year from my girlfriend, who was now at Berkeley. I drove up and visited her from time to time and, of course, saw her when she returned for holidays. Still, that year took a toll on us. We realized that if our relationship was going to continue, we needed to be together.

We decided for the next year to live together in the Bay Area. We found a place in Oakland and I transferred to Chabot College, another community college where I could complete the courses I needed to be accepted at a UC campus.

My decision to move out and live with my girlfriend caused some tensions with my parents, especially my mother. Although she likes to think that she's forward-thinking, she's still somewhat traditional. She did not care for my living with my girlfriend out of wedlock. I tried to explain to her how serious I was about my girlfriend and how under other circumstances I would already be engaged or married to her. My mom adjusted to my relationship and began to realize how serious I was and was further consoled that I was staying in school.

Going to Chabot was OK, but I didn't like Oakland. I didn't feel comfortable there. I knew that despite my girlfriend, I would not enjoy going to Berkeley even if I got in, which was a stretch. I had good grades but probably not enough to get into Berkeley. That year as I was finishing my AA degree, I applied only to UCLA, UC Santa Barbara, and San Diego.

My girlfriend supported me. She believed it was up to me; it was my decision. She knew that this was how I had supported her when she decided to go to Berkeley.

"Do whatever you need to do," she said. "We'll try to work it out and do whatever it takes to stay together."

In retrospect, she took this really hard. She thought it also had something to do with her, that I didn't want to live with her anymore. She understands now, however, that it wasn't her but it was that I just couldn't live in the Bay Area.

In applying to UC campuses, I still had the problem of my undocumented status. Fortunately, in the UC application there's a provision that if you're not a permanent resident but are in the process of becoming one that that you can not only be accepted but be eligible for in-state fees, which are much lower than out-of-state ones that I might have to pay if I was just considered a Mexican citizen. One of the accepted processes for becoming a U.S. resident, according to the UC application, was if you were going to get married to a U.S. citizen. My girlfriend and I agreed that I should put down that we were going to get married. We had talked about getting married, but we also knew that it was important for me to get into a UC school.

The next few months were anxious as I waited to hear about my applications. Starting in March I began to religiously go home as early as I could, open the mailbox, and hope to see something positive. I didn't even know what an acceptance letter looked like. I had never seen one.

"It's not a letter," my girlfriend told me, "it's a package."

So I looked for a package each day. One day, I got home, opened the mailbox, and saw this big package. It was from UC San Diego. I was thrilled. I was accepted. My dream of going to a four-year school, and especially a UC school, had come true!

I couldn't wait to tell someone—my girlfriend, my parents, my brothers, anyone—but my girlfriend was still at school and my parents were working. I had to hold it in until my girlfriend arrived. We jumped up and down in joy. Finally, I had one of the things I wanted in life.

In a day or so, I received even more good news when the package from UC Santa Barbara arrived. By then, I wasn't too disappointed when only a letter from UCLA arrived. I had a feeling that I wouldn't get into UCLA. But I wasn't sad because I had two other great choices.

I think I made my choice between San Diego and Santa Barbara primarily due to familiarity with the two areas. I didn't know San Diego very well but knew it was a beautiful city and that it might fit me very well. On the other hand, I knew Santa Barbara much better and had friends going to UCSB. The clincher was that Santa Barbara would make it much easier for me to drive up as often as I could to visit my girlfriend. The drive from San Diego would be twice as long. I accepted UCSB's offer.

That spring I received my AA degree from Chabot College. It was a wonderful graduation ceremony. My entire family from LA went up for it. They were very proud of me. I was the first to receive a college degree. My parents had always stressed the importance of education. They had not been able to acquire much, and my older brother had to start working much too early to obtain much schooling. As the youngest, I benefited from my parents' hope that I would be the exception. They didn't ask too much of me so that I could have the freedom to go to school. At the same time, they sacrificed themselves so that I could go to school and not have to drop out and go to work. My mother's biggest dream was to have at least one son who would graduate from a university and have a professional career.

My mom cried, and my whole family was happy. They were happy not only because I was getting my AA degree but because I was going on to UCSB. The Chabot graduation was one of the happiest times of my life.

My first year at UCSB took a lot of adjustment on my part. For example, I was in a committed relationship with my girlfriend, and yet UCSB is a very social place. At a community college, students just go to classes and then leave for their job. At a university such as UCSB, it's different. Students live on campus or in nearby Isla Vista. There are all kinds of social life. I've never been much of a social person. In a way, I thought UCSB would be the place for me to break out of my shell. But I came to know that I'm not that type of social person. I enjoy spending time at home and talking to my family. I also enjoy an occasional movie with my girlfriend. My roommates at UCSB couldn't believe I didn't want to go out partying. But I don't drink and I had no interest in meeting other girls. It was pointless for me to party, even though I went to a few.

My classes also meant an adjustment. I wasn't used to a fast-paced quarter system. You really have to stay on top of your classwork. I realized that you can't procrastinate. Still another adjustment had to do with the sheer amount of reading in my classes. At Cerritos and Chabot, I never really did the readings, and yet because I was interested in the classes and took good notes, I got good grades. But at UCSB, if you didn't do the readings, you didn't do well. In my first quarter, I read the most I ever had in my life. But it was a good experience.

That first quarter I got two Bs and a C. That pretty much was my average my first year. I got the C in a course on the ancient Mayans. I foolishly thought that with my Mexican background, I would have an easier time than other students. I underestimated how difficult the course actually was.

Fortunately, I didn't have to take many of the general education required courses since I had taken these in community college. I've been able to take more of my sociology major classes. Overall, I did well my first year despite the adjustments. Of course, I would have loved to have done better.

One of the things that hurt me a bit my first year at UCSB is that my girlfriend took a leave of absence from Berkeley and decided to spend a semester back in LA and fulfill some of her general ed classes at a community college. As a result, I went down to see her every weekend.

That was a poor decision on my part because it took time away from my studying. When she returned to Berkeley in her second semester, things calmed down for me.

Because I was traveling each weekend to LA, I didn't have much time to be involved in extracurricular activities. One of my best friends from high school who also attended UCSB suggested that I join his Latino fraternity, and I wanted to, but I realized that I wouldn't have the time. I didn't think it would be fair to them because I couldn't be fully involved. I hope during my senior year to perhaps become involved in some campus groups.

The one thing that continues to plague me is my undocumented status. This became a problem even before I transferred to UCSB. While living in Oakland, I got a job at the Berkeley YMCA as a lifeguard and swimming instructor. I enjoyed the job and things went well. After a while, I learned of an even better job with more pay at the downtown San Francisco Y. It was a coordinator's job. I applied and was thrilled when I got it. This was the Embarcadero Y with beautiful vistas of the Bay Bridge and the city. My job was to manage the day-to-day activities of the pool. I scheduled lifeguards, classes, and overall maintenance. I had a lot of responsibilities. It was also a full-time job, so I was getting paid a pretty good salary. I felt confident in doing my job, and my supervisor was very pleased with me.

But then things began to happen. After I had left the Berkeley Y, my supervisor there discovered that I had a phony social security number. They knew I had transferred to the San Francisco Y. This was all in the wake of 9/11 and the fear of terrorism linked with undocumented immigrants. As a result, Berkeley informed the San Francisco Y about my social security issue. My supervisor at my new job was nice and sympathetic but told me he had no choice but to release me. I didn't blame my supervisor, but I was angry at the Berkeley Y for releasing this information. I wasn't a terrorist and my supervisor there knew it.

After that, I found it difficult to get another job. I changed my social security number believing this would help, but it didn't. Then when I came to UCSB, I couldn't find a job on campus or off. Finally, I got a weekend job back in Montebello, where I had gotten my first real job. This only increased the pressure on me to commute each weekend to the LA area. However, after a couple of months, the Y told me that there was a problem with my social security number. My undocumented status kept catching up to me.

But my problem hasn't just been with trying to get a job. Not long ago on one of my trips back home, I was stopped by the Pico Rivera police for allegedly not stopping at a stop sign. I tried to tell them I had stopped, but you don't win such arguments. More seriously, since I don't have a driver's license due to my status, they arrested me and put me in jail. I had to spend the night in jail.

This was the last straw. I can't deal with it anymore. But the only recourse I have is to get married to my girlfriend. Since she is a U.S. citizen, this would start the process of regularizing my status.

My girlfriend had already talked about getting married. Actually, she's been more eager to do so than me. I've hesitated, thinking I should first deal with my status. But with all of these recent problems, I now see that marriage is the only way. I have two cousins who have gotten married to U.S. citizens, and they are now receiving their permanent residence papers, and so this is encouraging.

What's been great about all of this is how supportive my girlfriend has been. Her parents are also undocumented from Mexico, so she understands what I'm going through.

However, it gets more complicated. Even if we get married very soon, I still won't be able to process my request for regularization. After 9/11, the Congress—or perhaps it was an executive decision, I don't know—disallowed such requests based on marrying a U.S. citizen. The only way this can change, as I understand it, is for the president to open up this avenue through an executive order. I've learned all this from going to see an immigration attorney. However, we still want to get married and put in my application for regularization in case the president issues that order. At a minimum, my attorney tells me, I might be able to get a work permit, a green card. With that, then, I can also get an official social security number and a driver's license. It might also mean I can travel back to Mexico to visit my relatives there.

My parents, of course, face similar problems due to their undocumented status. Their hope is that eventually there will be another amnesty for the undocumented like there was in 1986. They had high hopes for this after President Bush and President Fox took office, but nothing came of it.

Although I am undocumented, I, at the same time, have grown up in this country. My cultural traditions have evolved as I have gone through different changes and experiences.

The issue of language is an interesting one. I grew up speaking Spanish. Spanish is still our home language. My mom for a while enrolled in

English classes after work in the evenings. However, she would come home so tired that she couldn't continue with them. She actually found that she really didn't need to learn that much English since where we lived, everyone spoke Spanish, and it was the same at her job. Actually, in a way, I'm glad that my parents don't know that much English because that has meant that we will continue to speak Spanish at home. This helped me maintain my Spanish at the same time that I learned English at school. I have some Mexican American friends who now speak mostly English at home, and they have lost a lot of their Spanish.

One of the results of my becoming bilingual is that I became my parents' translator. Whenever they had to communicate with an English-speaking person, I would translate for them. At first I found this intimidating, but in time I adjusted to this role.

Our diet and eating habits have also changed to an extent on this side of the border. My mother still cooks primarily Mexican dishes, but she has now included other ones as well from other cultures. She sometimes cooks pasta and other Italian food. She's added Salvadoran recipes. We've had Argentinean friends, and their cuisine has influenced us as well. We find common ground when it comes to food.

Going to school, I of course picked up the habit of eating fast food, such as hamburgers, hot dogs, and pizza. My mother doesn't object to me eating such foods because she's very open-minded when it comes to food. She does kid me about becoming too Anglo by eating such foods. I myself find that after eating too much of these fast foods, I really crave Mexican food. I love Mexican food and can't go too long without it.

One area where we might be different from other Mexican families is that we're not particularly religious. We are on one level but not on others. Actually, growing up I began to realize a contradiction with respect to religion, which in our case is Catholicism. My parents would tell me to do what Jesus wanted me to do, but then they didn't often go to church themselves. When I made my First Communion, I thought that now religion would play a larger role in my family, but it didn't.

I think that this is just a tradition in our family. In those years when I lived in Mexico, I noticed that my relatives there rarely went to church. Sometimes I say that my parents practice what I call a "commercial religion." By that I mean that they only observe particular feast days often associated with big community and even commercial interests. These would include Christmas and Easter.

On the other hand, my parents do participate in more popular religious practices. They become really religious during the feast day of La Virgen de Guadalupe on December 12. I remember that when we lived in Mexico, we would celebrate this day by making a pilgrimage to the Basilica of Our Lady of Guadalupe in Mexico City. At home, my dad has an altar to La Virgen de Guadalupe. He always says that she's the queen of Mexico. He has the utmost respect for La Virgen.

Another popular feast day that we observe is Día de los Muertos, or the Day of the Dead. To remember and honor our deceased relatives in Mexico, my mother that day, November 2, makes the foods that they enjoyed when they lived. This includes mole, tamales, and special desserts. If one of them liked to smoke, she buys that relative's favorite brand. All of these foods and favorite drinks are put up as offerings on our dining table. The tradition is that on these days, the spirits of our loved ones return to celebrate with us. My dad would contribute to these offerings by baking *pan de muerto*, or the bread of the dead. On the dining table, my mother also puts lighted glass candles with the images of the Sacred Heart of Jesus and La Virgen de Guadalupe. All of our family comes together on this special day.

Because of my parents' influence, I have mixed feelings about religion. Like them, I enjoy the more popular feast days, but I don't often go to Mass. I believe in some things and not others. I remember when I got my car, one of my brothers gave me a *santito*, or a saint image, to put on the dashboard. I didn't really know how to react to this. On the one hand, I didn't want to hurt his feelings, but on the other, I didn't really believe that the *santito* had the power to protect me. But I accepted it because I knew that it was important for my brother.

While I don't consider myself particularly religious, I do think that when the chips are down, we need something like faith. That may be selfish on my part, but I do believe that faith can see us through difficult times. I'm impressed, for example, by the faith that people have in the image of La Virgen de Guadalupe. They look at this image and pray to it, and it gives them hope. That's really powerful. I don't think anyone can deny that.

On the other hand, I have more difficulty with the established Church. I find too many contradictions sometimes. One in particular had to do with our local parish priest denouncing in one of his sermons homosexuals and their lifestyles. This especially affected me because one of my cousins is gay. I can't believe that God doesn't love him despite his sexual preference. I don't think that God would teach any individual to hate another person. So to hear a priest who claims to be religious talk about people that way was a really big turnoff.

Yet I have perhaps my own contradictions. While I'm not particularly religious and I have questions about the Church, at the same time, I'll get married in the Church. My girlfriend and I have talked about this as well as whether we would raise our kids in a religious way. We both agree that out of respect for our parents and for our cultural traditions, we would get married in the Church and our children, like us, will be baptized, make their First Communion, and observe other Catholic practices. But we're also going to do things because we want to. I think that we can find another meaning to these practices within ourselves—not so much what the Church makes it mean but what it means to us.

With respect to marriage, I think my parents are pleased that I'm marrying a girl of Mexican background. Perhaps they secretly would have preferred that I marry a girl from Mexico. I think my mother thinks that if this were the case, I wouldn't have lived with her before marriage. But my parents have adjusted to my relationship with my girlfriend. They know that I love her and that she loves me. What's also important to my parents is that my girlfriend is Mexican.

I know that they would object to me marrying a white girl. They would accept it, but they wouldn't like it. Perhaps they resent the way whites treat Mexicans. For sure, such intermarriage deals with their sense of cultural differences. That would make them uncomfortable.

Culturally, I've evolved in other interesting ways. As a kid and teenager, I was very much influenced by U.S. culture. I watched only English-language television. My musical tastes were American rock, and my lifestyle was geared more toward an American lifestyle. However, since I've been in college, I've been rediscovering my Mexican roots. I've begun to realize that I've neglected to really know and appreciate the entertainment that my own culture can promote. I'm now turning to more Mexican and Latino cultural influences, such as in music and sports. My favorite band is Café Tacuba from Mexico City. Their music is great. But I'm also into other Latino groups and singers. I didn't use to be a soccer fan before, but now I'm a huge soccer fan, especially of Mexican and Latin American teams.

I think in my life I've done a good job of including U.S. customs, Mexican culture, and world culture into my lifestyle. I've been able to expand my tastes.

Although I'm influenced by a variety of cultures, I consider myself to be a Mexican living in the United States. My Mexican culture and experiences are very important to me. The four years I spent back in Mexico were very important because it was the first time that I discovered where I was from, and I definitely enjoyed it. I know that I could be comfortable living in Mexico. But that's not possible. I live in the U.S., and it's important for me to open my eyes and my brain to everything that this country has to offer. I appreciate U.S. culture because I know it's not just white culture but everyone's culture, including the Mexican.

I prefer "Mexican" over the term "Chicano." I associate Chicano culture with one that is less Mexican or is trying to be Mexican. I don't fit into that.

If I can get my status regularized, I want to be able to help people who are in a similar situation. They're out there looking for help and for someone like me who has gone through a similar experience. This is especially true for young people like myself who are undocumented but want to go to college. I know how devastating it is to work very hard in high school and then discover due to your immigrant status that you can't go, or at least not to the school of your choice. I want to go into teaching at the high school level in LA, and preferably in my home area of Montebello. I know I can be of help there because I know the area and the people. That's my immediate future. But I want to continue my own education and eventually get a Ph.D. and teach at a university. That's my hope and my challenge. I know I can do it.

Álvaro Sánchez graduated from the University of California, Santa Barbara, in 2004. After marrying his girlfriend, he received his legal permanency in 2006. He divorced three years later and has a new relationship with his girlfriend of seven years. He obtained an M.A. in urban planning at USC in 2011 and is working in Oakland for a national nonprofit called Green for All whose mission is to create a green economy strong enough to lift people out of poverty. He is also a board member of the San Francisco–based organization Dolores Street Community Services, which advocates for immigrant rights, anti-homelessness work, and community development and organizing. He became a U.S. citizen in 2012 and is currently in the process of helping his father adjust his undocumented status. His mother, also undocumented, was deported after she tried to return to the United States after going to Mexico to visit her dying mother. Her status is more difficult to adjust.

NAYELI REYES

My mom was born in Tijuana. Her father worked in San Diego, where he managed a restaurant. He commuted across the border each week and would return on weekends. Because he made very good money, he and his family lived very well. They even had a maid that would clean and iron for them. Although they were quite privileged, my grandfather insisted that my mother still do some chores around the house. He believed that a household was a woman's domain. He was very old-fashioned and insisted that my mother had to learn how to take care of a future husband. He didn't believe in women working outside of the house. My grandmother Lidia never worked.

Because my grandfather had money, he would take the family on trips to places such as Disneyland and Knott's Berry Farm. My mother, Martha, was the only girl, so she was "Daddy's little girl." My mother had two brothers, my *tío* Bob and my *tío* Richard. My great-grandmother, Abuelita Martína, also lived with the family.

After some years of commuting across the border, my grandfather finally said: "We need to move to San Diego. This commuting is a big strain on me."

He didn't like not seeing his family each day. So the family moved in 1963 across the border. They didn't have any problems crossing over legally since my grandfather had important connections. He arranged for their papers. My mother was about five years old.

But my grandmother didn't like living in San Diego. She didn't like the smaller house they had to live in, so in two years she told my grandfather—and this must have taken a lot of courage—that she and the family were returning to Tijuana. And they did, including my grandfather.

However, in 1973, my grandfather finally had his way, and he convinced my grandmother to once again relocate to the United States. This time it was for good, and they moved to Los Angeles.

73

This move apparently further strained my grandparents' marital relations, and they soon separated. My grandma was left to raise three children by herself. My grandfather did not provide much child support, and he died shortly thereafter. With no prior work experience, my grandmother now had to find a job. She started working at a taco stand in downtown LA. She worked there for fourteen years. After I was born, I remember my mother taking me to visit my grandmother at the taco stand. Nacho, my grandmother's boss, would make me cheese tacos because it was the only thing I would eat.

My grandmother struggled for many years. She first received only the minimum wage, but her boss was good to her, made her a cashier, and paid her enough for her to provide for her family.

It wasn't easy for my mom, either. She started school in the United States in junior high, but she didn't know much English. She hated to speak English because of her very thick accent and because other kids would make fun of her. She started in ESL classes until she knew more English. She attended school in downtown LA for junior and senior high school. She really had to push herself to succeed in school. After high school, she attended junior college for a couple of years. My grandmother didn't support much education for my mother. She was satisfied with my mom just staying out of trouble. My mother was always a good girl. But my grandmother just expected my mom to eventually get married and have kids and that's that. My mother wanted a bit more. So she pushed herself in school and to go to junior college.

It was in high school that my parents met. The story of their meeting is quite beautiful. My mom danced in the school's *folklórico* group. At one performance, my dad in the audience spotted her and fell in love at first sight.

"I need to meet this girl," he told a friend. "Who is she?"

But my mom wasn't too interested in boys. She was very picky about boyfriends and had gone on only a couple of dates in high school. She would just concentrate on her classes. She would worry about boys later.

But my dad was determined to meet her. He asked a mutual friend to introduce them, but this friend warned him about my mother.

"Martha's not interested in having a boyfriend," he told my dad.

"But I have to talk to her," my dad responded.

So he cleverly joined the boy's Mexican singing group that performed with the *folklórico*. The boys sang and the girls danced. In this way, he got to meet my mother, and they started to see each other. Finally, my mom fell for my dad. The rest is history.

They both graduated from high school in 1977.

My dad's background is quite different. César was born in Guayaquil, Ecuador. His family was very poor. He remembers playing in the gutters when he was three or four years old. His mother would get very upset about this. He lived in an extended family with aunts, uncles, and cousins in a small house.

My dad never knew his father. He died when my dad's mother was one month pregnant with my father. My grandmother Lola decided a few years later to go to the U.S. for a better life. My father was four years old when they moved. It was my dad, my grandmother, and my aunt who left and went to Los Angeles. They didn't have any problems entering because my grandmother had a cousin already here who pulled some strings. After a couple of years, my grandma met my grandpa Jaime, and they got married. He was also from Ecuador but had grown up in the U.S. Grandpa Jaime raised my dad as his own. Grandpa Jaime was my dad's stepdad, but my father never referred to him as such. He always considered Grandpa Jaime his real dad.

Grandpa Jaime had permanent residency, and he worked at a lot of odd jobs for which he received less than minimum wage. He was a milkman once, a mechanic, and a distributor of ice cream cones, and he worked at a Tootsie Roll factory. My dad loved this last job because it meant that Grandpa Jaime would come home every evening with his pockets full of Tootsie Rolls.

My grandma also worked in LA. She worked at a garment factory sewing bathing suits. She got eleven cents per piece. To make extra money, each Friday she cooked an Ecuadorian *caldo* or soup made out of cow guts stuffed with cauliflower and green bananas. I think it sounds disgusting, but my dad says it was pretty good, although it stunk up the whole house. My grandma sold the soup to other Ecuadorian families who lived in the same neighborhood. She got a couple of dollars for each serving.

My dad, since he was still quite young when he came to this country, learned English as he started school. He attended a Catholic elementary school because his mother was very religious. My dad tells me how the nuns punished the kids, including him, by whacking them with rulers. My dad was actually quite *travieso* or naughty when he was young. Sometimes he would ditch school. But my grandmother believed in education and kept after my dad to do his schoolwork.

My grandmother wanted my dad to continue in a Catholic high school, but she couldn't afford to send him to one. Instead, she encouraged him to go to a Catholic seminary to become a priest. This way he could get a Catholic high school education and the archbishop would support him. My grandmother didn't want my dad to go to one of the public high schools, especially to a "Mexican" school. My dad didn't want to become a priest but went along with his mother's wishes for a couple of years. He was fourteen when he entered the seminary.

In the meantime, my grandparents decided to return to Ecuador. They were struggling economically here and felt that they might achieve a better life in Ecuador. Besides my dad, they now had three other children. They also believed their younger kids could get a better private or Catholic education that they could afford in Ecuador.

Later, my grandparents with their family returned to LA. My aunt and uncles, with the exception of one aunt, never returned to Ecuador. My grandma did again after her husband died. She's been moving back and forth ever since then.

My dad stayed in the seminary until he was a junior in high school. He moved in with one of his aunts who had not returned to Ecuador. This is when my dad started attending the public high school where he met my mother. It was here that my dad heard about the Chicano Movement, but he didn't want to be a part of it. He felt, "I'm an American and I don't need to go through that." He was losing his sense of ethnic identity. He remembers making fun of ESL students because they couldn't speak English very well. Students referred to these students as "wetbacks" and "beaners." None of these terms offended my father. I get very offended when I still hear someone talk like that. I'm just like, "Excuse me, you don't use terms like that!" If there are whites using such terms, I'm like, "I don't call you white trash or trailer trash, so why are you using these other offensive terms?"

My dad now regrets using these terms himself. He's brought me up to get offended when people say such stuff.

My dad's aunt was a nurse and worked odd hours, so no one really supervised him. As a result, my father didn't do well in school. He didn't care about school. He barely graduated. College was definitely not an option for him. One rainy day, he walked by an army recruiting office.

"I'm going to join the army," he told his friend.

Going into the military actually helped my dad a lot. Of course, by this time my dad and my mom were going steady. He loved my mother but felt he first had to do something about his life and felt that the army would help him. He joined without my mother's permission. But she also loved him and promised to wait for him. She waited four years.

My mom and dad's relationship was actually more complicated. My dad did ask my mom to marry him before he went into the army, but she refused.

"No," she told him. "I don't want to be left with a dead husband in the military."

My dad still kids her about that. But I admire her for doing that. In fact, my mom was very faithful to my dad. She would wait for his phone calls each weekend. She wouldn't go out at all.

In that time, my dad was sent to Kentucky and then Georgia, and then he spent a year in Korea. In his last year, he was stationed at Monterey, so he could now visit my mother on the weekends.

The army gave my dad certain opportunities he might not otherwise have had. He first had a job as a paper pusher, but in time he worked with the first army computers. He says that they were huge but very slow. It took seventeen minutes to print out a page, and if you messed up you had to start all over again. Fortunately, he never saw combat duty.

My mother, during this time, wrote letters to my dad in Spanish. She did that to force him to learn more Spanish. My dad had lost most of his Spanish growing up in LA, unlike my mother, who had retained hers. My mother told my dad, "You're going to learn Spanish." Through my mother's letters, he learned how to read Spanish and in time improved his speaking abilities. On the other hand, my dad wrote in English to my mom. He always complained, however, that he wrote these long fifteen-page letters, and in turn, he received from my mother these shorter two-page ones.

In addition, they would send each other tape recordings. She talked to him in Spanish. I've heard some of the tapes. They're so sweet but a bit corny. "I miss you so much," they would tell each other.

My dad also made these long distance calls to my mother, including when he was in Korea. My dad says that he would spend his entire pay-check on these calls. He called collect and then mailed my mom a check or sent over his paycheck to her to pay the phone bill.

During these four years, my mother, after graduating from high school, first attended a local community college, where she got training as a legal secretary. She then worked at a law firm as a legal secretary for a while until she landed another similar job at Security Pacific Bank.

When that bank closed down, she transferred to Bank of America, where she still works as a legal secretary.

My dad returned from the service in 1981, and one year later my parents got married. My dad actually wanted to get married right away, but my mom refused until he got a job. "I'm not going to marry a bum," she told him. I'm also proud of my mom for doing that!

At first, my dad didn't know what kind of job he could get. Because she had clerical experience, my mom, for some reason, suggested that he apply at the *Los Angeles Times*. He did and to his surprise was hired. At first he did rinky-dink jobs but after a few months was assigned more duties, including telecommunications work.

After my parents got married, they lived in an apartment in Montebello, east of LA. In 1984 I was born. In the hospital, my grandma saw my dad pace back and forth in the waiting room.

"Well, do you have a name for her?" she said.

"No, I don't."

My grandma always watched the Spanish-language TV show called *Sábado Gigante*, and on one program there was a three-year-old with a lot of talent. Her name was Nayeli.

"Well, what about Nayeli?" she asked my father.

"I like it," he replied.

So they gave me the name without knowing what it meant. It wasn't until recently that I discovered that it means "I love you" in the Aztec language. I've always thought it was a cool name. My family pronounces it "Nayeli," but my friends call me "Nayali." I respond to both.

Six months later my mom decided she didn't want to live in the large LA urban area. She didn't want to raise me, according to her, surrounded by cholos and *vatos* and the increasing gang violence in the area. She hated it. "I don't want to raise my children in the city," she told my dad.

So they moved to a more easterly suburb in San Bernardino County. My dad used his GI Bill of Rights plus some money from my maternal grandmother to buy a house there. We lived there for fourteen years. Six years after I was born, my brother César was born. There's the two of us and our dog, who's the baby of the family!

My first memories are of waking up in the morning and smelling cows, because this was still very much a rural area. I also remember playing with the little girl next door, Jennifer. She was very sweet. She was white, like most of the neighborhood except for us. I remember playing with my dolls and watching a lot of TV. I was always very smart, and

I remember that my parents never talked baby talk to me. They never talked down to me.

I also grew up speaking predominantly English. Initially my mother, who was fluent in Spanish, talked only Spanish to me. So did my dad. By this time, his Spanish had improved because my mother's mother, Grandma Lidia, only spoke Spanish, and for my dad to communicate with her, he had to learn Spanish. When I was three years old, I could speak both Spanish and English.

However, my bilingualism lasted only until I started preschool. Then, because all of the white kids only spoke English, I only wanted to speak English.

"Mommy, I don't want to speak Spanish anymore."

And so I stopped speaking it.

My mom would say, "Mija, háblame en español."

"No Mommy, I want to speak English."

So I lost my Spanish. And I now regret that. To this day I regret it. I can now speak some Spanish, but I jumble my words a lot. I stutter in Spanish.

I started in the public schools that were very good in our area. I attended an elementary school that was just five minutes away from my home. The school was right smack in the middle of our housing addition that was called Little Creek Loop. Our community was not a gated community, but it was very confined and safe.

From the very beginning, my parents encouraged education for me. My very first day of kindergarten, they gave me a bunny rabbit that I named Bouncer. This was to show me how proud they were that I was starting kindergarten. We did lots of crafts in kindergarten that I loved. Mrs. Jackson was my teacher, and she was very sweet. I liked her a lot. She never patronized me by talking to me like a child.

I did very well in elementary school. My parents helped by tutoring me at home, even though sometimes they would frustrate me because I already knew what they were trying to teach me at home. When I finished first grade, I was promoted to a combined second and third grade class. My parents were very proud of this.

One of my favorite elementary school teachers was Mr. Bourne, in fifth grade. I loved him and he taught me so much. He treated all of his students as equals. The whole class environment was very good. I still go back and visit him. He always makes fun of me because I've grown so much. It's funny, I go back to these classrooms and am amazed at how small they are, to match the smallness of the kids. The desks and chairs are shorter than normal. Of course, when I was in fifth grade, the desks and chairs seemed immense.

My elementary school was ethnically mixed, although the majority of the kids were probably white. Most of my friends were white, but I had one Asian friend, Jeni Lee. I also had another good friend, Stacy, who's black. My best friend in elementary school, however, was Heather, who is white. We've been friends since fourth grade. My dad calls Heather his "white daughter" and refers to the two of us as *café con leche* because I'm dark and Heather's very white. There were also other Mexican kids in the school.

My parents tried to involve themselves as much in my school as possible. My mother especially tried to attend PTA meetings and go to parent conferences. But that wasn't always easy because of my parents' work schedule. Throughout my elementary, junior high, and high school years, my parents still worked in LA and commuted back and forth. After school in elementary grades, I went to day care until my parents picked me up around 7 P.M. They'd be exhausted by the time we had dinner. Still, every evening my dad in the early school years would check my homework. He did that until I was in the eighth grade. By then he trusted me. He knew he had trained me to check my own work. My parents still do this with my brother. My father would tell me: "You got the problem wrong. You need to check this, please."

My mother would help me with my spelling. She would dictate to me while she cooked in the kitchen. I've always been a bad speller, but if I misspelled a word, my mom made me spell it correctly five times. At the dinner table, my father out of the blue would ask me: "What's five times five?"

If I hesitated, he'd say: "Come on, *mija*! Get up to speed!"

My parents instilled in me the importance of education. Ever since I was little, I was brought up to believe that I was going to college. It's not that I didn't have a choice, I just didn't have a choice! I knew I was going to college.

In junior high, my dad counseled me about which classes I should take that would help me get to college. I'd say, "Why do I have to take this math class?" My dad responded, "Because you need it to advance to the next math class that you'll need for college, that's why."

But my dad always told me that as long as I tried my best and if I knew in my heart that I tried my best, that's what was important to him.

If I didn't try my best, he would be disappointed. "I never want you to slack off," he'd tell me. He reminded me that in school he had slacked off and that he paid the price for it. He had to struggle very hard to get to where he was. He'd say, "A college education will help you get anything. It doesn't matter what you major in as long as you have a degree. I don't care if you have a degree in dancing, drama, art, or math. It doesn't matter as long as you have a degree."

There was only one junior high in our neighborhood, and we all went there. I had gotten all As in elementary school and accomplished the same in junior high. I was in all of the honors classes. I wasn't very athletic, but I did perform on the drill team in eighth grade. Drill team is not cheerleading. Drill team is a sport, and we participated in several competitions.

Following junior high, we all went to the only high school in the district. As a freshman, I'll never forget one particular incident. I had to go see my counselor, Mrs. Lodd, to get into honors classes. I knew I wouldn't have a problem because I had excellent grades in junior high. However, while I was on the way to see Mrs. Lodd, I overheard her and the principal talking about another freshman student by the name of Alejandra. They weren't aware that I was outside of the office with the door open. Mrs. Lodd said to the principal, whose first name was John: "By the way, John, this girl Alejandra came in to see me and wants to know why she's been put in preparatory classes and not college prep ones. What should I tell her?"

"Well," the principal said, "her last name is Hispanic. What's the big deal? You know that's where they belong. They're not capable of anything else."

I was so offended hearing this. I mustered up the courage, knocked on Mrs. Lodd's door, and entered after they acknowledged my presence. They seemed surprised that I was there.

"Excuse me, but I heard what you were saying about Alejandra. I'm from a Latino background and I'm Chicana. I've been in honors classes through junior high."

"Oh," the principal responded, "I didn't know you were sitting out there."

"I don't appreciate what I heard about Hispanic students," I further said.

I had never spoken like this to a teacher, much less to a principal. I was polite but at the same time offended.

I found out later that they allowed Alejandra to be in some of the honors classes. She and I became friends.

I continued to get very good grades in high school, although I had to work hard in some classes. If I got a C, I would freak out. Once I even got an F on a report, the only F I ever got in high school. My dad was furious.

"When did you do this report?" he demanded to know.

"The day before it was due."

"Why did you slack off?"

"I wasn't slacking off."

"Look at me. Did you honestly believe you did your best work? Is this your best work?"

I started crying.

"No, it's not," I admitted.

"OK, you know it's not my life," my dad lectured me, "it's yours, *mija*. Colleges look at grades. One F may not matter, but they all add up."

He just left it at that. I was so depressed the entire rest of the day. But I got all As in high school except for a couple of Bs.

I was fortunate because I was in the honors and later AP classes. But I became aware of the tracking system. There were only a few Mexicans, including me, in these advanced classes. I rarely saw an African American in them. The large majority were whites and Asians. There were few minorities in this track, which is probably why we're called minorities.

Most of the Chicanos and blacks were in the non-college track system. This included the ESL students. These students were always very quiet. That's the only thing I remember about them. I talked to some, but they were very shy and timid. I guess they were afraid to express themselves in English. I knew that they had thoughts inside of them, and I wanted to bring them out.

The tracking system in turn promoted a kind of ethnic clustering. The Asians always stuck together. They were all in tennis. In fact, they organized an Asian Tennis Club. The African Americans all hung out together. The basketball team was mostly black. The Chicanos, including the ESL students, also remained apart. Of course, the great majority of whites went off by themselves. They were just as clustered as anyone else. White students represented the most popular students, and some of them could be quite stuck-up.

Although I don't remember much obvious racial discrimination and I personally never experienced it, I would hear from time to time people using terms such as "beaner" and "wetback." When I heard these insults aimed at Mexicans, I would just go off.

"Excuse me," I would tell the student who used the offensive terms. "Are you joking? Don't you know those are racist terms? If some of these people had to cross the Rio Grande to get here, so what? At least they're here and they're trying." Or sometimes I would say, "They're the ones who pick and serve your food. You'd starve without them." I would go on forever.

The offending students would get all apologetic. "I didn't mean anything."

"OK, then don't say it again," I said.

What really also bothered me was when other students used the word "nigger." They picked this up from the hip-hop culture—"You be my nigger" type of thing. I know they weren't necessarily using the term in a bad way, but it still offended me. Even my friend David, who is white, used that word. Because he was on the basketball team, he tried to be black. He'd say to me, "Hey, you're my nigga."

I'm like, "No I'm not."

"I'm just saying you're my buddy."

"Well, then say I'm your buddy, not the other word. That bothers me."

I've never understood why, but I've always been very aware of my surroundings and the way people treat each other. If I hear something derogatory about a certain culture or race or gender, I just get very offended.

Even though there was a lot of ethnic clustering at my school, I personally had very mixed friends. Fran (Franciso) was from Chile. Sara is Korean. Rod is, I think, Filipino. Heather, Amber, and Decana are white. And Suti is black. Cindy was Chinese, and Diana was from Colombia. I also had Chicano friends.

Overall, I enjoyed my high school and I enjoyed my classes. My favorite classes were more in the humanities. I loved world history and learning about different cultures. It's fascinating to me. Art history was my favorite class. My teacher, Mrs. Upas, is awesome and beautiful. She would really get us to appreciate art not only by learning about it but by hands-on work.

"OK, so you think that impressionist painting is easy; well, let's see you do it," she would tell us.

So we had to do our own impressionistic painting as a way of appreciating this kind of art.

She was particularly sensitive to Latin American art. We had to do a Día de los Muertos altar to someone who had died. She taught us about Diego Rivera and Frida Kahlo. For an experiment, I did my impression of one of Rivera's classic paintings depicting an Indian peasant woman. I had never before painted in my life. Mrs. Upas thought my painting was very good, and without my knowledge she entered it into a school art contest, and I won first prize! It was a huge surprise. I learned so much from Mrs. Upas.

When the film *Frida* came out, I went and saw it and loved it. Not only is it a beautiful film, but I really appreciated it because I knew so much about the life and art of Frida and Rivera.

I was raised Catholic but mostly by my mom. My father isn't very religious, and he's always had reservations about the Church. My mother would take me to Mass on Sundays, and my dad would stay home. As I grew older, I began to think it unfair that he got to stay home Sunday mornings while I had to go to Mass.

"It's not fair," I would say. "I don't want to go to church; it's boring."

I didn't like the priest at our church. He made me feel depressed. "You're a sinner and you're going to go to hell because you don't pray enough." He would say things like that. I would live in fear of God. But I don't think that's what God is all about. God is supposed to be beautiful and loving. But that's not the God we got in church. As a little kid, I hated going to Mass. But my mom would make me go.

"*Mija*, God only asks for one hour of your time each week. You have to go."

So I went.

I made my First Communion but much, much later than other kids. I didn't receive it until I was in the eighth grade. This was because my mother couldn't drive me after school to First Communion classes due to her work schedule. Finally, when I was in eighth grade, one of my friend's mothers volunteered to drive me. I made my First Communion but only to please my mother, because I knew that she believes strongly in it.

I wear a cross around my neck that my mom gave me. I always wear it. I can't take it off. She gave it to me for protection.

"I can't always take care of you, but God will through this cross."

My grandmother and aunt are also very religious. They're always trying to get my dad to go to church, but he refuses. I did attend CCD [Confraternity of Christian Doctrine] classes before and after my First Communion, but I was never confirmed because by the time I would have taken all of the classes, I would have been out of high school and in college. I can't take these classes at UCSB either. My mother once thought of sending me to Mexico to get confirmed, because there you don't need to take all of these classes.

My mother is very, very religious. My dad still believes in God but doesn't like the Church.

At home, my mother has a huge cross in my parents' bedroom. It's about my size, and I'm 5 feet 3 inches. It's beautiful. It's Jesus on the cross. He looks real. When I see him, I want to cry. The cross hangs on the wall in front of their bed.

Before my mom goes to bed, she says the rosary. She also has a rosary in her car.

My grandma Lidia in her home has various religious icons. Her favorite is that of Our Lady of Guadalupe.

Before I go out of the house, both my parents bless me. They make the sign of the cross on me. If I say, "Bye, Mom, I'm leaving," she says, "No, no, come back here." And she blesses me. "Be careful."

Whenever my mom gets in her car, she makes the sign of the cross and says, "Pórtate bien, carrito" [Be good, little car].

This was her Toyota Tercel, which was my mom's very first car. She had it for many years and never wanted to get a new one because she believed the first was particularly blessed by God.

"We're in the hands of God," she would say about her car. "We'll be fine. He'll get us there safely."

She finally got a new car, but reluctantly.

My mother would also make me go to confession, even though I didn't want to.

"*Mija*, I want you to do this. It would make me very happy."

Since I love my mom, I'd say, "OK, Mom, I'll do it."

My parents have always been very strict with me. In high school, whenever I went out with friends, they had to have a phone number where they could call. Where was I going? Why was I going? When was I coming back? If I spent the night at a girlfriend's house, they first had to talk to my friend's parents. All this was embarrassing to me.

My friends would tell me, "I can stay out until 1 A.M." And I would have to say, "I have to be back home at 10 P.M." This would be on weekends. On weekdays, I'd have to be home, if I went to a school function, by 8 P.M.

My parents were very cautious, especially when it came to boys. This involved all boys, not necessarily boyfriends and not necessarily dates. If a guy friend came to pick me up to go somewhere, he had to first come in and meet my parents. He wouldn't really have to show a driver's license, but my dad would always say, "How long have you been driving?" They would give boys the third degree.

At the same time, after my parents got to know my guy friends, my mother always insisted that they give her a welcome hug and kiss. She would get offended if they didn't. Once my friend David came in, and he's quite tall, so he didn't see my mother, who is only about five feet tall. "Excuse me!" my mother scolded him, although, I think, with tongue in cheek. "Where's my hug and kiss?" David was so embarrassed.

My parents always insisted that my friends address them as Mr. Reyes and Mrs. Reyes.

I was not supposed to start dating until I was seventeen, but my parents decided that I was mature enough at fifteen to date. But my dad gave me a list of fifteen rules to abide by in dating. One of them was that I always had to remember that I was a lady and that I had to respect myself and to insist on respect by others. I could not walk home alone with a guy. I was never to go to a guy's house under any circumstances. If a guy came over, one of my parents had to be home. Inside my house, guys could not go upstairs. They had to be in the living room, where my parents could observe them. It was always very strict.

I'll never forget my first date. His name was Anthony. He arrived late because his mother had to use the car. He was a year or so older than me and already had his license. He came in very nervous, and it got worse when my dad started lecturing him on being punctual.

"We don't like tardiness in our family," he said. "We like people to be on time. We find it offensive when they aren't."

Anthony actually became my first boyfriend. My parents weren't too crazy about this. It had nothing to do with Anthony. They just found it hard to accept the idea that I had a boyfriend. My dad was kind of, "This is my little girl."

Despite this, my dad, more than my mom, has always been very straightforward with me about things like sex and drugs. At the same time, he didn't always want to confront the idea of me kissing a boy, for example. Once he walked in on me and Anthony kissing as Anthony was about to leave after a date. My father was totally embarrassed. Later, he apologized and said, "I knew you did this, but I didn't want to see it."

Now, of course, that I'm older and in college, my parents, especially my dad, give me more leeway. "When you come home, we can't exactly tell you not to do this or do that. You're eighteen now," my dad says. But my mom, on the other hand, isn't quite ready to give me full independence. "Excuse me," she responds to my father. "We still have a right to tell her about going out. We are the ones who, after all, are paying for her college, and she still lives at home when she returns."

My dad counters this by telling me, "*Mija*, we've raised you right. All we can hope now is that you make good decisions and if you make bad ones that you can learn from them."

Actually, both of my parents have a lot of trust and faith in me that I'll do the right thing.

In growing up, the only thing I didn't have when I turned fifteen was a *quinceañera* [celebration of a girl's fifteenth birthday]. I didn't really want one. My parents weren't into that. I remember when I was fifteen being taken to a *quinceañera* by my *tío* Richard and my *tía* Elizabeth. I think this was the first one I even attended. I was fascinated. It was elaborate and reminded me of a wedding. The girl turning fifteen wore a beautiful dress that resembled a wedding dress. Besides the church service, the reception was incredible with a band and tons of food. When I got home I said, "Mom! You didn't tell me that this is what I'd be missing!"

"*Mija*," she relied, "you didn't want one."

In fact, I didn't really want a *quinceañera*, and I don't regret it.

In our family, we eat mostly Mexican food. We always have Mexican rice. My mother makes the best tacos in the whole world. She makes *tacos de pollo*. She makes chicken tacos because my dad doesn't eat red meat. And my mom makes the best enchiladas ever. The green ones. Ever! She makes them from scratch. The house smells because she burns the chiles on the stove. This is deliberate, to cook the chiles this way. But it smells bad. It's worth it. It takes all day to make the enchiladas. She grates the cheese by hand. She makes the sauce. She boils the chicken. And then by the end of the day, it's just delicious! We eat this with Mexican rice.

My mother cooks other things like fettuccine and hamburgers, but my favorite is always her Mexican food. No one makes Mexican food like my mom. No one.

In my senior year in high school, I began to relax a bit academically. I had always worked very hard and been in honors classes and AP ones. I decided to take a break from these more rigorous classes and take regular classes, some that I needed anyway to graduate such as history, government/economics, and art history, an elective. I'm particularly glad I took art history because it made me love art. In all of my courses I got As. I was a straight-A student and graduated with a 4.12 average or something like that. I also graduated with honors. I was the first one in my family to do so. At graduation, I wore a white robe with a blue collar that symbolized that I belonged to the National Honor Society.

Needless to say, my parents were really proud of me. As a surprise, they rented a plane that flew over the graduation with a banner that read, "Congratulations Nayeli and Heather [my best friend]!"

I cried when I saw it.

My whole family came to my graduation, including my great-grandma Martína. She used to tell me, "*Mija*, I don't think I'll live long enough to see you graduate from high school."

"No, *Abuela*," I'd tell her. "You're going to make it."

And she did. She sat in the first row with the rest of my family and saw me graduate. She was so proud and so happy.

It was a great day.

When I graduated, I felt I had more of a sense of direction for my life than when I had entered school as a freshman. I always knew that I was going to college, but as a graduating senior I knew now that it would be a reality.

I wish I could say the same about some of the other Chicano/Latino students in my high school. Some, like myself, went on to college. But it's my sense that the majority did not, or at least not to a four-year institution. Many of them felt, "Why do I need to go to college?" I responded, "Well, to get a better life than your parents have. That's the whole point." They were going to stay home and find a job and work with their fathers. Some went to a community college, believing that's all they could aspire to. They'd say, "Congratulations, I'm really happy for you. That's great, but that's not for me." Some of the boys decided to go into the military.

When I applied to college, I had only two schools in mind: UCLA and UCSB. I preferred UCLA because it was closer to home and because of the prestige. However, I didn't get accepted there but did get admitted into UCSB.

I had visited UCSB sometime in my senior year with my dad. He really liked it. So did I. It also wasn't that far from home. This closeness to home was crucial for me because I need my family. I can't live without my family. My dad and I made the decision that I would go to UCSB. My mother didn't play that much of a role. My mother has always helped me in specific things like math because she's good at it. But for larger issues,

I usually rely on my dad. Of course, neither of my parents has a college degree, but they know the importance of college for their children.

When my parents drove me to UCSB to start my freshman year, I was very excited to move out of my house and to get away from the restrictions that my parents had put on me. At the same time, I was really scared. I had always been able to rely on my parents, and now I would be away from them. In high school and before, my parents would always be there when I came home from school. If I had a bad day, they could help me. If I had a problem, I could just call my dad: "Come pick me up" or "Dad, can you do this?" I wouldn't have this at UCSB. So when I arrived here, I felt like, "Hey, this is exciting but scary," because I didn't know my new setting and had to figure it out for myself. I couldn't go back to Mommy and Daddy for everything now.

My parents also took my leaving hard. Both of them cried when we left to go to UCSB.

When we got here, it was not a good situation. Everything went wrong. My boxes were all messed up. Everyone was in a bad mood. After my parents helped me move into my dorm room, we said our good-byes. They cried again. I was relieved when they left, but soon I began to feel lonely. I cried.

But I also realized that I had to adjust now to being on my own. Like, this is it. This is me, not my family. This is just my life.

On the other hand, I was lucky to have a really sweet roommate, Kristen. I was scared that my roommate would be some kind of weird person. I was also worried if my roommate would like me. But Kristen and I hit it off right away, and we've become really good friends.

Living in the dorms has its good sides and its bad. I like the freedom of being on my own, but I don't like the fact that I have to live in this tiny square room. At first it was OK because it was my space. But after several months, the room got smaller and smaller. It was driving me insane.

I live in the Santa Cruz substance-free dorm. In a way, I'm not getting the full college experience of students getting in at 3 A.M. drunk or using drugs like marijuana. Nothing like that happens in my hall, which I like because I don't want to be around students who drink or take drugs. The other dorms don't allow drinking or drugs, but it does happen. In my dorm, we have more serious girls and some who are quite religious.

One good thing about UCSB is that I'm not that far from home. In my first quarter, I went home a lot. I went by train and bus. However, in my second and third quarters, I've not gone back as frequently. The more I feel comfortable here, the less the urgency to go home.

One of the initial shocks I experienced at UCSB was the feeling of how "white" the campus is. At least, that's how I initially felt. I was used to a lot of diversity in my high school, including many Latinos. But I didn't find this here. I didn't see many Latinos, and there were even fewer blacks. The majority were white. I began to feel like a minority. In fact, I was a minority. The lack of diversity really bothered me. I'm not racist against whites, and in fact my best friend in high school, Heather, is white, but at the same time, I was shocked at how many white students went to UCSB.

However, after a while, I began to realize that there were more Latinos than I had first imagined. But I also realized that many of the Latinos here spoke more Spanish than my Latino friends in high school had. It seemed like they were perhaps more culturally aware and proud of their culture.

Being at UCSB here meant new academic challenges. It's very different from high school. In high school, I'd go home and maybe do an hour of homework. No reading. Assignments were not very difficult or long. I'd only stress out if I had a paper to do. I'm a procrastinator, so I'd wait until almost the last day or so. On the other hand, I work best under the gun. If I work on a paper with plenty of time, it doesn't come out as well as opposed to when I write it the night before. I don't know why, but that's the way I am.

But in college, things are totally different. I can't afford to procrastinate. The first day of class, you're already behind because you have reading assigned to that first lecture. I was freaking out right away. Perhaps the biggest change for me has been the amount of reading assigned. I've never done so much reading in my life. Each professor assigns about a hundred pages a week. So taking three or four classes per quarter adds up to three or four hundred pages a week. What? I freaked out! I found myself constantly reading and stressing out. I'm like, "OK, fine, I've done my Chicano studies; now I have to do my English. Oh, man!"

But after my initial quarter, I started to calm down. I've developed a strategy and routine to study for my classes. At the beginning of each week, I write down my assignments for each class. I then assign myself so much reading for each class per day. Then besides attending class, I'll study three hours a day for each class. That's my routine, and it's working.

The other big change is that you're on the honor system. You don't have to do the reading or studying. No one is looking over your shoulder. No one cares if you do or don't. No one is taking attendance. I don't have to go to class. In my first quarter, I didn't go to one particular class. I was tired and let myself sleep in. I paid the price. I missed an entire lecture that was crucial on the exam. I realized that I couldn't do that anymore.

My first quarter I only took three classes: Introduction to Chicano Studies, linguistics, and a drama class. In the second quarter I took art history, which I really loved. Then I had a women's studies class, psychology, and a writing class. I haven't declared a major yet, but I'm leaning toward global studies with a minor in art history. I thought about majoring in Chicano studies because I really love my culture. But I've realized that this would be limiting because I love all cultures as well as mine. Global studies would allow me to study a variety of cultures.

I decided to take the Introduction to Chicano Studies class my first quarter because two cousins of mine who went to community college had taken Chicano studies and told me, "Girl, you'll love it. It's your thing." I'm also proud to be a Latina. I know I belong to a wonderful culture. I'm a female and a Chicana. And I'm in college. I'm the first in my family to attend a UC campus. I'm very fortunate. I know I'm going to be successful, and part of this is to know more about my culture.

I appreciated the Introduction to Chicano Studies class, which had about 250 students, not only because of the content of the class but because there were so many other Latinos there. I felt that I wasn't alone at UCSB. There are other people of my culture here as well. I was proud that so many other Chicanos and Latinos, like myself, were in college. The stereotype is that Latinos mostly do menial jobs. We're laborers, janitors, cooks, et cetera. But here in that one class were all these Latinos studying to become professionals like teachers, engineers, lawyers, et cetera. This made me feel good.

I also enjoyed this class because in my linguistics class earlier in the day, there were mostly white students and only a few black and brown faces. I figured that what the professor was looking at was like a canvas. There were all of these white spots and then occasionally there would be a little black spot and then further down a little brown one. But in my Chicano studies class, my professor must have seen a different canvas. Here were all of these dark spots and then a little white spot here and there. I thought that was a really cool perspective. I felt more like one of the class. I felt like I could speak out more because I was more comfortable. Everyone in the class knew what I was talking about because they came from the same culture.

I've made a lot of new friends here at UCSB. I have more white friends than Latinos but that's because there are more whites here. But I have a really good Latino friend, Jessie. I met him at orientation. He's from El Monte, which is very much a Latino community. My cousins used to live there. Jessie just blows my mind. He's really smart and self-educated. Before he came to UCSB, he read tons and tons of books on all kinds of subjects. He's especially good at what's called intellectual rapping. It's like engaging in rhythmic verbal sparring. You have to be really on your toes. I had heard about this but never experienced it until I met Jessie.

I get into deep intellectual conversations with Jessie. He's always reminding me that I'm a Chicana and that I should be proud of that. I've never encountered a Chicano boy that I could really converse with. Our relationship is purely intellectual. But I've been impressed that I've also met some other Chicano guys like Jessie. They're serious and they've worked hard, like me, to get to college. They remind me of my dad.

I haven't been too involved in campus organizations. I went to a meeting of one Latino group, but I found it too militant. I don't want to stereotype the people in that group, but it seemed too militant for me. By this I mean that they seemed obsessed about their own ethnic identity and seemed to come down on other groups. I'm proud of my roots, but I want to experience and learn from other cultures at the same time. I didn't go back to their meetings, although occasionally I'll go with Jessie to some of their social functions.

My parents, of course, are very proud of me. They miss me, and I miss them. My mom calls me just about every day.

"*Mija*, what are you doing? Are you OK?"

My mother still can't accept that I'm an adult now with my own life. When I go home, she still asks me where I'm going when I go out and when I'll return. My dad is different. He tells my mom, "Just let her go. Do you think we can keep dibs on her when she's at college? I'm sure she stays out until two in the morning. We just have to trust her."

My dad has always treated me more as an adult, and that is even more the case now. I can be more open with him. He understands me. He gives me input, and we have intellectual conversations.

I appreciate both of their feelings. I still feel a little guilty about my new freedom. One night in my dorm room, I hung out with one of my guy friends. He was in my room until four in the morning. We were just having this long conversation, but I freaked out when I realized the time.

"Oh my gosh. My parents would have, like, a heart attack if they knew you were in my room right now," I told my friend.

I have no idea what I want to do with the rest of my life. I know I don't want to be like my mother, who put aside her life to wait for Father while he was in the army. I won't do that. I do have someone in mind whom I would like to marry eventually. But he's far away, so we can't be together now. I don't know what, if anything, will come of this, but I won't just be waiting around. I'm not concentrating my life on a man or on any man. I've always promised myself that I will never compromise myself or my future for a man.

I'm going to complete my college career and go further perhaps in my education. I'm going to have my career, whatever that might be. Before I marry a man, my career has to come first. I want to have an established career before I have children. I want a family, but I also want a good career. I want to be able to support my life if my marriage doesn't work out. I want to be able to stand on my own two feet. I don't want to have a man support me. And I don't want to have to support a man, either. He has to come to my level as well.

I don't feel that I have to give up a career for marriage and a family. My mom in the end didn't. Perhaps she never realized her own career dreams, but she's always worked. I feel I can do both also.

Since I'm the first one in my family to go on to a four-year college, I guess I do feel more pressure to succeed. But I know I'll succeed. But I've come to realize that I'll succeed not because my family wants this but because I want it. I'm going to college for myself. You shouldn't go to college for anyone else but yourself. I can make it. I have the patience. I always knew that I could do it, and look at me—here I am. I'm living out my dreams.

Nayeli Reyes graduated from the University of California, Santa Barbara, in 2006 and received an M.A. in education at the University of California, Riverside. She is a history teacher at Central City Value High School, a charter school in Los Angeles.

TANIA PICASSO

My father is the eldest of six siblings. He was born in Guanajuato, Mexico, in a small town called Acámbaro but was raised on a ranch called La Granja. All of my uncles and aunts, from my father's side of the family, were born in that *pueblo*. My dad is Sergio Picasso.

His father, my grandfather, is Jesús Picasso. He worked in the fields in La Granja. He owned his own house and a small plot of land where he grew maize, but he earned a living by working for a larger landowner. In the late 1940s, he started going to the United States to work as a bracero. He wasn't married at the time. But even after he got married to my grandmother, Celia Picasso, he continued on as a bracero. He worked in Texas, Oklahoma, and California. Sometimes he would stay for a month and sometimes for as much as six months. In between, he returned to La Granja and tried to find agricultural jobs there.

My grandpa's older brothers first went as braceros, so that by the time he joined them, they pretty much knew the ropes about contracting as braceros. My grandpa has told me that he was, for the most part, treated well by his Anglo employers. However, he does speak badly about Mexican Americans who, he says, didn't want to work and didn't work as hard. "Eran huevones [lazy]," he refers to them.

During one of his return trips to La Granja, he married my grandmother, Celia. They had been boyfriend and girlfriend before. Soon after they were married, she got pregnant and had my dad. Eventually there were four boys and two girls.

Because my grandfather would be gone as a bracero for different periods, my grandmother, mostly on her own, raised the children in addition to taking care of her own mother. She still has some bitterness about this. She says that when she and my grandfather were together, they were happy. However, when he was gone, things were very difficult. She had the whole burden of raising the family. At times she had no money and had to sell eggs from her chickens just to afford a piece of paper and a stamp to write a letter to my grandfather in the United States. My grandfather would send money, but that often wasn't enough.

Around the early 1960s, my grandfather decided to permanently live in the U.S. His older brothers had already done that by getting their papers. They helped him arrange for his papers also. He then joined his brothers who had settled in East Los Angeles. My grandfather first worked in a *panadería* [bakery] and then worked with his brother in a *carnicería* [meat market] in Culver City owned by Jews who treated them well. In the meantime, he left my grandmother and his family back in La Granja with a promise of bringing them once he got settled.

After working for a while, he bought an old, dilapidated house in the City Terrace neighborhood of East Los Angeles for $16,000. My grandparents still live there. He fixed it up and then arranged for his family to join him. He, with his brother's help, sent back enough money so that my grandmother could arrange for visas or whatever documents they needed to enter the U.S.

My grandmother still cries when she remembers the very hard and long trip with her children. They went from Guanajuato to Morelia to Guadalajara. From there they took a bus to Tijuana. During the whole trip, the younger children vomited the entire time. My grandfather met them in Tijuana, and they legally crossed the border.

Since so many family members came to the U.S., including my extended family, I don't have that many relatives anymore in Guanajuato. However, my grandparents still have their ranch in La Granja and over the years have returned to spend half the year there. This had much to do with my great-grandmother on my grandma's side still living there.

My dad was thirteen when the family came to East LA. The youngest sibling was one or two. My dad was born in 1951 or 1952.

My mother's name is Carolina Margarita Picasso, and she is also from a small *pueblo* called La Peñita de Jaltemba in the state of Nayarit. She is the third oldest girl in a family of eight. I don't know the exact date of her birth, but she's four or five years younger than my dad. Her father, my maternal grandfather, actually owned a good deal of land, and her family represented one of the two richest families in La Peñita. However, he lost the entire land when the other rich family threatened to harm him and his family if he didn't leave the area. I don't know all of the details about this except that it had something to do with gambling.

My grandfather and his family, including my mother, who was three years old at that time, left and migrated all the way to Tijuana. They wanted to get as far away as possible. It was in Tijuana that some of my mom's younger siblings were born. They lived there for several years, and my mother attended school up to the sixth grade.

From Tijuana, my grandfather started to work as a bracero. Leaving his family in Tijuana, he crossed the border to work in the lower San Joaquin Valley near towns such as Delano, Corcoran, and Bakersfield. This was a real come-down for him, since he had been a landowner. But he had no choice. He sent most of his pay to my grandmother in Tijuana. My grandfather used to come back from time to time to Tijuana, where he worked as a janitor until his next contract as a bracero.

When my mom was seventeen, she and her older siblings crossed the border and joined their dad working the cotton fields in Corcoran. By this time, my grandfather was no longer a bracero but didn't have legal documents, either. That was also true of my mother and her siblings.

On one occasion, the *migra* raided the fields where my mom was working. They didn't apprehend everyone at once but walked into the fields, asking workers for their papers. My mother kept on working, hoping they wouldn't ask her. She had a friend working alongside her, Gloria, who was a Mexican American from Texas. Gloria told my mother that if they asked her where she was from, she should say Texas. And if they asked her from where in Texas, she should say San Antonio.

Terrified, my mother kept working until the immigration people came up and asked her in Spanish: "¿De donde es usted?"

"De Tejas," my mother responded.

"¿Qué parte de Tejas?"

"Uh ... uh ..." My mother forgot what city Gloria had told her to say.

They took my mother and put her in a van filled with mainly men, all to be deported. My mother was very scared of being deported and more scared of being with all these men, so she decided to tell the *migra* that her father also did not have papers.

My grandfather appeared and told the *migra* that he was my mom's dad and that they were in the process of getting their papers, which was true. The *migra* told my grandfather that as long as they didn't have their papers, they had no choice but to deport him and my mother back to Tijuana. Fortunately, my *tía* Esperanza arranged for the papers for the entire family, and soon they all crossed the border legally and went to Corcoran, where they continued to work.

It was shortly thereafter that Tía Esperanza, who was married, moved with her family to Boyle Heights in East Los Angeles. She invited my mom to go with her to help take care of my aunt's two kids. My mom agreed, and they all moved into a one-bedroom apartment. My aunt's husband would later introduce my father to my mother.

For his part, my dad had a very difficult time initially adjusting to life in the United States. After his family settled in East LA, he started attending public school, even though he knew no English. He went to Belvedere Junior High. He has often told me how hard it was for him because of the language difference. It was like being submerged into a sea of people that spoke only English. He had no idea what he heard. He would get punished for speaking Spanish by being sent to a corner of the room. He doesn't recall being in an ESL class but does remember one class aimed specifically at teaching Mexican immigrant kids like himself English. That's where he started to learn the language. He was helped by a teacher whom my dad remembers as a really awesome person who never belittled any of his students or made them feel ashamed for speaking Spanish.

The one class my dad did very well in was math. This was because in Mexico, they had already taught him advanced math, so he was ahead of the students at Belvedere. The math he learned in Mexico was a bit different, but he adjusted to the change here. He really enjoyed math because, as he says, it was the only subject where he didn't have to speak English.

My dad also suffered at first because neither he nor his parents knew about getting free lunch tickets. They thought they had to pay for them. So at first my dad, along with other immigrant students, went hungry at school for lunch.

When my dad then started high school at Garfield High, he knew much more English. He and all his siblings went to Garfield High, where they all graduated. Although his English was better, my dad doesn't remember speaking up much in class. What he does remember is getting into fights with some of the Mexican American kids. The school was almost all Mexican, but it was divided between U.S.-born Mexican Americans and the immigrants like my dad. The Mexican Americans, or Chicanos, were antagonistic toward the immigrant kids and called them derogatory names such as "wetbacks," "tijuaneros," or "mojados." In turn, my dad and the other immigrant students retaliated by calling the Chicanos "pochos," "pochitos," or "gringos." My dad also recalls today with tears in his eyes how he and other immigrant kids were taunted by Mexican American students. When he first told my sister and me that story, we were in elementary school. We didn't know what it all meant, but we promised never to use those words, and to this day we never have.

My dad was at Garfield High when the 1968 "blowouts" occurred, when thousands of students walked out in protest in the East LA schools. My dad says that he doesn't really know what the walkouts were all about but that he walked out because everyone was doing it. He thinks that most of the students also didn't know what the meaning of the blowouts was—at least his circle of friends didn't. It was only the more politically active students who seemed to know what they were doing. Everyone else just got dragged into it. He didn't have to go to classes or do assignments during the walkouts. He and his friends, instead of going to the rallies, went off to shoot pool or go do their own thing.

My dad doesn't remember the issues involved in the blowouts, such as the high school dropout rates and low reading scores. He was too busy just trying to survive in school. What he does remember is some of the racism he experienced at Garfield. By racism, he means the way that he and the other immigrant students were treated and how they were ridiculed by the Mexican Americans, including by some of the few Chicano teachers. "*Órale*, wetback, *venga a sus clases*," the teacher would yell at them. He also remembers the shop teacher telling him and other students to pay attention because this was the kind of work that they would be doing after they left school.

I think my dad wasn't politically involved in the blowouts because he felt that the school didn't belong to him. He felt like an outsider because of his immigrant status. I think his parents felt the same way. Unlike the Mexican Americans who had been here longer and had laid a foundation out of which they could respond to discrimination, my grandparents didn't have this experience. They had just recently arrived. They felt lucky to just be here and that their kids were in school. They only had time to deal with their daily lives.

My dad also remembers the Chicano Moratorium of August 29, 1970 [the Chicano anti–Vietnam War protest of over 20,000 in East LA that was attacked by the police]. He was at the pool hall with his friends not too far from the demonstration and the riot. But he wasn't a part of it.

It was that year, 1970, that my dad graduated from high school.

My dad had some idea of going on to college, but it wasn't financially possible. He and my *tío* Lica, who were the two oldest brothers, went to work in a glass factory in Vernon right out of school. They both worked there for many years.

My father also married soon after graduating from high school. This wasn't my mother but another woman he knew from school. The marriage only lasted five or six years. My father doesn't talk much about this. They had two kids, but my father has never had much contact with them. The last time I saw my half-siblings was when I was in the second grade.

He met my mother in 1978, and they married that same year. At first they moved in with my dad's brother, my *tío* Lica, who had bought a duplex in Monterey Park. My dad and mom rented one of the units. We were living in that house when I was born in 1981. My mother named me after a popular Mexican singer—Tania Libertad. We lived there for a while until family politics forced us to leave. My uncle was having an affair with another woman, and when his wife found out, she accused my parents of knowing about it and not telling her. My aunt blamed my parents and forced them to leave.

We moved in with my dad's parents in City Terrace, the same house where my dad was raised. It was a big house, which was good because at one point eleven people lived there, including our family with three kids (my older sister and younger brother and me), one of my dad's sisters—a single mom—with her two kids, one of my dad's younger sisters, and, of course, my grandparents. It was a two-bedroom house. My family lived in the large den. My aunts each had a room, and my grandparents slept in the living room. Despite the number of people living in the house, we never saw it as a problem. We all simply adjusted. Besides, my grandparents once a year went back to Guanajuato.

My early school experience was in Monterey Park. This included preschool, kindergarten, and up through the second grade. I attended Robert Hill Lane Elementary School, which is right across from East LA College. It was a pretty diverse school with Mexicans, Asian Americans, and some whites and blacks.

When I started school, I could already speak English because my older sister had started before me, and through her I learned English. However, Spanish was my first language. But as we grew up, my siblings and I spoke English to each other. We didn't interact much in Spanish. We also started to respond to our parents in English. To this day, my parents speak Spanish to us and we respond in English, which they can understand. My dad, of course, speaks English, since he went to school here. My mom could speak some English but preferred not to because she was embarrassed by her accent. The only people I speak to in Spanish are my grandparents. But the younger generation, we all speak English to each other.

Because I knew English when I entered school, I was never placed in ESL classes. Later, when my younger brother, Diego, started school, they wanted to put him in an ESL class, but my mother wouldn't let them. He knew English but he was rather shy, so they thought he couldn't speak the language.

My memories of attending Robert Hill Lane are generally positive. But I switched schools when we left Monterey Park and moved in with my grandparents. My new school was Harrison Elementary School.

Harrison was OK but not as good as Robert Hill Lane, or so I thought. I especially remember how bad the cafeteria food was at Harrison. There I was first put into a regular third grade class but very soon switched into a gifted class. It was the only class that was diverse in the whole school, which was primarily Mexican. But in the gifted class there were Mexicans, Vietnamese, and Thai students. I remained in the gifted class through the sixth grade. All of my teachers were either white or Asian. The only Latino teacher in the school taught ESL.

I did very well in elementary school and received good grades.

Because my dad, unlike my mom, spoke English, he would attend the PTA meetings and conferences with my teachers. This changed a bit in junior high, but even then my mom wasn't too involved due to her lack of English.

It was in elementary school that I began to express interest in music. I started to play the violin in fifth grade and continued to do so for six more years. I loved it and played in the school orchestra in sixth, seventh, and eighth grade. I also played in several mariachi bands. My parents encouraged my music and paid for private lessons at the local music and art school.

Following elementary school, I attended Belvedere Junior High for sixth, seventh, and eighth grade. When I started, the school divided students into their core groups named after countries. There was the Jamaican core for "average" or "less than average" students. Then there was the Brazilian core for "gifted" students and the kids in the magnet program. They first placed me in the Jamaican core but then decided I didn't really belong there and put me in the Brazilian one. This is like the story of my life. I'm always being misplaced and then changed.

There were very few Latino teachers, but the one I most fondly remember is Mr. Velarde. He was my counselor. He really pushed for his students. He organized college workshops already in junior high! He would ask us, "What college are you going to attend?"

Whatever we said, he supported, even if someone mentioned a junior college. When he asked me, I didn't know what to say, but I had a cousin who attended Fullerton College, so I said, "JC Fullerton," not even really knowing the differences between a junior college and a university.

"Oh, that's awesome," he responded.

Mr. Velarde just wanted to already instill in us the idea of going to college, and he told us that all of us could and would attend college.

One of the things I'll never forget about junior high is when in 1994, most of my classmates and I walked out in reaction to Proposition 187, the anti-immigrant proposition on the ballot at that time. We frankly knew almost nothing about the proposition, only vaguely that it unfairly targeted Latinos like us and our parents. We had heard that Roosevelt and Garfield High Schools were going to have walkouts, and so some of my friends and I thought that we should do something.

"Let's walk out," we said.

We passed the word around and decided on this particular day in April 1994 to do it. We even called Channel 52, one of the Spanish-language TV stations, to tell them what we were planning.

On that day during nutrition class in the early morning, we secretly told everyone that we would walk out at 10:30 A.M. in the middle of third period and leave the school and go home. This would be our symbolic protest.

This was courageous on our part, as I look back on it. But I didn't discuss it with my parents. I didn't really interact with my parents much in junior high. It was just something that my friends Cindy and Sonia and I planned.

Third period came, and we were sitting in our English class. Everyone was looking at each other. The teacher had found out about what we were planning to do but didn't know just when it would happen. But Mr. Velarde found out that it would be during third period, so he told the principal, who at the start of the period went on the intercom and said that if any students walked out, they would be suspended. But that didn't stop us. I guess we felt that if all of us walked out, they couldn't suspend all of us.

Ten thirty came, and we got up and walked out. In fact, as students streamed out of their classrooms, they just started running out. It was more of a "run out" than a walkout.

We didn't have any signs or anything like that. We weren't political. We were only in junior high, but we had an idea that Proposition 187 was bad and was "anti-Mexican."

As we left the building, however, we discovered that the two main gates had been locked to keep us in. We tried to climb the gates but found it too difficult. So we tried lifting the gates up from the bottom, and this worked. We just went under it. In the meantime, the teachers were trying to stop us. "Get back to class," they ordered, but we didn't listen to them. Even Mr. Velarde, whom we respected, tried.

"Stop, children, stop!" he cried out. "We can talk about this. Why are you doing this?"

But by then we were committed and didn't stop.

Because we had been delayed by the locked gates, we missed the TV crew from Channel 52. They apparently had looked around, and when no one came out, they left.

Once out of school, we went to friends' houses and hung out.

Now that I am a college student and taking classes in Chicano history, I'm aware that what we did in 1994 was somewhat similar to what had happened in the famous 1968 blowouts in the East LA schools. Of course, my dad, even though he wasn't political, had participated in that walkout.

I also remember the reaction of my parents to Proposition 187. They were frightened of being deported. One day after class around this time, my mother told me in Spanish: "*Mija*, if one day you come home and I'm not here, I want you to live with your *tía* Esperanza. She has her papers." My mother, in fact, was legal, but she still feared that she might be rounded up and deported.

Because of Prop 187, my dad and other relatives, including my maternal grandparents, applied for citizenship and later became U.S. citizens.

Fortunately, there were no repercussions at school because of our walkout.

From junior high, I went to Garfield High School, still in East LA. What was unusual at Garfield were the different school calendar tracks. One track, Track A, covered the normal September to June schedule. But Tracks B and C started at different times and ended at different times. Everyone preferred Track A, but I was put in Track B. That meant I started school in the summer and ended in April. The tracks in different months overlapped. It was all very confusing, but it was meant to service more students.

But besides getting used to a different school schedule, I had other problems with this tracking system. For example, most of the Advanced Placement honors classes were in Track A, so I was limited in trying to be in AP classes. I lucked out my junior year when I wanted to take AP U.S. history, and for the first time it was offered in Track B. In my senior year, I wanted to take AP European history, but it was only offered in Track A. I was able to enroll in it, but it meant that I had to take some of these classes after my regular school year was over. This is called cross-tracking. Some of my friends cross-tracked several AP classes, and that meant they were in school the entire calendar year.

One other problem in taking AP classes in Track B was that the exams were given while we were on break. This meant that we took the exams two months after we had finished the course. It was hard to prepare in this way. As a result, I didn't pass my exam in AP U.S. history or U.S. government. I did pass the one in Spanish.

Besides the lack of AP classes in Tracks B and C, it appeared that Track A was geared to those whom the teachers and counselors believed were the brightest kids, although this wasn't always true. I had done very well in junior high but was not put in Track A. On top of this, or because of this, I had to constantly correct my counselor, who would schedule me for lesser academic classes or even vocational classes. I had to negotiate being in honors classes or stronger classes that I was eligible for. I qualified for geometry but only got pre-algebra. So I had to tell my counselor to change this until he did. Most other kids who could have taken stronger classes didn't bother to see their counselors, and most counselors just didn't care. Once I had to tell my counselor, "Why are you putting me in wood shop?"

During my vacation months, I compensated for some of the weak academic classes in high school by taking classes at East LA College. I even took a class there on Chicano literature. These classes were for college credit.

In high school I competed in sports, specifically in swimming and tennis. I had not been active in either sport until I went to Garfield. I did well in both. In tenth grade, our freshman-sophomore swim team won the city competition. Our biggest rivalry was against Roosevelt, Garfield's archrival in every sport. In tennis, I competed in doubles. We did well among the East Side schools, but at the overall city level we usually got blown away.

Although we did well in swimming, we had to overcome the problem of not having our own campus swimming pool. We had to be bused either to East LA College or to the YMCA in Boyle Heights. We'd practice for an hour and then jump back on the bus to return to school and then go home.

Besides sports, I also became active in leadership. While I didn't run for student body office, I was elected more than once as a class officer. One responsibility that I had in this area was to take care of certain activities, such as lunch dances and putting on fund-raisers for the school.

There was a MEChA club at Garfield, but I wasn't really involved in it. It wasn't very political, but that wasn't why I didn't participate in it. I guess I was just too busy with my classes and sports. I did go to some MEChA-sponsored meetings at Roosevelt, but that was primarily because my Spanish teacher, Mr. Hoppings, invited me and a few other students from his class to go with him.

Ethnicity or ethnic identity wasn't a big issue at Garfield, since 99.9 percent of the students were Latino. We had no white or Asian kids to compare ourselves to or compete with. Most of us were of Mexican background, but some were Central American, primarily Salvadoran. I had Salvadoran friends and even one white friend, an Anglo guy, who was bused in as part of the magnet program. Since we were pretty much all Latinos, kids hung around based on certain interests. So the basketball players hung out with each other and so too the cheerleaders, et cetera. My group of friends was pretty mixed. We were into sports, but we also studied together.

I did very well in my academic work, although I didn't particularly care for science and math. I was more interested in languages and literature, especially English. I graduated with a 3.9 or 4.0 average and was named to the Ephebian Society as a senior. The society included students who had excelled in academics but had also displayed leadership and contributed to the school. At graduation, Ephebian scholars wore black robes. Students nominated you for the award, but teachers selected you. I also graduated with high honors from the California Scholarship Federation.

I now think about how well I did in school even though I didn't have good study conditions at home. I never had my own room and desk. I shared the living room as a bedroom with my sister. If I wanted privacy, I'd retreat to the restroom. I had my radio there and would listen to music, read, or write in my journal. But there was no room to do my homework. So I'd go to the East LA Library, or to the East LA College library, or to the Anthony Quinn Library at Belvedere Junior High. Sometimes I'd study at a friend's house.

Actually, I didn't mind having to study elsewhere. As I grew up, I found my house too confining with so many people and so little room. I welcomed every opportunity to leave my house. I needed my space. Going out was an escape for me. This included trips with the tennis team or swim team or trips with friends. These were all ways for me not to be at home.

Overall, I had a positive experience in high school. I was very involved and had a strong group of friends who shared common interests. We called ourselves the "cool nerds." We were serious about our schoolwork, but we also liked to have a good time going to parties, dancing, and dating.

Part of my school life was having a boyfriend. My parents had been very strict with my sister, and she ended up dropping out of high school. They were less strict with me but at the same time were always cautioning me. They didn't want me dropping out of school, and they certainly didn't want me to get pregnant. They always kept telling me, "Be careful or you're going to end up like your sister," which was really unfair given that my sister could have had a fair shot at completing her education had she received the right amount of discipline and guidance.

Despite this concern, my parents gave me enough freedom. I had my friends, and my parents knew how important my friends were to me.

My mother, however, did insist on a curfew. "You know what time is a good time to come home," she'd say in Spanish. "You don't come strolling into the house at two in the morning. A decent woman doesn't do this."

But she didn't need to lecture me. I set my own curfew and never returned too late. I was very responsible.

My boyfriend was five years older than me. We had met when I was a sophomore and he had already been out of school for a year or two. We dated regularly until the beginning of my senior year.

Needless to say, my parents didn't like the fact that he was much older than me. They didn't like him. "Don't wind up getting pregnant," my mother would further warn me. "Watch out, he's going to pull you down and take you away from your studies."

"I won't let him do that to me," I asserted myself. "I'm going to prove you wrong."

With my parents' hatred toward my boyfriend, I didn't dare bring him home very much. He did attend a couple of family functions, but I tried to keep him away from my parents.

He was my first steady boyfriend, but I broke up with him. It was devastating. My mom got very worried. She thought I would drop out of school because of my breakup with him. But I didn't. Still, I took it hard, and my image of guys completely changed as well as my relationships. I think this has carried over until now. I've become very disillusioned about men. But it's OK. I'm sure one day this will change.

Although I had broken up with my boyfriend, I still attended my senior prom. By then I had a new boyfriend. He didn't go to my school but attended a highly gifted magnet program at North Hollywood High. Despite my misgivings about guys, I developed a compatible relationship with him. He remained my boyfriend until my sophomore year in college. Then we called it off completely. I was very serious about him, but it didn't work out.

One other change in my senior year in high school was that we moved to Whittier. There was a lot of tension, living in my grandparents' house. My aunt constantly fought with my sister. It became physical, and my mom couldn't take it any longer, which led us to move out of East LA. My mother told my dad, "I don't care whether you come with me or not, but the kids and I are leaving."

My dad agreed, and we moved to Whittier into the same apartment complex where my mother's parents lived. We lived upstairs and they lived downstairs in the same unit.

The one hesitation my mom had about moving was wondering what effect it would have on my education. She actually in a way sought my permission.

"Don't worry, Mom, let's move, but I'm not transferring schools. I'll commute for the rest of my senior year. It's only six more months."

And so I did. Each morning I'd take a bus from Whittier to East LA, crossing through Pico Rivera and Montebello. I adjusted, but my parents had even more of an adjustment because they also had to commute to work. My father had been laid off for a long time, but by the time we moved, he had found a new job at a *carnicería*, not as a butcher but packing and freezing the meat. But his job was closer to East LA. My mother also by this time had started working at a downtown garment factory operating machines and assembling parts. My dad got her a used car, and she commuted each day. The only one who didn't commute was my younger brother, who transferred to Katherine Edwards Middle School.

When graduation finally came, it was a big deal, a big family deal. Unfortunately, my grandparents were in Mexico at that time, but the rest of the family attended the ceremonies. Everyone was very emotional, including, of course, me. What made graduation even more special was that I graduated with high honors and wore a black robe to indicate this instead of the usual blue robe. Only twenty students graduated with a black robe out of over six hundred students. From that class, only a little over one hundred went on to a four-year college. Some, however, got into Stanford, Harvard, Yale, and a few other very prestigious schools.

During all of this time as I was growing up, my cultural tastes were affected by both my home and my friends.

Food at home was Mexican, especially because we lived with my grandparents. We always had frijoles and *arroz*. For special occasions, we'd have mole, enchiladas, menudo, or pozole. We'd have nopales from our backyard. My mom did most of the cooking. She learned to cook the way my dad's mom cooks. That's the only way my dad likes his food.

I never cooked. I picked up a few things from my mother, but she never asked me to cook. The only time I would help in the kitchen was at Christmas, when all the women in the family prepared the tamales. In fact, I did very little housework. I didn't really have the time because of my homework and extracurricular activities. My mother accepted this and supported my schoolwork and activities.

Outside of home, my friends and I would eat fast food like McDonald's or pizza. If at home I ever expressed a craving for McDonald's, my mother would get on my case: "What's the matter with you? Are burritos no longer good for you?" Now, living away from home, I really miss my mother's cooking.

As far as music was concerned, I was never much into voluntarily listening to Mexican music while growing up, although that was played at home and at family functions. With my friends, I liked more modern American music. I didn't even see it as American music but just as whatever appealed to me.

The only exception in my music tastes was mariachi music because I played it. I had asked for violin classes outside of the ones provided in school in seventh grade. My mother paid for the lessons at the local music and art school. I used a violin from my junior high. In high school, I couldn't check out a violin, so my mother bought me one for five hundred dollars. This wasn't a lot as violin prices go, but it still was a big sacrifice for my mom. Although I don't play the violin anymore, I still have it because it's special to me. I'll never get rid of it.

It was in high school that I heard a mariachi group in the community that met once a week at the art and music school. I asked my mom if I could go to the practices, and she agreed to pay for the lessons. It was called the Mariachi Heritage Society, and it was composed of people of different ages, including eight-year-old violinists and forty-year-old musicians. The director was José Hernández from the famous Sol de México mariachi based in Los Angeles. He wanted to start a smaller group to perform at parties and concerts. We traveled to Texas, Arizona, and other parts of California performing. My parents let me go to these events because other parents would always chaperone. At our performances, we'd wear these elaborate mariachi outfits.

I became very passionate about playing mariachi music. My grandparents loved hearing me practice at home and even hoped I would make this a career. My parents were also proud of my playing. But the more they encouraged me, the more I started to push away from it. I stopped later in high school. However, I still get emotional when I hear mariachi music. It was a nice time in my life.

Today my musical tastes are very modern and contemporary, but nothing specifically tied in with ethnic music.

As far as language is concerned, I feel more comfortable speaking English to my dad. I don't feel comfortable speaking Spanish with him. I just don't. Even though he'll respond to me both in English and Spanish, I won't do the Spanish thing with him. With my mom, I'm comfortable speaking both languages. Since I've been in college, I actually speak more Spanish to her. But as I was growing up, I would speak mostly English to her and she would respond in Spanish. In a way, this helped her understand and learn some English at the same time that I was losing my Spanish. My Spanish isn't all that great.

When I was in junior high and up to about tenth grade, I'd sit and translate English-language television shows for my grandparents. They especially liked the nature shows on PBS. On the other hand, they only watched Spanish-language news and movies in Spanish. We didn't have cable but only the basic channels. When my sister and I watched television, it was always English-language shows. The only program in Spanish I watched with my grandparents and parents was the popular *Sábado Gigante* every Saturday evening. My mother didn't watch Spanish-language soap operas because my sister and I would say, "Don't watch those *novelas*; they're awful." So she wouldn't. Throughout high school, I didn't watch much television because I didn't spend a lot of time at home, but even with my friends we didn't watch television. We'd listen to the radio and our albums. Even today, I don't watch much TV.

Although I'm not religious now, I did have a big dose of religion as I was growing up. My paternal grandparents are Catholic and very religious. My grandfather reads the Bible three times a day. He and my grandmother go to daily Mass at six in the morning. But both my dad and mom aren't very religious, especially my dad. My mom, however, made sure that my siblings and I went to Mass each Sunday. My parents would take us, but my dad would stay only for a little while and then go outside and wait for us. We attended Our Lady of Guadalupe Church near Belvedere Junior High.

Perhaps because my mother herself wasn't that religious, she didn't put me in catechism classes to prepare for my First Communion when I was young. Instead, I waited until high school to do my First Communion and confirmation. I was about fifteen years old at that time. I actually didn't want to go through this process, but my mom insisted. She threatened that if I didn't, she wouldn't support me doing sports or my music. I had no choice.

I remember, as I was growing up, being somewhat confused about religion. We're Catholics, but some of my relatives in Corcoran, on my mother's side, became born-again Christians. Another uncle is a Jehovah's Witness. I visited them each summer, and my aunt would take me to her church. I remember all this music, happy kids, and people falling on the floor feeling the faith. So I felt myself in the middle of my parents' Catholicism and my Corcoran relatives' born-again Christian religion. I didn't know what to believe. I think all of this made me drift away from my religion. I stopped going to Mass after my confirmation.

I also didn't have a *quinceañera* when I turned fifteen. I didn't want one, and besides, we couldn't afford it. I knew if I really wanted one, my mom would have financially sacrificed for it, but I didn't want one. I didn't like the idea of it. I thought, "Oh my God, what's the big fuss about wearing a white dress? If I'm going to have a big fuss, let it be when I get married." But I did have a big party with a deejay with all of my friends.

It was in my junior year that I started to think about attending college in a serious way. No one in my immediate family, of course, had attended college, so there was no prior experience to fall back on. At the same time, my parents supported the idea of further education. They would tell me, "Siga adelante"—keep going forward.

My friends and I started going to the counseling center at our school for advice. The director of the program, a white woman, didn't give us much attention because she was primarily favoring students in Track A. We did get some help from a student from UCLA named Beto, who was Chicano. He would come to our school every two weeks to encourage and advise students to apply to UCLA. We also got help from the secretary of our counseling center, a Latina.

My friends Cindy and Miguel and I initially only considered applying to UC Santa Barbara. We thought about how beautiful Santa Barbara was, and we also wanted to get away from home. I had never been to Santa Barbara but had only heard about it. We didn't consider UCLA because it was too close to home, and UC Berkeley was too far away. UCSB was just perfect.

Together, the three of us into our senior year devised a three-plan strategy about applying to college. Plan A was to apply to UCSB, UCLA, and UC San Diego, although our preference was UCSB. Plan B involved applying to all the Cal State schools, and Plan C was to go to East LA College, our local community college, and then transfer to a UC or Cal State campus.

I took the SAT exams but didn't do as well as I had hoped to. This hurt me in my applications. I was not admitted to UCLA or UC San Diego but managed to get into UCSB. This was great, except at the time I was graduating, I had changed my mind. I now wanted to go to UCLA! I had decided that I would prefer to be closer to home. Also, I felt that I was selling myself short by focusing on UCSB rather than UCLA. Part of my disappointment was that Cindy and Miguel both got into UCLA and decided to go there. But I got over my disappointment and realized that UCSB was also a major university and the important thing was what I put into my undergraduate education.

My parents were elated over my acceptance to UCSB. What was important to them was that a prestigious university had accepted their daughter! I still get emotional when I think about how happy they were at that moment.

When I decided on UCSB, my dad supported my going. My mother, however, began to have doubts. She wanted me to go to college and had expressed joy and pride when I got accepted into UCSB but then began to worry about my going away from home.

"Why are you going to Santa Barbara? Why do you have to go away? Why can't you go to UCLA? When will you be back? How often will you come home?"

I had to explain to her that UCLA hadn't admitted me, and since I wanted to go to a UC campus, my only choice was UCSB. She finally accepted my decision, and she, along with my whole family, was very supportive.

The summer that I graduated, I came to UCSB for the first time for the two-week STEP [Summer Transitional Enrichment Program], which is an orientation for mostly minority students. This was my first experience with Santa Barbara and UCSB.

"Wow," I thought to myself, "this place is beautiful!"

But I didn't think UCSB was for me. It was too white and too relaxed—it was just so different from what I was used to. On the other hand, I also thought of how UCSB wasn't too far from home and yet far enough so that I could become my own person and grow.

At first, I didn't like STEP because I felt that it pressured all of us to socialize and participate in group activities. I thought this was too much like high school. Despite the effort to bring diverse people together, I noticed that very quickly most everyone formed into cliques: blacks with blacks, Latinos with Latinos, and Asians with Asians.

I tried to avoid sticking to one particular group, so I floated around. What struck me was the diversity among minority students. First of all, I had never seen so many African American students. There really weren't that many, but compared to my high school that was primarily Latino, it was a lot. I also met Jewish and Asian students. I also realized that among Latinos, there were differences. Not all were Mexican. I met several from different Central American countries. I had never thought about this. In high school, we were all brown.

I also discovered that there was a certain amount of competitiveness and one-upmanship among the students in the program. People wanted to know your background, where you were from, what your GPA was, and what AP classes you took. When they would find out, sometimes some snobbishness would be expressed.

I was also exposed for the first time to students from other parts of California. I had never met, for example, students from the Bay Area. I was fascinated by the slang that they used that I was not familiar with. The fact was that I don't think I had ever met a person who lived past downtown LA!

One of the things I did like was meeting my roommate, Belén, for the program. She introduced me to some of her friends who would later play a huge role in my undergraduate experience and development.

Besides going to STEP, that summer I got my first real job. I worked at a Blockbuster video store.

September came along too fast, and it was time for me to start my freshman year at UCSB. I hadn't liked the experience of living in the on-campus dorms during STEP, so I chose to apply to live in the Fontaine-bleu off-campus apartments. Fortunately, I got my selection. It was a two-bedroom apartment with a living room and kitchen—although the building did have a cafeteria. It felt more like a home. I had to share it with three other girls.

I had lived at home in pretty tight quarters, so the living arrange-ments at UCSB weren't going to be a major change for me. What was a major change was that all three of my roommates were white. I remem-ber thinking, "This is not cool." But I also reminded myself that I was open-minded and that I was going to see this work out.

I tried but didn't get along too well with the student I shared a room with. Our personalities were too different. Among other things, she didn't appreciate my inviting my friends over. The same was true for one of the other girls. But I did get along with my fourth roommate. She was a bit older and a transfer student. She was very nice.

My living arrangement was helped by the fact that some of the friends I had made during STEP lived in the same complex. I often found myself over at their place. They kind of adopted me.

Like many other freshmen, I too suffered from homesickness. At first I fought against this and going home too frequently. I didn't want my family to think that I had made the wrong decision and that I should come home. Still, I found myself literally hungering for home. I craved my mother's tacos and enchiladas, and of course I missed my family. I ac-tually found myself returning home quite frequently. I felt guilty about this my first quarter, but then I decided that there was nothing wrong about missing my family, and so if I wanted to go home for a weekend, I should. I reconciled this feeling in the second quarter.

Another problem that I had to resolve concerned making friends at UCSB. I still believed that after my first year, I would transfer to UCLA. Feeling this way, I didn't want to develop too strong relationships at UCSB. But this changed in my second quarter when I found out about a Latina support group called Hermanas Unidas.

Actually, Hermanas Unidas started that winter quarter. The founders were some of my friends that I had met in STEP that previous summer. One day, my friend Veronica approached me and informed me that she was calling a meeting of Latina women who had been in STEP. She told me that she wanted to start this group of Latina students. I was a bit leery at first because I didn't like the idea of joining a sorority. But Veronica assured me that this wasn't a sorority. It would be a support group. I went to the first meeting, and it was really cool. There wasn't anything superficial because we all knew each other; we were friends before we became *hermanas*. We all agreed to form a chapter of Hermanas Unidas on campus.

I say a chapter because it was a statewide organization. The first and founding chapter was at UC Berkeley. They had started a few years before. We became the second chapter, and we've become the largest one. Other chapters exist at UCLA and St. Mary's. Hermanas Unidas focuses on three key issues: academics, community service, and social issues. For academics, we have study hours where we study together as Hermanas. For community service, we tutor Latino kids in Isla Vista, adjacent to UCSB, and we do outreach programs to some of the high schools to encourage Latinos to attend college. On the social side, we have food sales, car washes, and other events to raise money for our community programs. We started with about twelve to seventeen students, and we now have about sixty Hermanas.

Hermanas Unidas has been crucial for me. It gave me the motivation to continue at UCSB. I had a reason to stay. It provided me with leadership training. I've served as an officer by being a peer adviser for two years. Above all, it gave me a support network of other Latinas who cared for me and helped me when I needed help. Hermanas has been one of the most important aspects of my college experience. I don't think I would have stuck through college if not for Hermanas.

I think my biggest adjustment at UCSB was my academics. The workload was drastically different. It wasn't so much the classes as the pace of the quarter system of only ten weeks. I had no time for anything but studying, and I didn't like that. There were just so many different sides of me that needed to be fulfilled in order for me to be happy. But I wasn't happy just focusing on academics. It was driving me crazy. I didn't know how to manage my time properly. I was like, "This is due in two weeks? This is due in five weeks?" It was just too much.

What was also difficult was the size and composition of my classes. Two of my classes were in Campbell Hall, the largest lecture hall on campus, with an eight-hundred-student capacity. I always sat in the center middle and felt totally anonymous and intimidated. On top of this, I would look around me and see nothing but blond hair. The same was true of my other classes. My smaller discussion sections weren't very different, either. In my religious studies section there was only one other Latina—I didn't even know if she was Mexican—and one black girl. Everyone else was white, including the graduate teaching assistants.

I had never seen so many white people in my entire life. And they all wore flip-flops. I started to ask myself, "Should I be wearing flip-flops?" They all had their hair bleached blond. "Should I dye my hair?" I was stereotyping, but that's what I saw. It's raining. "Why are there people wearing sandals?" Everyone has a bike. "Okay, I need a bike." I got the bike, and it got stolen.

Under these conditions, I found it hard to speak up in my smaller classes and discussion sections. I felt very uncomfortable. But I thought, "No, I'm as smart as these people—so why am I so intimidated? Say something. You used to talk all the time in high school, Tania. Your teacher couldn't shut you up. You need to say something." I forced myself to say something but not often. I finally decided that I would speak up if I really had something to say and not because I felt I had to prove myself.

I didn't take any Chicano studies classes my first year. Many of my friends were taking Introduction to Chicano Studies, but I felt that they were doing so because they felt it was expected of them. I didn't want to do this. If I took a class, it was because I wanted to genuinely learn about it and not for another reason. To me, taking Chicano studies was narrowing myself and separating myself from everybody else. I didn't want to do that. I wanted to go out there and put myself with the rest of the students. I no longer believe this, but that's how I felt as a freshman. I also didn't identify as a Chicana but as a Mexican American.

That first year went by very fast. Where did all my time go? I did OK in classes, maintaining close to a B average. What was important was that I had made it through my first year. I had heard that if you survive the first year, then you'd probably stick out the rest of your college career. I had made it.

The next two years, I felt much more adjusted and comfortable at UCSB. I settled on a dual major of art history and film studies. I enjoyed most of my classes, but at the same time, it was hard to explain to my parents and friends who hadn't gone to college why I was majoring in these two fields. They wanted to know why I hadn't chosen something more like education, law, or medicine. Education to them was practical. You go to college to get a good job or profession. Why else go? What can you do with art history or film studies, they wanted to know. I couldn't really explain it to them, but this is what I liked, and I hoped it would lead to something I would enjoy doing after college.

One great thing about being at UCSB and at a UC campus was the opportunity to study abroad. The summer before my senior year, I participated in the Querétaro program as operated by the Center for Chicano Studies. This was a five-week program of UCSB classes in Querétaro, Mexico. We were placed with a host family and got to interact with them. My host family was very hospitable and warm. They treated me like their daughter. They had a son my age who attended the local university, and he took me and some of the other UCSB girls out to clubs and local events. We also went on family trips to other towns.

The fact that I knew Spanish was an advantage, or so I thought. I had learned my Spanish at home from parents and grandparents who were from the ranchos in Mexico. By contrast, the Mexicans in Querétaro were urban and more sophisticated. So I would say certain things in Spanish, and they would correct me. "No, that's not how you say it in Spanish." Despite these differences, I enjoyed my experience in Querétaro, and it prepared me for my next experience abroad.

That fall I went to Spain for the UC program there. I had wanted to go to Spain since I had heard about the program in my freshman year. But my mother wouldn't hear of it. She forbade me to go. I told her that this only made me want to go even more. And I finally did.

Spain was totally different. It was a dramatic change of people and culture. I had a hard time adjusting. One adjustment involved the fact that the Spaniards whom I met couldn't or wouldn't believe that I was American. They saw me as a Mexican. Some even thought I was Persian or Chinese. They couldn't understand that I was Mexican American. I learned that many other Latino students in Spain encountered the same reaction. The Spaniards had a stereotype of who was American, and we didn't fit it. Another UC student and I lived with six Spanish girls. When I would call my mother and speak to her both in Spanish and English, the Spanish girls couldn't understand this: "You speak to her in Spanish and then in English!"

At the Universidad de Alcalá in Alcalá de Henares, I took classes in Spanish feminist literature, Spanish cinema, and the geography of Spain, plus a grammar and conversation class. The classes were composed only of UC students but taught by Spanish professors. All of the classes were in Spanish.

The classes were quite mixed ethnically, although we were all from the United States. What was interesting was that our Spanish professors had high expectations of the Latino students. They assumed that our command of Spanish was stronger than the Anglos', and so they expected much better essays and exams in Spanish. But this was another stereotype. The fact was that many of the Caucasian students wrote better in Spanish than we did. This is because, although as Latinos we could speak Spanish, we couldn't write it very well. We hadn't mastered Spanish academically, especially in writing. By contrast, the Caucasian students couldn't speak Spanish as well, but because they had studied it more academically, they could write it better. Some of us Latinos got our essays returned with all of these red marks on them correcting our Spanish.

But the language issue wasn't just in the classes. I encountered it with some of the Spanish students. For example, on one of my first visits to a Spanish bar, I started talking to this guy in Spanish. I thought I was talking perfectly well in Spanish, only to be shocked when he rudely interrupted me.

"Háblame en español. Eso no es en español."

I was shocked and offended. How could this guy tell me I couldn't speak Spanish? "Excuse me," I thought to myself and had to just walk away.

By the end of the semester, I became more used to all of the stereotypes and expectations and just concentrated on having a good time in Spain. One benefit of the program was that we could travel to other European countries. With some of my UC friends, I visited Paris and Amsterdam.

I could have stayed for a second semester, but like most of the other UC students, I was ready to come back home. I'm glad that I went. I missed my family and felt deeply sad when my maternal grandfather passed away while I was gone, but overall, I grew a lot from the experience, both academically and emotionally.

I'll be graduating in a year, but already I feel that my life has changed quite a bit. I feel more assured of myself. I don't know yet what I'll be in life, but I'm not afraid of the future. I'm looking forward to graduating, and I can't wait to get out. I want to go to New York and get an internship there and see what happens. Then I want to go to graduate school within two years. I don't know yet what I would study, but I'll settle on something. Right now my goal is to go to New York. I hope to get an internship at the Metropolitan Museum of Art in the Latin American section. I've told my mom of my plans, and she's not in favor of my going to New York.

"Why are you going?" she says. "Why can't you come home?"

But I can't go home, not anymore. This isn't an option for me anymore. I can't imagine myself living there. I've changed too much. Even though I can't live at home anymore, curiously I've become even more family oriented. I have a better relationship with my parents and siblings. I've also learned to appreciate my culture a lot more. Definitely my trips to Mexico and Spain contributed to this. Those trips really gave me a better understanding of who I am and have helped me appreciate my family and background more.

This sense of not being able to go back home to live is part of my change. Change is definitely a process. I can't pinpoint big changes; some I'm probably not even conscious of. When I came back from Spain, I remember all of my friends saying, "Whoa, you're different."

"What do you mean? I feel like I'm the same person."

"No," they told me, "you don't even joke around the same way. You don't do the same things anymore. You're a different person."

I thought that maybe that was true, but then I think we've all changed. People are always changing.

I've also changed in my relationships with men. I've become more skeptical of relationships. At UCSB, I started analyzing relationships and concluded that there's no way one can have a faithful relationship here. No way. The climate supports too much fooling around. It's not the place for fidelity.

You also come under various pressures about dating. There's no specific pressure about dating a white guy, but the fact is that it seems that minorities here tend to date only within their own group. So if you dated outside of it, it would be rare and quite noticeable. I don't necessarily support this type of dating only within your own ethnic group. I've dated whites and blacks. However, I have to say that I've concluded that I can't imagine myself in the future marrying a person who is not of my same cultural background because I want my future kids, if I have kids, to be raised with similar cultural values.

But marriage, as far as I'm concerned, is not in the near future anyway. All of my cousins who are my age are either now married or single moms with kids. That's not for me. I don't consider myself better than them, but I don't want to be married now with kids. That's my decision. My mother seems to be OK with this. She says, "You keep going as far as you can." Still, part of her wants me to eventually have kids. She's worried about who would care for me later in life. But I tell her that I'll decide when and if I'll have kids. I believe that as a woman, I shouldn't be expected to have children. It's a choice, and I'll choose not to, at least for several years. It's not like my parents are waiting for me to give them their first grandchild.

If and when I get married, I don't see this affecting whatever career I'll have. For one thing, I won't get married until I'm already settled into a career. Even if I have children, I'll still maintain my career. My future husband will just have to accept that.

I consider myself a feminist, although it's only been recently that I've embraced that term. I don't like labels, but based on the way I think, I see myself as a feminist. I identify more with being a woman, being a feminist, than with being a Chicana. To me, the woman part of me is more important than ethnicity, although they are all truly connected.

Tania Picasso graduated from the University of California, Santa Barbara, in 2004. She worked for two years for Artnet in New York City before returning to California, where she received a master of public art studies degree from the University of Southern California. She works for the City of Los Angeles Department of Cultural Affairs within the Public Art Division and is happily married.

SANDY ESCOBEDO

I don't know very much about my parents' family background. They never really told me much about it. My father was born in Guadalajara, Jalisco, in Mexico in 1960. My mother is from El Salvador, having been born there in 1958. She was born in La Union, but her family moved to San Miguel. She eventually moved to San Salvador, the capital, as a young woman. My father's name is Javier Escobedo, and my mother's is Elizabeth Escobedo.

Both of my parents have limited education. My father got the equivalent of a middle school education. My mom has mentioned to me that what education she received was largely on her own. She enrolled herself in school. It wasn't her parents' priority to educate her. My mom had an innate interest to be educated. Unfortunately, she didn't go beyond the sixth grade. However, later in the United States, she took a GED preparation exam at Ford Park Adult Center in Bell Gardens in the greater Los Angeles area.

Because both my parents were from poor families, they had to work at an early age. My dad's father passed away when Dad was only six years old. That immediately forced him to start working to help his mother. In my mom's case, her mother was a baker and sold bread in the streets. At age nine, my mom assisted her. My mother is very proud of this. She loves to work, just like my dad.

Both of my parents entered the U.S. in 1979. My dad wasn't nineteen yet, and my mom was twenty-one. My dad came because he had an uncle who had already been working in the U.S. On a trip back to Mexico, he invited my dad to join him when he returned north. My dad readily agreed. Finding work in the U.S. was his big motivation for his decision, but it was also a sense of adventure.

My mom also had an uncle who influenced her to go to the U.S. In her case, her uncle was a well-to-do businessman in El Salvador with business contacts in the U.S. Her uncle knew that the political situation in El Salvador was only going to get worse. He advised my mom to leave before things got worse. She did. She took a bus through Mexico all the way to Tijuana. There, her uncle's Anglo business partners met her, and she got into a 1979 red sports car with them. My mom has fair skin, so when they crossed the border, the inspector didn't pay much attention to her. They assumed that she was American.

My dad also crossed without papers, but in his case he either crossed a desert or crossed a river. I don't know.

Coincidently, my parents wound up living in the same apartment building in Los Angeles. It was near USC around Vermont and Hoover on 20th Street, right off the 10 freeway. Both of them had aunts there who housed them. It was a two-story building, and my dad lived on the bottom floor and my mom on the top. This is how they met and eventually married.

After they met, they didn't date too long before getting married. I think my dad was first attracted to my mom. He then asked my mom's aunt for permission to date her niece. What my mom most liked about my dad was how responsible he was, especially toward his mother in Mexico. He regularly sent her money. They got married in June of 1980 by a justice of the peace. They wanted to be married in the Catholic church, but my dad's family wanted the wedding to be in Mexico and my mom's family wanted it in El Salvador. To ease the tension, they just got married by a judge. Nine years later, on a trip to Mexico, they got remarried in the Basílica de Zapopán. Then they got their own apartment in the same building where they lived. After I was born on March 29, 1981, this is where we lived. But we soon moved out because it was too noisy.

We moved to Bell, just south of LA. A friend of my dad's cousin lived there and rented a guesthouse to us.

Although my parents were from different countries, they shared many similar Latino cultural traditions. The only area that concerned my dad was food. He loved his Mexican food. My mother actually didn't know how to cook any kind of food. Fortunately, my dad's aunt showed her how to cook Mexican food. She can't cook Salvadoran food.

My dad at first worked a number of jobs. He worked in upholstery making furniture. He also worked as a busboy in restaurants. After I was born, he had to work two jobs to make ends meet since my mother had to stop working.

My mom first worked as a babysitter in Beverly Hills. She took care of two children. She didn't work when she got pregnant with me and later with my sister, but after giving birth she resumed working.

When my parents came to the U.S., only my mom knew a little English. In El Salvador she had met some American missionaries and from them picked up some English. She also learned a few English words by listening to American pop music on the radio. Once in LA, they both in time took ESL classes and learned enough English to get by. My dad, however, still isn't very comfortable with the language, while my mother is more fluent.

After they arrived in the U.S., some of their other siblings also left from Mexico and El Salvador to live in different parts of the United States. My grandmother on my dad's side moved permanently to the U.S. in the early 2000s. My grandmother on my mom's side moved to the U.S. in 1997 but passed away in 2003. My maternal grandfather never immigrated.

I grew up in Bell until I was twelve. We then moved to Bell Gardens, which is only about ten minutes away. I think I had a pretty good childhood. I specifically remember Christmas, when the city of Bell put up Christmas lights throughout the city. I remember the huge pine trees by the public library that were all decorated. They would also have a Santa Claus there. My mom would take me and told Santa what I wanted. I was an only child for almost ten years, until my sister was born. We were the only kids in the family.

My neighborhood in Bell was predominantly Latino, mostly Mexican, but some neighbors were of other Latino backgrounds. For example, the person who took care of me before I went to school and while my mom worked was Cuban, Juana Álvarez. I grew very close to her and considered her like my grandmother. She lives in Miami now, where I have gone to visit her.

My mother continued to work while I grew up as well as after my sister was born. Before she was pregnant with me, she worked in a cookie factory run by Asian people, perhaps Korean or Chinese. After that she worked at Sears. Then she became a home care provider for senior citizens. She worked at that for quite a while until she left to work for Mission Food Cooperative, a large tortilla company. She packed tortillas until she injured her arm and had to stop working for a long time. She stopped in 1992 and didn't work again until 1996. She then went back to being a home care provider in 2000.

My dad has had various jobs as well. When I turned seven, he went to work for Alcoa. I don't know specifically what he did, but it was a company that built airplane parts. When it closed in 1991, he went back to doing upholstery. In 1994, he got a job as a machine operator for Kaiser, and that's where he works now. Sometimes, however, he's been laid off, like in 1994 and 1996.

Both of my parents are now documented, and they are U.S. citizens. This was the result of the 1986 amnesty law. They became citizens in December of 1994.

My mom is especially proud of being a U.S. citizen. She loves this country. She really believes that anyone who wants to become something has every possibility and opportunity to do that here. I respect her for her view but don't completely agree. My parents have been fortunate, although they have worked hard to achieve a better life than the one they had in their respective countries of origin. But many other Latino immigrants haven't been as fortunate. I really don't think that my parents have confronted some of the abuses that other immigrants experience.

I started my education in preschool. This was a school run by the city called the Bell Tiny Tots Program. I was in the class of '86. By going to preschool and watching television shows like *Sesame Street*, I learned English. When I went to kindergarten at Corona Avenue Elementary, I had to take a placement test that was given in both English and Spanish. I took both and did better in English than in Spanish. So I never went through ESL.

Right away, my teacher told my mom that I was going to be a special kid. I could have skipped kindergarten and gone directly into first grade, but my teacher felt that it would be better for me to stay with my own age group.

In the second grade, I was nominated to take the gifted and talented test. I took it and passed. So starting in third grade, I was separated and put in the more advanced classes. I learned Greek mythology in third grade. My teacher, Mrs. Hare, took us on a field trip to the Getty Museum that was still in Malibu then. We had to choose our own favorite Greek god or goddess and explain why. I chose Apollo because I liked music. At that time I also joined the orchestra and played the flute. I only played it for two years.

Mrs. Hare also helped me when I struggled. My mom would speak to her in her halting English, and if worst came to worst, I would translate for her. She had to see Mrs. Hare various times because I wasn't doing well in math. But Mrs. Hare was encouraging and got me to come in early to school to be tutored in math.

My school and my classes were mostly Latino, although there were still a few whites. But there was also a strong Middle Eastern presence, specifically Lebanese. Our neighbors were from Lebanon. In fact, there was one street, Otis Avenue, where many Lebanese lived. We called them "Arabics," not knowing any better.

I attended Corona Avenue through fourth grade until they redrew the school boundaries and I had to enroll in the Nueva Vista School. It didn't have a gifted program, but they did put me in a group with fifth and sixth graders. It was as close to gifted as possible. We were basically taught sixth grade material. This was also a predominantly Latino school.

As I began to go through my school years, I increasingly became more English-speaking, especially with other students and my friends. The students at my school were, like me, mostly U.S.-born Latinos, including some whose parents had arrived from El Salvador, Guatemala, or Nicaragua. At home, however, I still spoke mostly Spanish to my parents, although sometimes I would respond to them in English. I didn't call them *mamá* or *papá* but Dad and Mom.

Because of my home environment, I developed a bilingual ability. This allowed me to become literally a translator for my parents. For example, when my mom got injured and had to hire an Anglo lawyer, I wrote the letter to him, read every document he sent to my mom, and explained to her what these documents meant. I was eleven or twelve at the time.

After I graduated from Nueva Vista, I attended Chester W. Nimitz Middle School in Huntington Park. This was the middle school in my district. At first my mom didn't want me to go there because she thought there were gang problems at the school. But it wasn't really that bad. There were a few minor gang types but nothing like you see in East LA. It was a perfectly safe school.

Because of my academic abilities and achievements, I was placed in the honors classes through the eighth grade. The school was all Latino, but we divided ourselves between the honors students—the nerds—and the non-honors students. We in the honors classes thought ourselves better than the others. We saw ourselves as "smart" and the others as the problem kids. Looking back at it now, this was wrong, but that was the attitude at the time. There was no friction or fights between the groups, just a differentiation and clustering. I hung out only with the other honors students.

One way that we separated ourselves had to do with the music we liked. At the time, I didn't like hip-hop or rap at all. This was the music of the "stupid" kids. I wasn't stupid, so I didn't listen to that music. I and the other honors students preferred alternative rock and music like that. It was grunge culture versus hip-hop culture.

Within our group of honors students, we had a pretty good balance between boys and girls. It wasn't primarily girls.

In middle school, I participated in student leadership. I was elected to the student council and represented the council at the monthly meeting of the teachers. One issue that I differed from the teachers on had to do with mandatory school uniforms. The teachers supported the idea, but I opposed it, arguing that it stifled individuality. They didn't adopt the policy until I graduated, but now I think it's a good idea. My school also prohibited piercings.

Despite the fact that I was in honors classes in middle school, I didn't do as well in my classes as I should have. Middle school was a point in my life in which I wasn't focused on school. I began to develop other interests. I liked school, but I wasn't passionate about it. As a result, I got mostly Bs and Cs. I also had mostly substitute teachers in my seventh grade pre-algebra class. My parents, however, always encouraged me to do better, especially my mom. Even though she still couldn't speak English very well, she would go to parent conferences.

One thing I remember very well when I was in eighth grade in 1994 was Proposition 187, which was passed that year. It was against undocumented immigrants and their children. It didn't affect my parents because they had already legalized their condition and had become U.S. citizens. But it affected many in our community. I was actually quite vocal about it at school. A few students walked out of school in protest to Prop 187. I didn't because we were prohibited from doing so. Of course, we learned that in East LA, many students walked out.

I was particularly devastated that one of my mother's friends, a Salvadoran married to a Cuban, supported the proposition. She told us that with pride she voted for it. I thought to myself about her: "You didn't come here legally. How could you forget where you came from?"

My parents were concerned but not very vocal about Prop 187. But deep down they were troubled because there were others who would be affected by it.

Because my mom was concerned that I do well in high school and that I get a good education, she arranged for me to attend a magnet school that brought students, mostly minority ones, from different sections of the school district to a more advanced academic program. I enrolled in Francisco Bravo Medical Magnet Senior High School. It was named after a Mexican American doctor who had been very active in the community.

At first, I was pissed off that I had to attend this school. I wanted to go to school with my friends and not with strangers. I also resented having to take an honors test to see if I placed in the honors program at Bravo. I had been in honors classes all through school and felt that I shouldn't have to take these tests. But I did pass them and was placed in some of the honors classes and later AP ones. The other thing that I resented was commuting to the school. It was in East LA, and this meant a very long commute on the bus. This was further complicated in my sophomore year when I became a cheerleader and had to go to practice before school started. I'd get up at 5:30 in the morning, get ready, and take the bus at 6:30 A.M. One hour later, I'd arrive at school, practice for half an hour, and start class at eight. Of course, I'd have the long commute back home in the evening.

Despite my resistance, I adjusted and got to appreciate the school. I'm glad I went there. I don't think I would have been able to go to college if I hadn't. I learned how to be a better student there. The other advantage of Bravo was that it was much smaller than the regular high schools.

My magnet school functioned like a regular high school except that it had an emphasis on encouraging students to consider a medical career. It had a specific program in the sciences for such students, which included assisting graduate or medical school students in doing research. I didn't want to go this route, but fortunately, the rest of the curriculum was excellent as well. For example, I was able to take AP art history, which excited me enough to major in that subject in college. I was also in AP English literature my senior year of high school. My junior year, I passed AP art history and AP Spanish language exams. I thought about also being in AP U.S. history but was kind of intimidated to do so. Instead, I took the U.S. history honors class. The same teacher taught both classes, and so I asked her if I could still take the AP exam. "Go for it," she said. I did and passed it. I graduated with twenty-four AP units to apply toward my college work.

Unlike my other school, Bravo was not mostly Latino. It was about 50 percent Latino and the rest a mixture of Asian Americans, Pacific Islanders, African Americans, and whites. However, the whites weren't what I considered to be full whites. They were white ethnicities, such as

Armenians and Russians. Everyone got along well on a superficial level, but if you looked in the school cafeteria, you would see Latino kids hanging out only with each other and the same for the blacks, Asians, and whites. I had a good friend whose parents were from Syria, but most of the students I hung out with were Latinos. Some of this ethnic grouping also could be seen in classes. In our AP calculus classes, for example, we had mostly Asian Americans and ethnic whites.

Despite some level of ethnic separation, most of the students were bright and hardworking. Of my class of three hundred, something like 97 percent graduated. And of those, forty were accepted at UCLA alone. Others got into other UC campuses or top private schools, like our valedictorian, who went to Cornell.

It was also at Bravo that I began to differentiate among Latinos. There were the Chicanos—and I learned this term there—who were the more acculturated kids and who didn't speak much Spanish anymore. Some were children of immigrants, but most were children of U.S.-born Mexican Americans. I had one such friend, Jacob. He didn't speak any Spanish.

"Why don't you speak Spanish?" I once asked him.

"Well, my mom wasn't allowed to speak Spanish in the schools and got punished if she did. So she didn't teach me Spanish so I wouldn't get punished."

Then there were some of the students who had been born in Mexico and perhaps came at a later age. They were very much still Mexican and preferred to speak Spanish outside of school. They were into *ranchero* music and all that I didn't identify with, and so I didn't hang out too much with these students.

Finally, there were Latino students such as me who were in the middle. We were much more a product of dual cultures, Latino and American, and we were very much bilingual.

Actually, high school was a period when I was trying to deal with my ethnic identity. For me, I didn't recognize my Salvadoran part until someone pointed it out to me.

"What are you?" this student asked.

"I'm Mexican."

"Is your dad Mexican?"

"Yes."

"Is your mom Mexican?"

"No."

"What is she?"

"Salvadoran."

"Okay, then you're not Mexican."

"Well, then I'm not," I concluded.

My dual Latino background obviously complicated matters for me.

I think that because of this confusion, I tried to see my world as race-less. I tried to not care or to associate with it at all. I didn't want to be stereotyped as a Latina. I didn't want people to think I had to look or act in a certain way because I was Latina. I knew that I was ethnic, but not in terms of my education and the cultural changes I was undergoing. There was a La Raza student group at Bravo, but I didn't join it.

I didn't participate in too many extracurricular activities. There were the usual high school clubs and teams except for football. I decided to become a cheerleader only because some of my friends tried out. I did this only for a year. I didn't like it, and besides, it only made me have to get up earlier and sometimes after games return home later. In my senior year, I participated in a program called LAMP (Latina Academic Mentorship Program). But this didn't work out too well because there were problems in arranging mentors for us. We never met them, and that was a bummer.

I didn't work while in school but did during the summer before my junior and senior years, respectively. I was in a program called Med Corp during the school year. I had been in this program since the eighth grade. I gave up my Saturdays and would go to USC to be exposed to the medical field. It was a great program. Even if we didn't go on to medicine, it exposed us to college. Because of this program, I worked as a nursing assistant in high school for two summers. I worked as a translator for the doctors. That's when I really got exposed to injustices and inequality. It was a shock for me. I would go into the hospital and see patients there, and the next day they would be gone. I would ask why. Well, I was told, one patient was homeless, so he had to be thrown back into the streets. This was an eye-opener for me. When you're sixteen, you're just concerned about the mall and clothes or whatever. I learned that I was worried about the wrong things. I learned a lot through this experience.

Part of my growing up, of course, had to do with religion. It was very important in my upbringing. We're Catholic and do the Catholic thing. I didn't have a strict Catholic upbringing, but it definitely was a big part of my life. Every night I would say my prayers in Spanish. I still know them and hope to pass them on some day to my children as a way for them to learn Spanish. We'd go every Sunday to Mass. Both of my parents attended, except when my dad had to work Sundays. I've been baptized and took my First Communion, but I haven't been confirmed.

Unlike some of my friends, I didn't have a *quinceañera*. I didn't want one, but if I did, I told my mom, I wanted to wear a black dress and not a white one. My parents wanted to give me a *quinceañera*, but they respected my wishes. One of the things that turned me off was the expense. I participated in some of my friends' *quinceañeras*, and they were very elaborate and expensive. I didn't want my parents to use their salaries for something like this. My younger sister, who is twelve, doesn't want one either.

At home, like in most other Latino homes, we had a home altar. I should say my mother had an *altarcito*. It was filled with various icons, but the most prominent has always been the Virgen de Guadalupe. We also didn't eat meat on Good Friday and things of that sort. There was a time when as a family we would all pray the rosary together. We also always attended Spanish-language Mass.

Yes despite this Catholic early influence, I have to say that I'm no longer a practicing Catholic. That just came about. Once I hit high school, I started doing the questioning thing: "Is there a God?" I found that once I started questioning, things were never the same. I couldn't go back to believing the way I did before. I think I started questioning because of the music I was listening to and other influences. It was almost like a form of rebellion. To not believe in God was rebellious.

Dating in high school was affected by my parents' views on such matters. It isn't so much their Catholicism as their Latino culture, especially as immigrants. This proved to be annoying to me, and it's still annoying. They somehow expect my potential boyfriend to come to my house and ask my dad for permission to date me.

"No," I still tell him. "He doesn't have to ask you. He has to ask me."

But I couldn't convince my parents that in this country, dating isn't done this way. In any event, they didn't let me date anyone in high school. I got around this by going behind their back. I had one boyfriend my freshman year, but he was stupid and it was a negative experience. I'm glad I went through it because I've learned a lot from it. After that, I didn't have any boyfriends until college. Actually, I've had two boyfriends. The first one also didn't work out, and now I'm with someone. My parents know of him and that he's my friend, but I've never told them that he's my boyfriend. When I graduate from college, they can't bug me about this anymore.

My parents prohibited boyfriends in high school, but they did allow me to go to dances and parties. I didn't go to many because they wanted me to take my little sister along. My friends would tease me: "Want to know what happens when we ask Sandy to go out dancing? She'll ask, 'Can I take my sister?'"

I did go to my senior prom. This involved going with a boy, but my parents allowed this because they didn't regard it as a real date. This was because they selected the boy, the son of a close friend. Actually, it turned out OK because he was cute.

Family visits to Mexico and El Salvador were also a part of my growing up. Prior to my starting high school, we went three times to Mexico and once to El Salvador. I was much younger for the first two visits, but for the one in 1992, I didn't want to go. I hated going to Mexico, and I also didn't want to go to El Salvador that year. I had felt out of place in Mexico because it didn't seem very Americanized. However, the trip to El Salvador in 1993 wasn't too bad because my cousins there, who were my age, were very much into the same kind of U.S. music I was into. They went out of their way to make me feel comfortable. They took me to Pizza Hut and things like that. But since then, I haven't gone back with my parents to either country.

My graduating from high school was a major event for my family. My parents were very proud of me. They felt that everything they had done for me, all of their sacrifices, hadn't been in vain. I had taken advantage of everything they had provided me. I felt so fortunate. In a way, I benefited from being ten years older than my little sister. By this I mean that my parents never felt the pressure that if they did something for me, they had to do it for other siblings closer in age. They could concentrate their resources on me, knowing that they still had plenty of time to do the same for my sister.

I always had a sense of going to college. That was my goal. I especially wanted to go to a UC campus. But I had to stay committed to the goal. One counselor at UC Irvine, after I applied, told me that my personal statement was excellent but that my GPA wasn't high enough. "I would encourage you to apply to a Cal State campus or community college."

"No," I replied. "The worst your school can say to me is no. I have more to win than to lose."

So I applied to other UC schools and was admitted into UCSB. That's how I decided to come here. Now I'm in the honors program and doing pretty well.

UCSB was an appealing campus for me because it looked like a beautiful school. I hadn't seen it in person but had the brochures. I also had heard good things about it. And just it being a UC school was like, wow, that's cool! I knew I didn't want to go to a Cal State school or a community college. I thought I was too good for that. I felt I was more than capable of succeeding at a UC school. That's why I chose to come here.

My parents agreed with me. They had no problem with me going away to school because it was for my education. That's what's interesting. They wouldn't let me date, but they were willing to let me go away to college, including an entire year in France! I guess they were just afraid that if I dated in high school, I would fall in love and drop out. They still felt a little of this my freshman year, but now that I'm close to graduating, they no longer fear that I'll drop out.

I was hoping to move out. I wanted to experience something different. It wasn't like I was going away too far. Besides, I talk to my parents almost every day.

I was excited about starting at UCSB. But, like all freshmen, it was an adjustment process. I had a lot of free time now on my hands and had to decide what to do with it. I'd stay out until three in the morning—not necessarily at parties but sitting outside talking with friends. Coming in and out of the dorms, doing what I pleased was really cool. I could order pizza at two in the morning! That was the best. But then came the "freshman twenty," and that wasn't good. I gained twenty pounds my freshman year. There was too much cafeteria food and just food. So my body began to change. When I was in high school, I weighed about a hundred pounds and could eat anything. It's not that way anymore.

I lived in the Anacapa dorms. At first that was cool. I really tried to mingle a lot with some of the Anglo students in the dorms during my freshman year. But now that I look back on this, I feel that their attempts at talking to me were very superficial. They didn't really make the effort to be friendly.

I had better luck with my roommate. She was Asian. We got along great. She had taken Spanish in high school and so occasionally would say a word here and there. She spoke Cantonese. We could relate on a lot of things.

Academically, UCSB was kind of a big change. Although I came well prepared from Bravo, I came in with a determination to do well, and I was very afraid to fail the first quarter. That fear motivated me to work hard. I would study well in advance of my midterms. I was studying all the time. It paid off. I did well that first quarter and my first year. In fact, I received an Educational Opportunity Program academic excellence award.

It also helped that I didn't have to work, so I could focus on my studying. I got a pretty good financial package. It covered a little more than half of my expenses. So my parents had to cover the rest. Fortunately, they didn't have to take out a loan. They just saved. But this wasn't easy for them. It required a lot of overtime work for my dad.

I didn't have to think much about my major. I always knew since high school that I wanted to major in art history. I've enjoyed my program, although I noticed a difference with the Anglo art history majors in my freshman honors section. Some of them would talk about their experience of having visited major art museums not only in this country but in Europe. I felt a bit different in this, although I had visited some of the art museums in Washington, D.C., in high school. This was through what is called a Close Up program that teaches students about the U.S. government in Washington, D.C., for a week. The only problem is that it costs $2,000 per student. Here again, my parents supported me. They paid for my trip, even though given their low income, this was an exorbitant amount. My dad had to take extra jobs to pay off the costs.

UCSB also exposed me to Chicano studies classes. I first took Introduction to Chicano Studies and then a few upper-division courses. Taking these classes has affected me tremendously. If anything, they've made me definitely become more critical. I've learned a lot more critical thinking skills in my Chicano studies classes than in other ones. Chicano studies classes have also made me question my own identity. I didn't do that before. My parents told me that I was both Mexican and Salvadoran but born in the U.S., so I was an American. But now I was thinking about what all that meant. In addition, I was now exposed to the term "Chicano." I really believe that the term Chicano is like a process. You don't become Chicano overnight, especially someone of my background. This is especially true if you don't grow up with that term, as I didn't. I understand now through my Chicano studies classes the meaning of Chicano; although I'll use it for myself at times, I don't use it most of the time. It can be confusing because sometimes it's used to refer to someone's Mexican background, but then also to someone's politics. If someone calls me a Chicana, I don't have a problem with it. However, I prefer the term "Latina." If someone were to call me Hispanic, I would have a problem, but I would explain why I had a problem.

One of the highlights of my UCSB years was going abroad to France my junior year. I went to Bordeaux. I was the only one from UCSB that went there. I loved it. I love French culture. I've always been interested in it. I remember that when I was a child, my mom bought the *Childcraft: How and Why Library*. There was volume 10, *Places to Know*. It had a lot about France, and I read it. So I always wanted to go there. In high school, I took French instead of Spanish because I already knew Spanish and wanted to learn French. I took additional French classes at UCSB. In art history, I've always been interested in French art, especially that of the second half of the nineteenth century. My favorite painter is Manet, and my favorite painting by him is *Olympia*.

Studying in Bordeaux was awesome. I loved it and miss it. All of my classes were in French and with French students. My French really improved. I got along just great with the French people. Life was so much more intellectual than in the U.S. I really appreciated the differences. For example, here when you go to a bar, it's a social and dating event. But in France, you can go by yourself and just sit and read or engage with others about ideas and politics. The French considered me American but a Latino at the same time. Because they appreciated my Latin American background, they seemed to have more of an affinity with me. We were all Latin.

Going to Bordeaux for a year also meant that I could and did travel to other parts of France and Europe. My favorite city was Paris. I visited it five times and loved the museums such as the Louvre and the Musée d'Orsay. I was almost in tears seeing all the magnificent art. I was so excited. I also visited Rome, Venice, Florence, Madrid, Barcelona, and Amsterdam. I loved Europe. If I could get a job over there, I wouldn't mind moving.

Being abroad for a year really changed me. I can't even explain how much it changed me. I lived by myself for the first time, so I actually got to know myself. I also learned so much. Everything was a learning experience.

No sooner did I return to the U.S. than I went off for a quarter internship at the Smithsonian in Washington, D.C. I did it through the UCDC program. Academically and professionally, it was one of the best experiences of my life.

I'll be graduating this year, and my hope is to go on to graduate school in American studies with an emphasis on ethnicity. I think I would have a core emphasis in history but with interdisciplinary training. Looking down the road, ten, twenty, thirty years, I can't really say what's in store for me. Hopefully teaching. I would love to be a professor. But we'll see. I do know that I really want to do something that will change people's lives for the better. Life is so unpredictable, and unfortunately, we're living in a time that's scary when you think about the decisions that a few men with power are making.

Sandy Escobedo graduated from the University of California, Santa Barbara, in 2003 with a degree in art history and minors in French and history. She taught for a bilingual prekindergarten classroom through Teach for America in the Bronx in New York City and obtained a master's degree in teaching and curriculum from Fordham University. In 2007, she graduated from the University of Pennsylvania with a master of public administration degree. She has worked in philanthropy and now works as a senior policy analyst for the Advancement Project, a civil rights organization in Los Angeles. She also serves as the board chair for the Los Angeles Junior Chamber of Commerce.

DAVID GUERRA

My father, José Meza Guerra, is from Jalisco, Mexico. He was born on January 30, 1938, on a rancho called San José de Gracia. It was in a poor town. His parents had twelve children. My grandfather worked as a campesino. He could barely provide for his family. My dad received only less than a second grade education because he had to work as a child on the rancho. The same was true of his siblings. Some of them couldn't even read or write. My dad learned a bit more because he began to travel around as a young man.

His traveling had to do with him joining a small *teatro* or theater group. He became an entertainer. His *teatro* put on *comedias* or comedies performed as *actos* or skits. He also learned to play the trumpet and played in a mariachi. I'm a drama major and hope to become a professional actor, and so I guess I inherited this from my dad.

My father was a really handsome guy. He's fair-skinned and looks very European. He has green eyes. I guess he thought that his looks would help him make a life as an actor, but it didn't work out that way. He couldn't make a living in this small *teatro*. He continued to travel about, but this time looking for jobs. After he left with the *teatro*, he never really returned to the rancho. I think he only went back when his mother died.

Part of his traveling took him across the border into the United States. He crossed without papers and went all the way to Chicago. He worked in a restaurant or hotel, primarily with Polish Americans. He felt that he blended in well with that community because of his fair complexion and green eyes. But he would also return to Mexico for work. This included working in the oil fields of Veracruz, where he met my mother sometime in the 1960s.

My mother's story I know even less about. She, Evodia Tejada González, was born on May 6, 1941, in Oaxaca, but her family moved to Veracruz, where her father operated a billiard hall. Unlike my father, my mother is much more Indian. In fact, my paternal grandfather spoke Nahuatl in addition to Spanish. My mother also received more education than my dad. I think she went through the sixth grade. She couldn't go further because she had to help take care of her younger siblings.

Part of my mother's side that I know very little about is that she was married to another man before my dad. Out of this marriage, she had two sons. But the marriage didn't work, and she divorced or left her husband. My father was also previously married, and a daughter was born. I don't know much more other than that. It was sometime about then that my mother met my father while he was working in Veracruz.

My parents started their relationship, and before getting married, they decided to migrate to Los Angeles, where my dad, they hoped, could find a better job. They came over to the U.S. with a special visitors' permit. Once in LA, my parents got married and then tried to bring my mother's sons over as well. I'm not sure whether my half-brothers had documents when they came over. It's possible that by then my parents had acquired their papers and had established residency in LA. They lived in Lincoln Heights.

On this side of the border, my father held down various jobs. Nothing steady. I know he worked for a time in a restaurant. My mother also worked from time to time. I know she had a job for a while as a housekeeper in Bel Air. Not only did they have to provide for my mother's two sons from her earlier marriage, but then they started a family of their own. My older full brother was born in 1970, and then I came along in 1976.

It was in Maywood where I started preschool and kindergarten. I'm almost sure that I knew some English by then. My older brothers, of course, were already in school, so I picked up some English from them. Watching English-language TV obviously also had an influence. I know that in elementary school, I was never put in ESL classes, where the predominantly Spanish-speaking students were sent. However, I remember that even though ESL lessons were not required for me, I wanted to take them anyway as an extracurricular activity. But they wouldn't let me.

My schooling started in Maywood, a suburb of Los Angeles and south of LA, because we moved there for a couple of reasons. My dad was working in a Mexican restaurant with several chains, and one was either in Maywood or close to it. Then we had our aunt, Marina, who along with some of our other relatives on my dad's side had also migrated from

Jalisco to Maywood. Moving to Maywood reunited us with our relatives. In fact, a large group of people from Jalisco lived there in an enclave. I call it Little Jalisco. We actually bought a home there since my dad had been able to save enough for the down payment. It was in what I would call a half barrio—about half white and half Mexican, but increasingly becoming Mexican.

My elementary school was Fishburn Elementary, and it also was already completely Mexican. I remember having close ties with my friends and also with some of my teachers. I had really close ties with my black teachers. I don't think I was conscious of being colored myself, but somehow I just really connected with my black teachers. I had a great relationship with them and felt like they were mother figures. They seemed to understand me and made me feel comfortable. I remember their warm hands on my shoulders. I had one Latina teacher, Miss Mendoza.

One of the black teachers, Mrs. Green, had two nephews and a niece at the school. One of the nephews, Curtis, was my best friend. This was in first and second grade. I adjusted well to school. I was a few times chosen as student of the month in my classes. I struggled more later in math but did well in my other classes, especially art. I liked to draw, although this sometimes got me in trouble. When we had to practice writing our letters, I would try to be a bit artsy and write them with some flair. I didn't want to draw the letters like the other kids. This didn't go well with my teachers. I guess it exposed not only the artist in me but a kind of individual rebellion. Not a cultural rebellion but just me.

I, like the other kids, sometimes got into fights. This was to show our toughness. I didn't want to fight and I wasn't tough at all, but sometimes a guy would pick on me too much, and so I fought back.

My parents, due to their lack of education and inability to speak English, couldn't help me with my homework. My mom did go to PTA meetings, but my father couldn't because he was working.

At home, we spoke Spanish with our parents, but to friends and brothers, I spoke English. My parents over the years managed to learn some English.

As a kid, I played the usual games,—some tennis, basketball, handball, and baseball. I also liked music a lot. I always had this idea of playing the drums but never did. I liked the arts, including drawing. The arts have always been my strongest point.

What was interesting as I was growing up was that my two older half-brothers were well past high school. Both completed high school, and one went on to college. I really looked up to them as examples of men and adults.

For middle school, I attended Chester W. Nimitz Middle School in adjacent Hunter Park. It was, of course, a much bigger school. Mostly Latino students attended with some Asian Americans, blacks, and a few whites. The Latino students, like me, were mostly children of immigrants. I can look back now and recognize the ethnic composition, but at the time I was totally ignorant of this. It had no direct relevance to me. We were all just kids.

Some of the kids were older and tougher. Some were already quite mature with hair in places I didn't have. As a result, I was shy about showering after PE classes.

I did satisfactorily in classes. Not great, but OK. I was always on the edge, meaning I would do my work but could easily be distracted.

One big change in middle school was that I became more aware of gangs. I didn't get involved with them, although some of the kids were my friends. They were pretty tough, including the female gang members. I wasn't in a gang, but their style and culture affected me. I dressed in a "conservative" gang style. I also got into hip-hop, which I loved. I loved dancing to it and was even in a hip-hop dance group. We sometimes would dance during the lunch break on a stage in the middle of our school quad.

While speaking more English in school and being influenced by mainstream culture, I still lived in a Mexican American family. But my family was also changing. My mother, for example, cooked mostly Mexican food, but she also learned how to cook stuff like spaghetti with a Mexican touch. She even cooked her version of Chinese food. What was interesting about my parents is that they were also influenced by the American good life. Since my mother was a maid and worked in Bel Air, she picked up a lot of American ways and saw the good life there. I only went to Mexico twice as a youngster. I visited family in Veracruz, Tabasco, and Mexico City. I've never been to my father's rancho. He's probably been back himself only twice in twenty years or more.

Like in other Latino families, religion played a role but not necessarily a dominant one. My mother was religious, and she had her favorite saint, La Virgen de la Caridad de Cobre, who, I believe, is actually a Cuban saint. She took us to Mass when we were young, but as we grew up she didn't insist on us going to Mass. Perhaps this was because we were boys and she was more lenient with us. My dad was not religious at all. So we grew up in a Mexican American culture but one that was not isolated from other influences.

After middle school, I attended Bell High School. I did pretty well in my classes except for math. I got Bs in most classes. I was also introduced to drama and took it as an elective and participated in a couple of plays, although I later dropped out of drama.

My first play was *A Funny Thing Happened on the Way to the Forum*, which is a musical. I found that being in a play really tests your courage. I was only a freshman. But it's also a place where you meet other people who also feel insecure, and so you develop a bond with them. I had an OK role. I played the part of an old man named Erroneous. I enjoyed being in the play and being with the other kids. You have fun. You flirt. My parents saw the play but separately due to my father's work schedule. My older brother Tony was instrumental in my exposure to the arts and theater, as he would take me to plays and museums.

My second play was more like a Broadway revue that included different presentations. I didn't enjoy this as much. By this time I was also getting a bit more rebellious.

My freshman year was the most difficult one in high school. I was getting into some recreational drugs like marijuana. This began to affect my schoolwork a bit. I found that in my English class, my writing became more poetic. I thought it was good writing, but my teacher wanted a more traditional style. I failed this class as well as World History I. I later had to make them up in order to graduate. I later improved in my classes and eventually graduated with a 2.5 GPA.

My extracurricular activities, besides being in those plays, included playing tennis for a while. I also played music and was in a small band. I was the guitarist and sang a bit.

I didn't have a girlfriend until my junior year. I was a really shy boy. I liked my girlfriend a lot. My parents never put any restrictions on my dating. But I was also still smoking weed. I could also go to gigs in places like Southgate, South LA, and Watts to see certain bands.

Smoking weed caught up to me when I was found doing it on campus. That was the only time. My counselor called my parents, who were very upset with me. This was in my senior year, and I almost didn't graduate because of this. Somehow, I made it.

While I was into weed, other kids both on and off campus used harder drugs. In that part of the county where I lived, there was a lot of drug selling and use. There was one particular little corner where people could buy crack and other stuff. This corner was called "The Curve." I never used those drugs. Unfortunately, my brother who is six years older than me and who dropped out of high school got into some very heavy drug use. He was still living at home then. This really set him back until he finally got his life together. I think seeing the trouble he was in influenced me not to use hard drugs and to make sure I finished school.

I had some good friends in high school, but they tended to be like me—kids who always seemed to be on the edge. I discovered that many came from broken homes and dysfunctional families. This would make me realize later how lucky I've been to have both my parents and to come from a healthy home. By this time, my dad worked as a janitor in my old elementary school. This was a big step forward for him because he became a member of the union and secured adequate pay and benefits, including a retirement pension. My mother doesn't work anymore. She worked for many years at Sears. My father is still working.

I myself didn't have a job while in high school. My parents gave me a small allowance. I actually got more of an allowance from my brother Tony.

I thought about going to college as I neared my senior year. I wasn't sure where. However, by the time I was a senior, I decided that I wanted to take some time off from school, perhaps work a bit, and then later go to college.

I graduated in 1994 and decided to work before possibly going to college full-time. I think that decision to work after school had something to do with my developing philosophy of life. I've always been on the brink of freedom that would, for me, include the outside world and academics. That's how I interpreted freedom. I have to have both, not just one. My goal was to have the best of both worlds or as much of both worlds as possible. I still feel that today. Once I graduate from UCSB, I want to be living in the world without dismissing academics but retiring from it.

After graduating from high school, I got a full-time job at UPS. What I thought was going to be a short stint turned out to be several years with odd jobs and long stints working in the apparel industry of Los Angeles.

However, I also began to take some classes at East LA College, a junior college. I took a couple of classes a semester. This really delayed my AA degree. My friend Ricardo Molina and I were at East LA College for so long that we kidded each other that we would eventually get our Ph.D.s from there.

One of many good things about East LA College is that I resumed acting. I did a couple of plays. I was also introduced to an American method of acting that stressed passion and getting into the soul of the character through personal life experiences. One play in which I played the role of an old man was called *I Hear You*. It was written by an Asian American playwright and dealt with the LA fruit market. Then I did an experimental play with two other actors. I would have liked to have done more acting, but my full-time job wouldn't allow it. I began to realize that I needed to go to school at some point full-time.

During those years, I continued to live at home. I gave a lot of my salary to my mom, although I paid for my particular bills plus my clothes.

Despite working full-time, I did fairly well in my classes. More important, East LA College convinced me that I would get a degree in acting and some day become a professional actor. I decided that all these experiences that I was having at work and at school, working in the services, using my body as a tool, all of these were important for my acting. I could bring these experiences to my roles. Part of these experiences had once again to do with how I interpreted the dualities of my life. I worked and I studied. I was seeing the world through the eyes of art. I was seeing life as a form of art, either through signs or whatever.

As I finished at East LA College, I knew that I wanted to continue my education. My older brother Tony had attended UC Santa Barbara, although he didn't graduate from UCSB but from Cal State, Long Beach, with a degree in civil engineering. He works for Caltrans. I asked Tony for his advice.

"David, you don't want to go to a UC school. It's too complicated, and I don't think you'll like it there. The student body will be much younger. In the Cal State system, you'll meet more students like you who have had more life experiences."

I listened but still decided to apply to a UC school. I liked the prestige of the system. I applied to Berkeley, UCLA, and UCSB. But to be safe, I also applied to some of the Cal State schools.

Of all these schools, Berkeley was my top choice. I had visited the campus when my sister-in-law attended, and I loved it.

I also wanted to transfer as a dramatic arts major. This is what I wanted to do. I didn't want to do English or global studies. I wanted to stick with drama. But to get into a drama program in the UC system, you had to audition. I'll never forget those experiences. At UCLA, I remember a lot of kids, some with their parents, in the auditorium. I must have been the oldest because it had been a few years since I had graduated from high school. I wasn't very confident. I wasn't fresh with my audition pieces. I had to do a Shakespeare monologue and a contemporary one. I didn't do very well, and so I wasn't surprised when UCLA turned me down.

I didn't audition at Berkeley but didn't get in there either. I did go up to UCSB for an audition. Here I had to do a contemporary dramatic monologue and a contemporary comedy one. Again, I didn't think I did very well, but to my surprise, I was accepted. I think part of it had to do with my ethnicity. The B.F.A., the bachelor of fine arts program, didn't have many minorities, and so I think this helped me. This plus the fact that I had some theater experience probably played a significant role. I didn't mind being considered a Chicano actor. I had seen Chicano theater, especially Culture Clash, and thought it was great. Political theater is the best theater. It can stimulate people. I wanted to do this.

My transition to UCSB involved getting into a program where I could question a lot of things. I wanted to question issues, authority, the position of Chicanos. I wanted to engage in dialogue with my fellow students. But I was disappointed. This didn't happen. I found too many of the other students not very serious. There was too much partying. This was OK, but I already had done a lot of partying. I wanted to study and discuss serious issues. At least I didn't live in Isla Vista, where so much of the partying went on. I lived in El Dorado, a university-owned apartment complex.

One thing that at least helped was that I was able right away to plunge into my major. I had already completed many of my major prerequisites at East LA College. However, I still had to take some core classes in drama at UCSB. This meant that I was actually starting as a sophomore because the B.F.A. program is a three-year one. The core classes consisted of acting, movement, and voice. There's a lot of pressure this first year because you're still on probation in the program and can be cut from it. Fortunately, I made the cut.

I also had to adjust to being part of an ensemble in class. You go through the program with the other students in your class. You develop a close relationship with them. This wasn't at first easy for me because it takes a while for me to make friends. I first analyze people I meet, and it takes me time before I decide on a friendship. It didn't help that most of them were white kids. I don't have any problems with them except that I wasn't used to being around mostly whites. East LA College was almost all Latino. The white kids also showed a lot more *ganas* or confidence when they took the stage. I was much more quiet and, I guess, insecure.

My personality at first affected my acting. People see me as shy but then are startled when I finally express myself in a scene. It seems out of character for me. I'll never forget one of my first acting exercises when this happened as my scene partner and I were rehearsing a scene in front of our peers and professor. There's a moment when her character starts bugging me. I'm a Vietnam War veteran, and she mentions one of my war buddies who was killed in Vietnam. She's trying to get something out of me, using this reference to my dead friend. She's bugging me so much that I finally say, "Stop saying his name!"

But she continues, and so in anger I grab her and say, "Don't say that again!" I displayed such anger that I actually scared my fellow actor. But that was part of the character that was in me.

I don't know if I impressed my teacher, but I showed my classmates a part of me that they hadn't seen before. I probably drew from my earlier experience of working or from something in my background. But I didn't know if the other students fully appreciated my performance. Perhaps for them it was too conventional.

But more difficult than adjusting to my program was my age. I found it difficult to tell other students my age, since I was a few years older. I was self-conscious about this.

I was also self-conscious about the fact that I was the only Chicano, Latino, in my class. I started with some other Latinos and Chicanos, but they didn't make the early cuts. There were only four other minorities, three blacks and a Filipina. There were two Latinas in the class ahead of me, and I looked up to them. They encouraged me, and I encouraged them. Still, I would have liked another Chicano in my class. I wish there was a beautiful Latina actress in the program whom I could admire and in whom I could see a reflection of myself. But I guess this lack of Chicanos and other minorities is a microcosm of where we are as a society in the entertainment industry. This challenges me more. I feel I have to represent other Chicanos and do well.

On the other hand, we do have two Latino professors: Carlos Morton and Leo Cabranes. This helps a great deal.

But overall, the program has been very important to me. You learn about classical plays, American, British, Scandinavian, Russian. You learn various forms of acting techniques traditional to American theater. You have great, amazing teachers. All of these things have had a huge impact on me. At the same time, I have to remember that it's all about me, David Guerra, interpreting Shakespeare or any other playwright. I'm getting directions from the director, but I'm also David Guerra's body. If I'm doing *Richard III* or *Hamlet*, it is my interpretation of Hamlet, the way I see Hamlet. It's not necessarily the way Hamlet sees it but the way my body reacts to Hamlet. But I'm still doing it in a way that the audience can comprehend and say, "OK, I can understand Hamlet like this."

Of all the acting techniques that I've learned, the most difficult has to do with accent. Some of my professors, especially my voice teacher, made me realize that I have somewhat of an accent. "Damn, I have an accent, really?" I never realized I had an accent until I came here. But accents are related to acting. We learn phonetics, how words are spelled and said. This really messes with your mind, especially when you're bilingual. All of this is to be able to do a character with a standard American accent or to learn a British accent or an Irish or Russian one. I would never lose my heart for my culture or lose my tongue either. But in order to become a skilled actor, a multidimensional actor, you have to be able to control and master accents and dialogue.

In my program, I've been in several plays, both on and off campus. In my sophomore year, I did a play called *Fun*. I played this drunken guy. It was a pretty good experience. It wasn't a great role, but it gave me experience. It gave me the opportunity to get into a role. The character was a drunkard, but there was more to him. I had to develop his mannerisms, the way he speaks, and what his life was all about.

I also did a play for the Unitarian Society. It was a small role, but again it gave me experience. Then I did an original play written by one of the students. I played an expressionist artist, Antonin Artaud. It was very gratifying. One of the best roles I've done is in a play called *The Trestle at Pope Lick Creek*. It deals with the Great Depression. At first, I wasn't sure I wanted to audition for the play because I thought all of the characters were Anglo. This was my ignorant side. Still, I auditioned and got the part. I played the main character's father. What was interesting was that even though the play is set in an Anglo family, the cast wasn't. Besides myself, there was another Chicano guy, Freddy Gaitán, who actually played the lead role. Then there were two Jewish American girls in the play, one of whom played my wife. It was wild! So this contradicted my ignorance. I could play any role.

I approached my role as a method actor. I developed my character introspectively. I took examples from my father, the way he worked, the way he got angry, his passion, and his failures. I really enjoyed the role.

Another play that I did was written by my movement professor, James Donlon. It's called *Caliban's Dream*, which is an adaptation of Shakespeare's *The Tempest*. It was mostly a physical play. My professor is a movement teacher, and he concentrates on movement and improvisation. I played multiple characters, but my specific role involved a Latino taxi driver named Miguel in Mexico. Within this cab driver, I put in different aspects of being Latin American. I used some Argentinian idioms, such as the term "che," and some Puerto Rican, Cuban, and even Chicano lingos. I really identified as Latin American.

All these productions made me mature as an actor. I did well in these plays and have developed a good reputation. I kind of set a name for myself—David Guerra. If you say "David Guerra," they know who I am. I'm not being too bigheaded or anything. I'm just saying that I set out to develop a name for myself. Have I been successful? Yes, I have. But I've been fortunate in my training, and I feel good about going into the world to make it as an actor.

I'm looking forward to my senior year and hope that I can audition successfully to be in a play or two. But whatever happens, I already feel good about my experiences here at UCSB. I know I haven't reconciled everything within me, especially that sense of duality—of being part of the academic world and of just wanting to be in the reality of life outside campus. But I hope to be able to do this after I graduate.

What I want to do in theater is to be able to do classic roles by such playwrights as Shakespeare, Chekov, or Arthur Miller. I want to see me, David Guerra, in a title role with an ensemble of actors of whatever background. On the other hand, I want to be part of a Chicano ensemble doing these classic plays. These plays are not just classical ones; they have a lot of life and struggle. Take Chekov, for example: he lived through the Russian Revolution. In a way, the Chicano Movement is similar. People struggled and even died for the cause. At the same time, I have a passion for something like Teatro Campesino, something comedic, big, boisterous, organic, spiritual, and so indigenous.

But I'm not there yet. After I graduate, I may go for an M.F.A., master of fine arts, perhaps at New York University or Juilliard. There's also ACT in San Francisco. Or I could just go ahead and try to make it as an actor in the "real world." I'm even thinking of contacting Luis Valdez and seeing if I can join Teatro Campesino.

I have different options to think about. It's frightening but worth it. I'm inspired by César Chávez, who told the farmworkers that it was going to be a long struggle, but the end would be worth it.

I also feel good that my parents have reconciled themselves to my decision about wanting to be an actor. They've seen some of my plays and were impressed with me. They said, "OK, David, you can go ahead and try it." Of course, I was going to do it anyway, but I feel good about their acceptance.

But whatever my future is, I also know that I will never lose my Chicanismo; my ethnic identity is embedded within me. If I do a role in a Chekov play with an Anglo ensemble, I don't want my Chicano community saying that I sold out. But I want my community to be proud of me that I can perform Chekov. I haven't had the time to be involved in Chicano issues on campus. I work twenty hours a week at Home Depot. But this doesn't mean I don't support Chicano issues. I do.

I know what I want to do with my life. I want to act, and hopefully I will. I love it.

David Guerra graduated with honors from the University of California, Santa Barbara, in 2004. He is an actor, director, and teaching and performing artist in Los Angeles.

GABRIELA FERNÁNDEZ

I don't know much about my father's family in Mexico. He comes from a *pueblo* or small town called Purépero in Michoacán. He was born in 1951. He's the oldest of thirteen or fourteen children. It's sad to say that I don't know my father's family as well as I should. My father's name is Artemio. I know very little about my paternal grandfather. I only met him once, when I was very little. My understanding is that my paternal grandfather wasn't around much; he would stay a while with the family but would then leave for another period of time. In the meantime, the family got bigger and bigger. My dad and his siblings were raised by my grandmother and two aunts, though I'm still not sure if they were sisters of my grandmother or my grandfather. I never really asked.

What's funny is that I also don't know much about my dad's life in Mexico. I think that he didn't even finish elementary school. I don't think he liked school very much. My dad doesn't talk a lot about his early life. As a boy he did odd jobs to help his mother. I remember him telling me of a time when he worked making shoes when he was just a boy and being a complete *vago* [good-for-nothing] and being out on the street or the *cerro* [hills] with his friends. He's told us he used to give his mom and aunts a headache because he would get himself into so much trouble sometimes.

On my mother's side, I know much more. She was also born in Purépero in 1956. I grew up with my mother's family. We actually have some French background. Part of my mother's family name is Sahurat, which is French. My mother's name is María Leticia. We have blue-eyed and green-eyed children in the family because of that French influence. Most of us are *güeritas* or light-skinned. As a kid I was blond, but as I got older, my hair got darker and I am now a brunette. I found out about the French ancestry when I had to do a family tree in junior high. My dad is darker, but I don't know much about his ancestry.

My mother is the fifth of ten children. I think both of my grandmothers had miscarriages, although I'm not sure how many.

My maternal grandfather was a truck driver or *trailero*, as they were called. He traveled a lot carrying large loads of livestock, especially *puercos* or pork. Although he died when I was in second grade, I remember him fondly. Everyone loved him.

Both of my parents grew up not having much but having just enough to get by. They weren't poor, but they didn't have lots of luxuries, as I recall. My mother tells the story of her and her siblings along with other kids going to hear the radio or to see television in the only home in the *pueblo* that had these luxuries.

My mother also has more education than my dad. She has the equivalent of a junior high school education. She went to both *primaria* (elementary) and part of *secundaria* (junior high school). After completing that education, my mother lived in the *pueblo*. She had studied secretarial work in school and got a job as a secretary at the local police station. She lived at home until she was twenty-four, when she married my dad.

Before my parents got married, my dad had already been going to work in California. He'd work for a while and then return for a while. He was in his late teens when he first went to the United States. He lived and worked mainly in Wilmington, which is south of Los Angeles. He lived in an apartment that interestingly is just a few blocks from where we live today. I think he worked at a variety of jobs, including being a busboy at a restaurant in Palos Verdes—that's a very nice area.

My dad is five years older than my mother, and they both knew each other faintly in Purépero. However, when my mother got older, she had all kinds of boyfriends. Everyone says that she was a beautiful young woman. Even today when we return to Purépero, people will remark that my mother hasn't changed at all. On one of my father's returns, he took notice of my mother. He started talking to her and asked her to date, but my mother says that at first she wasn't interested. She thought my dad was too arrogant or something. Her friends and even family members, however, encouraged her to become friends with my dad. They kept telling her what a great guy he was. My mom was reluctant at first but eventually gave him a chance.

They dated for a short period of time before my dad asked my mother's parents' permission to marry their daughter. They approved, although my grandmother said to my dad: "You know that she can't cook, right?" My dad responded, "That's OK. I know how to cook. I'll teach her." My mom used to tell me how much she hated the kitchen. If given the choice, she would rather do any other chore in the house than go into the kitchen. She bartered with her sisters and exchanged chores for favors.

My parents got married in 1980. My father was twenty-nine, and my mother was twenty-four. Although my mom was still young, well before she got married she was mocked by friends and family who told her, "Te vas a quedar cotorra" [You're going to wind up as an old maid]. The expectation among Mexican families is, if you're a girl, you finish school, get married, and then have kids.

Shortly after they married, my parents left for California. By this time my father had his green card, and my mother, his wife, could cross legally as well. They went to Wilmington. The move was very traumatic for my mother. She had never before been in the U.S. She knew no English. On top of that, she resented just staying at home being a housewife. Since she was older, she had worked outside the home in Purépero. She had her own income and independence. Now she was totally dependent on her husband. But she had no choice. The Mexican tradition, at least in Mexico, is that you go wherever your husband goes, and you accommodate his needs. So my mother did.

The only person my mother knew in Wilmington was my *tía* Silvia, my mother's eldest sister, who had already been living there with her husband for a few years. They owned four small apartments, and my parents moved into one of them.

It's funny, Wilmington was such a Mexican town. It was primarily Mexican, and most were from Michoacán and from Guadalajara. In fact, in time other relatives from Purépero migrated to Wilmington, and so as I grew up I had all of these *primos*—cousins—living there. Some I didn't even know were my cousins were going to school with me, and at some party or event someone introduced us as cousins. "I didn't know we're related," I would say.

My brother, Fabián, and I were born in the same year. We were the only two children, although my mother lost another young baby. I remember my early childhood in that one-bedroom apartment, growing up surrounded by other relatives who lived in the same complex owned by my *tía*. Because our one-bedroom apartment was so small, my brother and I shared a sofa bed for several years while my parents were in the one bedroom.

My brother and I were close in age, and I grew up with mostly boy cousins. I remember that as they later went into junior and senior high, they would take me to the football games at Phineas Banning High School, where I later went to school and graduated.

One other advantage of growing up with older cousins was that I learned English from them before I started kindergarten. I knew English and Spanish perfectly because my cousins spoke English with me and my brother. Before I started school, I knew the alphabet and could count to twenty in English. I also knew how to read a little bit. I remember sitting in my kindergarten class and the teacher passing around a book and asking us to sound out the words one by one. I read the whole sentence, and my teacher asked me to stop and later asked me, "Who taught you to read?" I told her, "At home. My cousins did."

I started kindergarten at Wilmington Park Elementary School. It was right down the street from our house. It was a huge school with 99 percent Mexican and Mexican American students. You started either in Spanish classes, bilingual classes, or English classes. According to my mom, the school wanted my brother and me to be put into English courses, but she fought and asked that we be put into bilingual ones. Eventually, we were both put into bilingual classes, where we learned, spoke, and wrote everything in both languages. After a few years, we ended up in English-only classes, but if the teachers knew Spanish, my mom urged them to practice it with us as much as possible.

My mother from the beginning was very active in our education; my father, not as much. During our first year in school, she would come and do arts and crafts and be like a parent TA for the teacher. At first it was a way to help my brother get used to being at school and not get so anxious. She would eventually be there less and less until he was comfortable being there. My kindergarten class was just a few doors down, but I didn't have any trouble with school like my brother did.

As we went beyond kindergarten and started getting grades for our schoolwork, my mother always wanted to see our grades, and if we got anything other than As or Bs, she asked if we were having particular problems. She helped with our homework as far as she could. My mom also always went to the open houses to meet with our teachers.

I was a very good student in elementary school. I loved school and still do. I think it's because of my mother. For both my mom and my dad, it was always education, education, education for me and my brother. "Your only job as a kid is to be a good student," they would tell us. Their encouragement started in the early grades, and then by the time I was in junior high, they started putting into my head that I was going to college. I became the first in my family to both graduate from high school and go to college. My brother followed me.

Elementary school was also a lot of fun. I loved every single teacher for different reasons. Miss Thompson was my first and third grade teacher, and I became one of her favorites. She also knew how dedicated my mom was to my education. I had both Anglo and Mexican American teachers, although the principals in elementary school were always Latinos. What was interesting is that almost all of the teachers knew Spanish and were bilingual. The few who didn't used us as translators for our parents. But most of the time the teacher could converse with my mother in Spanish.

In the summer after I completed the second grade, my parents made the decision to return to Purépero. We had never lost contact with family back there, and even though I was a child we went there each summer. I came to enjoy these trips and getting to play with my cousins. I came to love Purépero, my *pueblito* or village. During these years, my father was actually constructing a house there for us to eventually live in. After my second grade year, we received notice that the house was done, and so that summer we decided to move there. My father didn't go with us but would join us later and bring down furniture for the new house.

However, when we got to Purépero, we discovered that the house had not been completed, and I later learned that the person who was building the house in fact stole most of the money and had only constructed the frame of the house. We didn't know what to do, so we stayed at my maternal grandmother's house, where we usually spent the summer anyway.

Because my parents had not yet decided what to do, my brother and I were enrolled in the elementary school in Purépero that fall. This was a different experience for me and not particularly pleasant. The school was very strict. I had to wear a uniform consisting of a skirt, knee-high socks, black saddle shoes, white blouse, sweater, and gloves. Some of the homework was oral. There was no playground but a short recess. On top of this, all of the students in my class hated me. They made fun of me as a "gringa," calling me "la güerita" or "the little blond." I cried every day when I got home. Fortunately, my parents, after my first few weeks in school, decided to return to California. On his own from time to time my dad has continued to build the home in Purépero. He still believes he'll return there for good. Maybe he will.

We also continued to return to Purépero each summer. We usually saved during the year to fly to Guadalajara, and then someone would pick us up and take us to my village. I continued to love these trips. I'm very grateful to my parents for that experience. I want my future kids to have this as well. It's culturally enriching and has kept us in contact with our families there.

After we returned to the U.S. and I started third grade, my mother began working because my dad was laid off from his job with a company that made garage doors. My dad did manual labor. The company folded, and so my dad was out of work. My mother filled in by first getting a job in an athletic clothing factory in Wilmington.

My father after about six months finally got another job working in the *yarda* or the yard of a company where he did a lot of the heavy lifting of material. It was a company that filled up gas tanks for hospitals and clinics. He had done that kind of hard manual labor for years and is still doing it. He's changed companies but still does the same kind of work.

After my dad went back to work, my mother gave up her job but took up doing sewing at home for other people. She took in work. At her job at the factory, she learned to operate large sewing machines, and so she applied that experience to become a seamstress at home. She purchased a large industrial sewing machine. People in the neighborhood started asking her not only to mend clothes but to actually make special clothes for *bodas* [weddings] and *quinceañeras* and costumes for other occasions. So my mother had her own little *negocio* or business. She's very enterprising.

It was around this time—after we didn't permanently move to Mexico—that my parents moved us to another apartment. So we moved to a smaller one-bedroom apartment but still in the same general area so my brother and I wouldn't have to switch schools. My brother and I still shared the sofa bed. However, by the time I got to fifth or sixth grade, my parents felt we had outgrown the sofa bed, so they moved out of the bedroom and let us sleep in their queen-size bed while they took over the sofa bed. By the time I finished elementary school, they bought me my very own twin bed while my brother occupied the larger bed. After elementary school, we moved to a two-bedroom apartment. I shared a bedroom with my brother, so we never really had privacy, but we were comfortable with each other. Sharing a space was a normal thing for us. We were taught to appreciate and make do with what we had. Some friends, when I tell them this story, think that it's a weird experience, but I don't think so. It was a lot better than in other large families we knew. Some of my friends whose parents had as many as eight kids had to share a two-bedroom place. At least there were only two of us.

Overall, I had a very good experience in elementary school. I became very proficient in English and loved all of my classes. I was also very interested in other school activities, especially being on the drill team (a form of gymnastics).

I then went to Wilmington Junior High. It was also just a few blocks from my home. Although junior high had been ordinarily seventh through ninth grade, this was changed after I got there to include sixth, seventh, and eighth graders. I was there for only seventh and eighth grade. Even though it was only two years, I hated junior high. I had so much drama there. I had bullies, or at least other students who didn't like me. Some of them I had gone with in elementary school. These were other Latino kids—mostly girls.

A lot of this animosity came out in my eighth grade year, especially in my drill team. I had decided not to be too active in seventh grade in order to adjust to junior high, and so I didn't do drill team that year. However, I picked it up again the following year. I had been doing drill team since I was a little kid, and so I had a lot of experience and was pretty good. This made many of the other girls jealous, I think. Then when the coach made me captain of the team, these resentments against me escalated. They put in my locker zigzags, the paper used to roll up marijuana cigarettes, to get me into trouble. They spread all kinds of negative rumors about me. Fortunately, my coach knew me and knew I wouldn't do such things, and so she supported me. In fact, one day my coach had had enough and brought the whole team together and warned that she knew those responsible and that I should be left alone. It didn't keep the girls from not liking me, but they at least left me alone after that.

All this affected me, but I tried to shine it off. I never told my mother or anyone in the family because I knew my mother would confront the school, and I didn't want that. The fact is that I continued to do well in school and got all As in my final year.

Because of this friction with other students, I pretty much kept to myself except for my best friend from elementary school, María, and a couple of other students. We had lunch together and pretty much kept away from the other students.

My junior high was predominantly Latino. Overall, kids got along fine except for the occasional fights, mostly between boys. I wasn't aware of tracking in my school, but I was mostly in advanced classes. AP classes weren't offered in junior high. But tracking, if that's what it was, wasn't very clear-cut. I do remember a lot of trouble with math classes. This was a time when they were introducing a lot of the pre-calculus classes such as geometry and trigonometry. It was very confusing. When I took Math I, it was a disaster. We had, like, five different teachers in that class because even the teachers were confused as to what they were supposed to teach. One teacher left after only three weeks because she got so frustrated. There were both Anglo and Latino teachers.

On top of this, every other class was overcrowded. In the Math I course, there were between fifty and sixty kids. There weren't enough desks in the science room where the course was taught, and so some students sat on the floor and on the laboratory counters.

Although my mother had been very active in my elementary school, she was much less so in junior high. This wasn't because she didn't want to be but because I—and later my brother when he entered junior high—didn't want my mother around. We were embarrassed. It wasn't because of her; it was because of us. She did go to parent-teacher conferences and open houses. And she always inspected our report cards. She was also particularly strict on attendance. She expected us to get perfect attendance each year, and we did. Up until I was in high school, I never missed a day of class except in elementary school for two weeks when I had the chicken pox. As long as I could walk, breathe, and eat, I was in school.

My mother also expected us to do our homework. We didn't have a particular schedule, but we just knew we had to do our homework. We went to school, went to practice right after school, got picked up by our mom, got home, took a shower, ate, and did homework. Our homework was just a given. Doing what we had to do when it needed to be done was drilled in us by our parents. So they never had to ask if we had any homework or if we had finished it. They knew that we were responsible and would get it done.

Following junior high, I went to Phineas Banning High School, named after the founder of Wilmington. It was the only high school in town. It was huge and mainly Latino. It was built to house twenty-five hundred students, but it was always overcrowded. Every year it would get more crowded. You couldn't even walk down the hallway. Every class was crowded, averaging between forty and fifty students. If you didn't have a seat, you weren't going to have one for the whole year, and you'd either sit on the floor or try to find another class.

Because of the overcrowding, there also weren't enough books. Some-times you had to share books with another student. And the books we did have weren't in good shape. Many had pages and corners missing. We did have computer rooms and at least one computer per classroom. When I started high school, we didn't have a computer at home. I was still using an electric typewriter my parents had bought me in junior high. But as I had to do more reports and essays in high school, the typewriter became inadequate. If I made a mistake, I would have to retype the page. I started using a computer that my cousin Rosa had bought for her home, but my parents didn't like my doing that. They were very much against borrowing anything, and so they bought me and my brother a computer.

High school was OK as a whole, but I wasn't too involved in extracur-ricular activities except for drill team, which was outside school and not a school sport. I went to a few games but not many. I honestly didn't care about this sort of stuff. Instead, I focused on my studies. I was placed into college prep classes and did very well. I didn't ask for these classes, nor did my mother. I was just placed in them due to my junior high grades and my grades in high school. In my junior year I had almost all AP classes, and in my senior all of my classes were AP. I got As in almost all of them, except for AP calculus. That was more difficult. I think I got a C+, which was one of the few Cs I've ever had in any school.

Because there were so many students in the school, there were also tensions—not all of the time but enough. There was maybe a fight every week. Then there were the gangs. Some of the kids belonged to one of two gangs, the Eastside Wilmas or the Westside Wilmas. In either my sophomore or junior year—I can't remember—we actually had a riot between these two gangs at lunch period that continued for about three days. Because of these tensions and just the large number of students, Banning had its own police force in addition to "yellow jackets," the school staff wearing yellow jackets who helped to patrol the school.

Gang activity plus other school problems also led to my school having a very high dropout rate. I think my freshman year class had about fif-teen hundred students, but only five hundred to six hundred graduated. My senior year, I would see a lot fewer people who had come in with me.

"Oh, where did he go?" I would ask.

"He dropped out," would be the response.

Although I didn't participate in too many extracurricular activities during my first three years in high school, this changed my senior year. I became more involved. I was a reporter, artist, and editor for the school newspaper. I was also a member of a club called Friday Night Live that focused on community outreach activities such as drug prevention. Although I had been on my independent drill team my first three years of high school, I couldn't continue into my senior year because the team folded that year.

The sense that I would go on to college after high school didn't diminish. It was still a given. This came from my parents but also from the fact that I was taking all of these college prep courses. My school also had a college office that contained information on a number of colleges, principally in California. This included scholarship information. Even more important, representatives from different colleges, especially alums from my school, usually were in the office to consult with students. All of this complemented my goal to go to college. It was never a decision. It was like, I'm going to college. There were no ifs or buts about it.

As I began the college application process, I focused only on the UC system. I never thought of going to a state university, much less a community college. In my junior year, I visited UCSB and UC San Diego, and these became my two major goals. Of these two, my preference was UCSB because I didn't want to go to school in a big urban setting. UCSB was not urban; it was a lot more spread out, more peaceful, and less fast-paced. I applied to backup schools as well and to UCLA to make my parents happy (they wanted me closer to home) and to UC Berkeley to please some of my teachers who felt I could get into Berkeley.

Actually, the fact is that initially I didn't want to stay in California to go to school; I wanted to go as far away as possible. I thought of places such as Virginia and Montana. I didn't see the point of experiencing college while still living at home. The way I saw it, if I had the opportunity to go someplace new and experience new people, why not? I saw it as a chance to have a clean slate and do things my way.

My mother wanted me to stay close to home so I could live with my parents while going to school. But I knew that unless I left, I wouldn't grow as a person and would miss out on something big that I would surely later regret if I didn't pursue it. So our compromise was that I would go away to school but stay in California.

Growing up, we maintained and adapted Mexican cultural traditions at home and in the community. First and foremost was our annual trip to Purépero, especially the times we visited for the December and Christmas holidays. If we went early that month, we participated in the celebration of the festival day of Our Lady of Guadalupe on December 12. Then there were the *posadas* that lasted from December 12 to Christmas Eve. The *posadas* reenacted the search by Mary and Joseph for shelter. Then, of course, there was the Noche Buena, or Christmas Eve. These visits and celebrations reinforced our Mexican Catholic identity and culture.

On this side of the border, we try to maintain these and other traditions. My mother and aunts are the key to all of this. They are the ones who arrange for the *posadas* and cook the tamales for Noche Buena. The difference between here and Purépero is that in my Mexican village the whole community participates, while here it's only the family. There isn't that community participation.

Religion—Catholicism—is very important to us. My mother is very religious. Both of my parents and my brother and I as we grew up went to Sunday Mass. We were baptized and made our confirmation. We also always went to the Spanish-language Mass. I learned all of my prayers—*oraciónes*—in Spanish. When I would go to an English-language Mass, it was weird. The last apartment we moved into was almost next door to our church, St. Peter and St. Paul. My mom just loves that church. She told us that we had no excuses to go to Mass because the church was next door. My brother and I also attended catechism class every Saturday when we were in third or fourth grade.

Today in college, I don't go to Mass every Sunday unless I go home. But I have a lot more going on in my life. I also don't feel comfortable in English masses at the local St. Mark's Church. I'm just not as strict about Mass as my mom.

At home, my mother has her share of religious icons. She doesn't really have an *altarcito*, a home altar, but she places different religious images right next to her large sewing machine. This includes Our Lady of Guadalupe and St. Judas Tadeo, who is the saint of lost causes. She also has holy water and in her bedroom above the bed a crucifix. She's had that crucifix ever since she got married. I think it's a tradition to give a newlywed couple a cross as a kind of blessing.

Another tradition that very early on impressed me was when we all went to church on New Year's Eve and walked on our knees all the way from the back of the church to the altar. Lots of other Mexicans did the same thing. You pray as you go on your knees. You're dying of pain by the time you're halfway to the altar. You're giving thanks for living another year, and you're sacrificing as a way of thanking God.

Religion extended into our car rides to school. As soon as we got in the car for my mom to drive us to school, she would have us pray while we warmed up the car. We would do the same when we took trips, for example, to visit relatives in Oxnard. My mother would also always bless us anytime we left the house, even just to walk to the market.

In high school I didn't date. My parents didn't forbid dating, but they asked that we not date until we were eighteen and instead concentrate on our studies until then. I never dated in high school, not so much because I didn't want to but because I never found a boy who would like me in that way. So I poured all of my energy and time into my studies and decided that dating would be something I would do after high school. I was too busy anyway.

I also didn't go to many parties or drink. Even my small group of friends weren't too much into partying. We were all very school-oriented. It's not that we didn't want to party, but the fact is that we either weren't invited or we just did our own thing. I didn't even go to too many movies or visit my girlfriends' homes. I was just too busy studying or by my senior year involved in school events.

In my senior year, I did go to my school's winter festival dance. Everybody gets all dressed up. I went, but I didn't take a date. I went by myself. I didn't expect any boy to ask me. But I had a great time. I did go to my senior prom, and this time I asked a boy who had dropped out but whom I had known since elementary school. I liked him. I had had a huge crush on him since junior high. I wound up having an awful time, but that's a whole other story.

Unlike a lot of other Latino girls, I also didn't have a *quinceañera* or a coming-out fifteenth birthday fiesta. This is very traditional among Mexican families, but it's one tradition I didn't want. My parents and my relatives wanted me to have one because I was the only girl at that time among my extended family who turned fifteen. But I said I didn't want one. I saw no point in wasting thousands of dollars on one stupid party when I was just going to turn one year older, especially since I knew that my family didn't have that kind of money.

"Just give me a cake and my family," I told my mom. "That's all I want."

My mom kept pressing me, and I finally compromised. I agreed to have a Sweet Sixteen party one year later. But it was just for family. My mother also wanted to make me a fancy dress, and I agreed to it.

"But if you're going to give me a dress, don't get me a *salón* [ballroom] or a seven-layer cake. If you want to take me to Mass, we'll go to regular Mass. Don't get a whole Mass just for me. Don't make a big deal out of it. Just keep it simple. If you want to make me that dress, OK, but don't make it white. I don't want to look like a bride. I want to pick the color."

My mother agreed, and she ended up making me a peach-colored dress (which I chose despite her wanting something different for me).

At home we all watched Spanish-language television, especially shows like *Sábado Gigante* and *Siempre en Domingo* and comedy ones like *Chespirito*. We also watched old black and white comedy movies of Cantinflas, Capulina, Los Polivoces, La India María, and many other famous Mexican comedians. We grew up appreciating Mexican comedy and cinema. My mom would sometimes watch *novelas*—the Mexican soap operas. My brother and I watched English-language programs. I always thought the *novelas* were stupid, and I still do.

Going to UCSB in the fall after my high school graduation was a shocker. It was an educational and cultural shock. I quickly realized that there was no way my high school had prepared me for college, even though I was in AP and college prep classes. I didn't feel prepared at all when that fall I started classes. I had been told that college was going to be a lot of hard work, but I really had no idea just how demanding it would be. I found it very fast-paced. I had to get used to it immediately. It was stressful. But the biggest shocker was the amount of reading involved in college. I wasn't used to reading so much, at least for academic purposes. I loved reading but mostly for recreation. I would read in one week in college what we read in a whole semester in high school!

As a result, I didn't do very well my first quarter and, in fact, was put on academic probation. I got a GPA of 1.94, and that put me into trouble. "I need to try much harder than I've ever done in high school," I told myself. I was always such a good student that I didn't think I could ever fail. Fortunately, I recovered during the next two quarters as I became more adjusted.

Initially, I was also very homesick. I called my mother many times and told her I wanted to go home. I missed my brother dearly; he'd been my best friend and roommate up until I left for college. In turn, my mom became very depressed as well. She blamed my father for driving me away. She also started questioning whether she was a good mother. She herself had not left home until she got married at age twenty-four, and here I was leaving home at eighteen. Once I realized that expressing my homesickness to my mother was making her depression worse and giving her false hope that I would come back, I stopped doing that and started being a strong person, the person I sought to become for myself.

Of course, it helped that I returned for the holidays and the occasional weekend.

Another big change for me was being in the dorms and having a roommate. My roommate was Elizabeth, and we didn't get along at all at first. For one, I was terrified to live with another girl. I didn't know how to handle this. On top of this, we had to live on a whole floor filled with girls. I was in a theme dorm that was filled with all Latina women. On the floor above were all Latino guys. I became very close with the guys; it just felt more comfortable, more natural than hanging out with the girls. I also spent as little time as possible in my room. I slept and showered there, but that's about all.

The next year, my sophomore year, I moved into the adjoining Isla Vista community and rented a one-bedroom apartment with another Latina girl, but this also proved to be difficult. It was too much roommate drama.

Despite my living problems, by the end of my second year I was more stable academically. I started thinking of becoming a biochemistry major because I loved science, but I found it different from what I thought it would be, so I switched to psychology. I soon discovered that this wasn't for me either. So I finally settled by the start of my junior year as a double major in sociology and global studies.

I also worked on campus and outside of campus to help with my expenses. I first did babysitting in family housing and then worked in one of the dining commons and later in the university center kitchen preparing catered orders. All of this was work-study. I'm now working off campus at an Allstate Insurance Company where I do all kinds of clerical work, including handling policies. I was able to work off campus because my dad bought me a car during my junior year.

As I've improved my grades and settled on a major, I've also begun to think of going to graduate school. I especially want to go to La Verne College in Southern California. I've always heard that it's a good school. I want to get an M.A. in health administration so I can become a health care administrator. My parents have always expressed concerns about my getting a good-paying job. But this doesn't influence me. Don't get me wrong. I want to make good money, but above all I want a professional position where I look forward to going to work each day, not where I'm counting the days before the weekend and my next vacation.

So I plan after graduating to move back to LA. This summer before my senior year I'm planning to rent an apartment somewhere in LA and work. I haven't told my parents this, nor have I told them that this plan involves my living with my boyfriend, Ernie, this summer. I know my mother will have a heart attack when she hears this. I think my dad will understand. But I'm not looking forward to telling my mother this, if I decide to tell her at all. Here I'm up against one of these Mexican traditions. It's one of those things you can't mention in a Mexican family. Anything nontraditional is a big ugly issue to face in a Mexican family, especially one with a religious parent.

But then again, my mom and I once bumped heads about a lot of things. When she found out I smoked marijuana in college, she freaked out. I told her I had a chance to smoke it as early as junior high, but I didn't. I didn't try it until my sophomore year at UCSB. I did it because I was curious. I wanted to try it out. Somehow my mom found out, and she completely flipped.

"What else are you doing that I don't know about?" she quizzed me.

I told her that I was an open book and she could ask me anything she wanted, but she would need to face the possibility that she was going to hear something she was not going to like. She never took me up on my offer. I'm very open-minded and straightforward. My mother doesn't like people like this, and she especially doesn't like that her own daughter is like this. She's very traditional. She's complained already that Ernie and I don't have a traditional relationship.

"What do you mean?" I asked.

"You go and pick him up when you go out sometimes."

"So?"

"Don't you get it? The woman should never go after the man. The man should always come after the woman."

"Mom, things here are not like in Mexico. The girl doesn't always have to wait for the guy to make the first move. If I like a guy, I'm not going to wait for him hoping he'll notice me. I'll ask him out, and that's OK."

But I can't make her understand this. It's very hard to even talk about these things because she automatically assumes the worst possible thing is going on. She was shocked when she learned that some of my cousins were sexually active before they got married. I told her that I didn't think premarital sex is a bad thing. But there's no way you can talk about sex with my mother; she's really private about such things. As I said, my mother didn't leave her home until she was twenty-four, and that was to get married. On the other hand, my dad was twenty-nine when he got married. I really doubt that he was a virgin when he got married. My mother was. My mother has never been exposed to new and untraditional ideas. Time and time again she would hope that I would come around and magically become the daughter she wanted me to be, but that's never going to happen.

Although I plan to live with my boyfriend, I'm not thinking of getting married, at least not right away. I want to graduate, go to graduate school, and start my profession. Ernie feels the same way. He's going to med school.

While I don't call myself a feminist, I'm very open to a lot of things. Unlike my mother, who is always worried about what people think of her and her family, I frankly don't care. I'm a very matter-of-fact type of person, speaking my mind without fear of what those around me think of me or of what I've got to say. I'm blunt and don't sugarcoat things either because that's how I expect others to treat me, without games or pretenses. I can't stand fake people, gossip, or any sense of not being honest, like when some people speak just to be heard—it makes me twitch.

As far as my ethnic identity, I've always seen myself as Mexicana or a Mexican. I accept terms such as "Hispanic," "Latino," or even "Chicano" and respect those who use such terms, but at a personal level I don't use them. The term "Chicano" for me is a political term, especially if you're in MEChA or you're involved in political things. That's fine. I understand that. I haven't been too involved in such organizations, only in a group called Hermanas Unidas. This is a female Latina group, and there's a male group called Hermanos Unidos. We're a community service organization. We do a lot of outreach with Latino high school kids in Santa Barbara. We have a program called MENTOR [Making Educational Networks That Open Doors] where we bring a number of high school students to UCSB for about three days. We house them and introduce them to campus life, including taking them to classes with us. Our main concern is to encourage them to graduate from high school. If we can, we also encourage them to go to college; that's great, too. But for sure we want them to finish high school.

I know I appreciate having graduated from high school and going to college. I know I made the right decision to come to UCSB. Just going to college has been great. I wouldn't exchange this with anything. Just moving out of the house, I needed to do that. In contrast, my brother didn't leave home. After high school, he went to Cal State, Dominguez Hills, but he still lives at home.

As I've said, I want to graduate, go to grad school, and then start my career. I can see myself teaching, especially in high school, because I want to encourage kids to graduate and go to college. In the long run, I want to work in a hospital or clinic where I can help other Latinos who especially need help, because most don't have health insurance. I'd say that only 5 percent of Mexicans have health insurance. They can't afford it, their jobs don't offer it, or they don't want to spend the money. My parents never had health insurance, though I was never sure if it was because it was too expensive or because my dad didn't see the need to waste money on something that may or may not come to pass. As a result, we never went to the doctor unless it was absolutely necessary. Otherwise, it was home remedies. If we went to a doctor, we always paid in cash. The only time I recall going to the doctor was when we were little either for our shots or because of my brother's ear infections. We periodically went to the dentist when we were kids, but as we got older, if we needed any work done, we'd wait until we went to Mexico to get it done. My brother and I wanted braces, but we couldn't afford this. I only recently got health insurance because all students at UCSB have to get it.

I have plans, though not that clear, but for sure I want to have my career. I don't know about marriage and kids; neither is a priority. I don't care to be a housewife like my mom; I'd go nuts. That's not to say that being a housewife is not rewarding and a respectable job if one decides to care for her family 24/7. I just feel like I can do that while still being my own person and remaining independent and self-reliant. Growing up with a mom who was a housewife, I know how there would have been an obvious difference if she had had a career as I hope to have. I've just never been convinced that she was ever really happy just being a housewife.

As far as marriage is concerned, I'd prefer to marry someone who is also Mexicano. My boyfriend is Mexican. I want someone more in tune with my own culture, as I am.

Although I identify as a Mexicana, I do feel the pull of both cultures and both countries. I feel like I'm on the borderline of both. I don't feel much more over here than I do over there. If I have any kids, I want them to have the same experience I've had. I want them to have their life here, but I also want them to have their life over there too. I want them to experience how it is in Mexico. It just teaches you a lot more to appreciate who you are and what you have. It's very important to me that they travel so that they know there is more than what we're exposed to growing up in the U.S. It ends up enriching your life in so many ways when you experience another country, culture, and language and learn a new language and about your roots. I feel comfortable on either side. It's just that economically I'm better here. But I definitely want to raise my kids bilingually and biculturally.

Gabriela Fernández graduated from the University of California, Santa Barbara, in 2004. She now works at the University of Southern California's Marshall School of Business. She is married to Ernie Vázquez; they have no children.

CINDY ROMERO

My father is from Puebla, Mexico. He was one of three children but also had some stepbrothers and stepsisters that I know nothing about. His name is Jesús Romero, and he was born in 1955. I know very little about my dad's past because either he doesn't talk about it or it has just oddly never come up in conversation. But what I do know is that my paternal grandfather first came to the United States in the early '60s for a more fulfilling life for him and his family. He had worked in a textile factory in Mexico but felt that job was not going to get him anywhere, so he legally migrated to the United States while my paternal grandmother, father, and his siblings stayed behind in Mexico. He had taken classes through some correspondence school through which he learned a trade and eventually began fixing appliance fixtures in restaurants.

During this time, he traveled back and forth from the United States to Mexico to obtain legal paperwork for the rest of the family to come. My father said that process took two years, and in 1968, he and the rest of his family came to the United States. My grandmother worked as a babysitter and previously worked as a seamstress while in Mexico. None of them knew English. My father remembers being placed in ESL-type classes that he didn't like because he felt they prevented him from learning better and more English. He said he experienced culture shock. He eventually went to Garfield High School in East LA, where he became friends with a close-knit group of other students; they ultimately formed a band. Three years ago, my dad became a U. S. citizen.

On my mother's side, I know a bit more. Her maiden name is Martha Romero, and she was born in 1958. Her family is from Torreon, Mexico, and her family is much bigger. My grandmother gave birth to a total of thirteen children; however, three of them died as babies before my mother was even born. My mother is the third youngest of the bunch. They didn't always live in Mexico, and actually the youngest child was born in Texas (the only one born a U.S. citizen). From what my mother told me, my grandfather had a good-paying job in Mexico but chose to bring the family to the United States in hopes of providing them with a more fulfilling future, like my paternal grandfather had done. People had apparently thought he was crazy for willingly giving up so much for such uncertainty. He legally came on his own while he got everyone else's papers in order. He got a job working in a cafeteria and making much less. It was a sacrifice, but my grandfather knew that it would ultimately pay off in the future.

After spending some time alone in the United States, my grandfather went back and got my grandmother, a few older kids, and the baby of the bunch, while the middle siblings and my mother stayed behind with my great-grandmother. The firstborn was already older and Mexico had become his home, so he decided to stay behind. My grandfather had only brought back a few at a time because they were such a big bunch and he wasn't able to get everyone's documents at the same time. During this time, my grandmother worked as a housekeeper for some rich man while the kids began school. So while half the family was in the United States getting settled, my mother and the rest of her family lived in Tijuana with their grandmother so their parents and siblings could visit every other weekend.

It wasn't until a year later, when my mother was about six years old, that my grandparents were able to bring the whole family to the United States. They must have had the idea of migrating to the U.S. early on, because when my mother turned five, they didn't start her in school because they wanted to wait until they went to the U.S. My grandmother eventually switched to working as a seamstress. They also settled in East LA in the Boyle Heights area. At first they all lived in a one-bedroom apartment and eventually moved into a two-bedroom home, where my grandfather still lives today. They struggled to have enough to eat and clothes to wear but relied on each other for help and never saw themselves as poor.

My mother finally started her education in East LA and eventually went to Roosevelt High School. She graduated in 1976 after she already had her first child, my older brother Sergio. She was seventeen when she had my brother and actually married my dad the November before graduating high school. My parents met at a wedding, so love must have been in the air. Before my brother was even born, they lived on their own in a small apartment, then moved in with my paternal grandmother once she arrived so she could help. After some time, they moved to their own apartment in East LA and then bought a duplex in Huntington Park. This is where my first home was, but I was so young I don't remember it. My mother eventually wanted to get out of Huntington Park, so when I was three, my parents bought a home in Pico Rivera, California. This is where my memories really began.

Seven years after my brother Sergio was born, they had my other brother, Ruben, then two years later on March 22, 1984, they had me, and one more child followed in 1986—my sister, Stephanie. Although my parents were young first-time parents, I applaud them for waiting seven years and stabilizing their lives a bit more before having more children. My mother tells me that I was the easiest birth of all. She said they got to the hospital around 1 A.M., and by 1:30 A.M. I was out on the second push. My paternal grandmother had only just arrived at the hospital and was starting to pray her rosary when my dad came out of the delivery room.

"What happened? Is there something wrong with the baby?" my grandmother nervously asked.

"Oh no. The baby's already born."

"But I'm not done with my rosary," my grandmother replied. "I'm not done praying. How could she be born already?"

My parents named me Cindy after one of my mother's favorite dolls. To this day I joke with my mother that she owes me thirty dollars for being born in thirty minutes, saving her hours of potential pain. I have yet to receive that money.

My father has always been a hard-working man and pursues opportunities that would be best for the family, just as his father had done. But as a result he isn't home much, working various jobs at a time. For example, right now he's working three jobs. He works with the LA County sheriff's department sending court orders to people and delivering court papers to attorneys and judges. He also works at two clinics on the weekends, alternating clinics every other weekend. He never talks much about his jobs other than how stressful they can be at times, but he works very hard. Like my grandfathers, all the sacrifices he makes, he makes for his family. Although he works nearly every day and we don't see him all that much except in the evenings, we still appreciate everything he does and cherish the moments we can spend together.

My mother has always worked as well. She has been a clerical worker at the LA County USC Hospital for years dealing with patients' bills.

I think my parents have been good parents for my siblings and me. They have always told me not to curse, for example, and to this day I never do. I feel those words have been so nonexistent in my vocabulary that there's really no reason to use them. I guess you could say I've found other more appropriate words to express how I feel. My parents also told us not to drink, smoke, or use drugs. I never do, even though in college people are always offering me liquor. It's funny because people always think I chose UCSB for the party atmosphere, but partying is really the last thing I do. I do occasionally go to parties with the others in my dorms, but I don't drink and still manage to have fun. Interestingly, even though we were raised the same, one of my brothers has had more trouble due to poor choices, but overall I think my parents have been great parents to us.

Although my parents are bilingual, we were raised speaking primarily English. I can't say I know for sure what their reasoning behind this was, but I think it had to do with them using English on a more regular basis since they learned it at such young ages. In fact, I would say my parents have mastered the English language and really have no accents. But because Spanish wasn't spoken much in my home growing up, my Spanish isn't very good. I can understand it OK but have difficulty speaking it and reading it. My oldest brother actually knows Spanish fairly well, and I think it has to do with him growing up around Spanish-speaking family members, since my parents had him young and lived with or in near proximity to family. But when it comes to my other brother, my sister, and me, our Spanish-speaking abilities are lacking.

Actually, Spanish was my and my other brother's first language, but what my mother said is that when he started school, he struggled because he didn't know much English, so they emphasized talking to me in English fairly young so I wouldn't have the same problem. So by the time I started school, English became my primary language. Since Spanish really wasn't used much in the home by the time my sister grew up, she only knew English. The only time my parents speak in Spanish is for work or when mingling with family who only speak or prefer to speak Spanish.

I do wish my parents had spoken to us using both languages so I could be bilingual. I almost feel ashamed when people automatically assume I know Spanish just because I'm Hispanic, but it's especially embarrassing when they find out both my parents are actually fluent in Spanish and I don't know it. Other Latinos seem to get offended by my lack of Spanish-speaking abilities, and I have been told I'm "one of those Mexicans."

Growing up, I really only remember living in Pico Rivera and my current hometown of Chino. Pico Rivera is a primarily Hispanic neighborhood and where I began my education. My elementary school was predominantly Hispanic, yet my best friend was African American, the only black in my class. The teachers were Hispanic and white. Although I entered school speaking English, this wasn't true of other kids. I remember that some were put in ESL classes, and students who were not in those classes would tease them and called them stupid. One of my older brothers actually was put in an ESL class because, unlike me, he was still learning English when he entered school. He had a rough time dealing with both languages in class, and that affected his schoolwork. Because the school was primarily Hispanic, there was a *folklórico* dance group that I participated in. It was a fun experience to do something that appreciated my Mexican heritage.

We only actually lived in Pico Rivera for about four years before my parents felt the neighborhood was going downhill and wanted to make sure my siblings and I didn't fall into the wrong crowd. My family eventually settled in a larger home in Chino when I was seven years old. At the time, Chino was still very much a small farm-town community and semi-rural. You could see dairies and cows. The city is also known for its state prison. It's a quieter city. There were cows at nearly every corner, and the smell of them was something we had to get used to. I remember thinking how "white'" Chino was compared to Pico Rivera, as there weren't many brown people like me. In fact, I believe we were the first minorities to move into our street.

Even though we moved to Chino, we still went to elementary school in Pico Rivera. This was because my parents felt it was easier for them to drop us off on their way to work in downtown LA, and then the local park's after-school program could watch us. It took an hour to get to Pico Rivera and one hour back. I remember my dad losing his temper because of the heavy traffic.

I was a very good student. I was the best reader in my class, probably because I entered school already knowing English. I was always the "smart little girl." I always got on the principal's honor roll and usually got straight As. My parents always expected me to get straight As. That's why today in college, when I get some Cs or Bs, I feel that I've let them down.

It wasn't until it was time for me to begin sixth grade that my parents decided to enroll us in school in Chino. The problem I had with starting school in Chino was that my elementary school in Pico Rivera only went up to the fifth grade, while the elementary schools in Chino went up to the sixth grade. So I had to be enrolled in the elementary school again and wound up graduating from two elementary schools. Although Chino felt very much like a white community, to my surprise, the school I went to was nearly all Hispanics. It was as if I found where all the brown kids were hiding. It was also in the more rundown area of Chino. I guess the white families were able to send their kids to the mostly white elementary schools. Surprisingly, though, I managed to become best friends with the three seemingly only white girls. It's as if I was always searching for diversity in my friendships. Still, I hated the school in Chino. Aside from these three girls, I didn't make many friends and felt very lonely

Much of my junior high and high school experience was very typical and average. My junior high was mixed with about half white and half Mexican American kids. I didn't care for middle school either. I still didn't know many people, and because I'm shy, this made it more difficult to make new friends. But my teachers were nice; I liked them. I did really well in my classes and got straight As in both seventh and eighth grade. I did well academically but not socially. I joined the flag team thinking it was going to be fun, like cheerleading. The flag team performed at football games and wore uniforms. However, most of the girls were white, including the older ones who were the captains, and they were very stuck-up. They thought they knew everything better than everyone else. Because of those girls, I didn't like it. I just performed.

At school, kids tended to stick with their own ethnic group. You could see this at lunchtime when you saw tables filled with whites and tables filled with Mexican Americans. This separation later carried into high school. But the more Chino became diverse, the more diverse my group of friendships became. So by the time I got to UCSB, the culture shock that so many of my Latino friends experience is something I have not felt; nothing is new to me.

I went to Chino High School, which was the one, out of two high schools, closest to my home. I wasn't very social in high school, but I established a close-knit circle of friends. I didn't join any clubs except the yearbook one. I did very well overall in my classes. I mostly got As, a couple of Bs, and one C that I anguished over. It was my AP history class, and my parents were very disappointed in that grade, and so was I. Still, I managed to graduate with a 4.28 GPA because I took several honors and AP classes. My graduating class consisted of 550 students, and I was ranked eighteenth. My parents were happy about this but felt I could have gotten a higher ranking, perhaps in the top ten and even valedictorian. I felt like, "Mom, I'm not that smart. Other people are smarter."

My high school was about half white and half Mexican American. I had two sets of friends. One consisted of all Mexican American girls, and the other was of students from a variety of backgrounds: African American, Japanese, Vietnamese, white, Indian, German, and Dutch. In freshman and sophomore year, I hung around with the more diverse group. However, by junior year, most of these girls now had boyfriends, and so they spent their time with them. This is when I hung around the Mexican American girls.

In high school, I didn't have a boyfriend. In fact, I never dated. For one, my dad didn't want me to date. Even now he says I can't get married until I'm thirty. I think it's just a dad kind of thing. Since I didn't date, my parents didn't have to worry about this.

I don't recall that there was a specific tracking system in high school. We were all encouraged to do our best. At first I had no idea what honors classes were about, but my counselor explained this to me and encouraged me to enroll in them because of my good grades. There were vocational classes, but these were for kids who didn't want to do well academically or had bad grades. I never really associated with these students. It was always me and the kids who wanted to go to college.

We grew up Catholic but not necessarily in a completely strict religious family environment. My mother, for example, was not very religious, even though she had been raised Catholic. She doesn't really believe in religion, although she does believe in God or at least a spiritual force. She doesn't believe in heaven or hell. On the other hand, she still participates in some Catholic traditions, such as Ash Wednesday, but she doesn't push us to go to Mass every Sunday.

My dad is just the opposite. He's very religious. He's always made us go to Mass. After we were baptized, it was my dad who later enrolled us in CCD [Confraternity of Christian Doctrine] classes to prepare for our confirmation. When we would express a reluctance to go to Mass because it was boring, he still insisted on taking us. But sometimes if my dad worked on Sundays, we would go out to the mall with my mother. My dad at one point wanted me to go to a Catholic school because he believed they were better. This never happened. My cousins went to Catholic schools, but they haven't done as well academically as my siblings and I have, so I question that theory.

We don't have any religious statues at home. My mother doesn't care for that. Once someone gave her a clock of the Virgin Mary, but she didn't display it. Even though my dad is religious, he also doesn't like to put up religious images. However, he does pray each morning and evening.

My dad would always say that when we turned eighteen, we could decide whether we wanted to continue going to Mass or not. My brothers stopped going when they became eighteen, but even after I turned eighteen my dad still insisted that I go to Mass and still does.

At home, we also always eat Mexican food. We always have rice and beans and use tortillas as utensils. On special occasions, we have carne asada, especially when other relatives visit. I always used to say to my mom: "Can't we have lasagna or hamburgers or other American food? Can't we go to McDonald's?"

"No, I don't want to do that."

So we had more rice and beans.

Although we are of Mexican descent, we didn't have too many other Mexican traditions, other than things like piñatas for birthdays. My dad always says he wants to go to see his dad in Mexico, but he never goes. On a couple of occasions, his father has visited us from Mexico, but I really don't know him, so it's been kind of odd. I've only really been to Mexico twice that I can think of. Once was a family trip with other relatives to Ensenada. The other was a visit to a cousin in El Paso; we then crossed over to Juárez to visit other relatives. This was awkward because I didn't know these people and I didn't know what to say. I also felt too "Americanized" to blend in, and because I didn't know Spanish, I felt very out of place.

My parents never emphasized or talked about ethnic consciousness. It was just part of our life but not in any overt way. My dad, for example, only listens to Spanish-language radio and watches Spanish-language television such as Telemundo. But my mom doesn't. She listens to oldies music and watches English-language television. I'm more like my mother in my cultural tastes. In fact, my mother says I try to be white, but I don't think I do. I just never grew up listening to Mexican music or watching Spanish-language TV because most of my friends didn't, and I guess you could say my tastes were influenced by them. Although I acknowledge myself to be Mexican American, I don't let it become my identity because I feel I've always just been me.

"No, I'm not trying to be white," I tell my mother. "It's just the way I grew up."

I knew that I wanted to go to college ever since I was quite young. I wanted to go, but I didn't really know what it was. By the time I was in high school, I had a much better idea. I also knew that I wanted to go to a UC school. I didn't want to go out of state. Because I didn't know which UC campus I preferred, I applied to all of them. I got accepted into Riverside, Santa Cruz, Davis, and Santa Barbara. Riverside was too close to home, so I didn't want to go there. Someone told me Davis was in the middle of nowhere. And one of my teachers said Santa Cruz wasn't that good of a school and that Santa Barbara would be better. So I decided on UCSB.

My parents actually wanted me to apply to schools like Princeton and Stanford. I was like, "Mom, I doubt I'll get into those schools." I had a lot of doubt and never applied. They would have also wanted me to go to Berkeley or UCLA, but I didn't get accepted there. We went to a workshop at a high school in West Covina where representatives from all the UC campuses came and talked. From this meeting, my parents warmed up to my going to UCSB. In April we drove up to visit the campus, and they thought it was very nice and liked its proximity to the beach. This settled it.

As the months went on after graduation and it came closer to going to college, I began to feel sad because I would be leaving home and my friends. Some of my friends went to UC Riverside, Cal Poly Pomona, Chino Community College, and even USC. Three other students and I went to UCSB from my high school.

Before I started that fall, I came to participate in STEP [Summer Transitional Enrichment Program], which is an orientation for minority students. It was for two weeks, and we lived in the dorms. I came with my friend who also was accepted, and we shared the same room. The first week was kind of boring. We had to go to different lectures and do certain assignments. The second week was much better because there was more socializing. But I learned a lot and especially got an idea of the campus and where certain buildings were, like the library. This made it easier when I came back in September.

College in many ways has been an adjustment for me, especially since I'm only a freshman. The most significant part is how much reading I have to do. I have never read this much in high school. I also have a lot of free time now between my classes. I don't have to wake up at six in the morning anymore to get ready to go to school. College is not every day from seven to three. I've never had midterms or a quarter system. Here, everything is condensed and more fast-paced.

Living in the dorms, in Anacapa Hall, on the other hand, has also been an adjustment. I always relied on my mom to do everything for me. She got my food, my shampoo, and other daily stuff. I was always shy about shopping on my own, and so my mother would also go with me. But coming to college has also made me realize that I can do things for myself and that I can live on my own. Coming to STEP really helped me in this area. Initially I was homesick in STEP, but I soon got over it. So in the fall, it was easier to move into my dorm and not have homesickness. Also, living with a roommate wasn't hard because at home I had shared a room with my younger sister. Besides, my roommate, who is half Asian and half white, is never there. I have the room to myself a lot. We talk when we're in the room, but we don't do things together. Since school started in the fall, I've gone home a couple of times, especially if there's something there I have to do.

Although I've just started at UCSB, I've declared myself as a psychology major. I knew I didn't want to major in math or science. My older brother who is in graduate school is a psychology major, and that has influenced me. When he returns home, he tells me about his work and I flip through his books, and it intrigues me. On the other hand, my brother and his fiancée, who have their graduate degrees, can't find jobs in psychology, so I do worry about this. My mother is concerned about me majoring in this field for this same reason.

One of my initial courses has been Introduction to Chicano Studies. I took this course because I wanted to find out more about my culture and to understand it better, since I feel my culture was never something that was emphasized in my life. One of the last lectures was on César Chávez and the farmworkers' movement. I had heard about Chávez but didn't know why he is important historically. I learned a lot about him and found it interesting. Now I know why Brooklyn Avenue in East LA is now César Chávez Avenue. I had never learned about him in high school and, looking back, feel it's because I went to school in a predominately Caucasian city. I had also heard the term "Chicano" before taking this class but never really used it because the more common term used instead was simply "Mexican." I did have one high school teacher, a young teacher from Berkeley, who did talk a bit about the Chicano Movement and even showed us a documentary on the 1968 East LA school walkouts. But other than that, I knew almost nothing about Chicano history, and it was never really taught in school. So I am glad that I get to learn about my identity, background, and heritage.

As far as my future goes, I'm not sure what the future holds in store for me. I know I want to get my degree and get a good-paying job so I can help my parents. I don't want my dad to have three jobs the rest of his life. I want to help them and give back in the way they sacrificed so much for me. I just hope I can make them proud.

Cindy Romero graduated from the University of California, Santa Barbara, in 2006. She worked for two years in Southern California with foster children and teenagers on probation. She obtained a master of social work degree from the University of Nevada at Las Vegas in 2010. She is currently working as a children's social worker for the County of Los Angeles.

ADRIANA VALDEZ

I know more about my mother than my father. She was born in a small town called Tepetongo in the Mexican state of Zacatecas. She comes from a large family of five sisters and five brothers. She's the oldest sister. Her parents had actually been in the U.S., I think prior to my mom's birth. They were in Pasadena and then returned to Mexico, but I don't know the details. I do know that we don't discuss very much our family history. My mother's name is Hortensia. My father, Juan Valdez, also was from Tepetongo, Zacatecas, but I don't know much of his family background. My parents met in their town and later were reunited in Pasadena. My mother crossed legally in 1969 with one of her brothers who had papers and lived in Pasadena. She stayed with him and his family until she married my dad in 1975. Prior to her marriage, my mother worked in a factory. My parents got married in Pasadena. They then rented a home there in the foothills near Fuller Theological Seminary. I was born on August 10, 1977.

I don't have good memories as a young child. The one thing that comes to my mind is my parents fighting and my not liking school. I hated school. I also remember talking back to my older sister, Cathy, who's two years older. But above all, I remember that my parents weren't happy. They fought all of the time. My father was an alcoholic, and he abused my mother both physically and mentally. One incident that I'll never forget is when my mother served my dad a bowl of pozole. He took a sip of it and didn't like it, and so he threw it on her. I remember that so well. I also remember my mother keeping a knife on top of the fridge, probably because she feared what my father might to do her. Sometimes the police would come to our house around three or four in the morning after my mother called them because of my father's attacks on her. My dad drank at home. He always hid his Budweiser in this brown bag. I remember that white and red Budweiser can and him drinking all of the time and his breath smelling like alcohol. He worked in and out of restaurants, often being fired for showing up drunk or for fighting. One of the reasons I didn't want to be in early school was because I didn't want to leave my mother alone at home with my father. My mother didn't work then.

My home condition also wasn't helped because my sister and I didn't get along. We're totally different. She's really quiet and does what she's told. She was the good girl. I, on the other hand, became the black sheep of the family. I was rebellious.

Our home was in a predominantly white neighborhood, mainly with students studying at the seminary. However, after my parents divorced when I was six, my mother, my sister, and I moved.

I somehow realized that my parents got divorced or that something was wrong when this one day I was waiting after school—this was first grade—for my mom to pick me up like she normally did, walking because she didn't know how to drive. As I was waiting, my uncle's truck pulled up with a bunch of our stuff. I looked at him and wondered, "What's going on? Why is our furniture in your truck?"

"You're moving into a new home," my uncle said.

That same day I found out that my dad wasn't coming home with us. We moved next to my maternal grandmother, who also migrated to Pasadena.

My mother tells me I had a very difficult time adjusting to the divorce. I was worried that my dad wouldn't get enough to eat because my mother wouldn't cook for him anymore. I don't know why I felt this way since I wasn't close to my father. My mother never talked to my sister or me about the divorce.

Because of my parents' divorce and our move, I attended three elementary schools. I started in kindergarten close to where my parents lived before the separation. School from the start for me was a difficult experience. For one, I knew no English since neither of my parents spoke it. I learned a little from my older sister but not enough. I found the adjustment very traumatic. I have three specific memories of kindergarten, and they're all bad. The first was after my mother and I were called into the principal's office over my not wanting to be in school. After my mother got up to leave, I wanted to go with her and not back to class. The principal grabbed me by the arm and dragged me back to class with me yelling, kicking, and screaming. I ended up spitting in her face. They sent me home. The second experience I remember was waiting for the school bus with my mom to go to school. When the bus arrived, I refused to get on. The driver tried to help my mom put me on the bus, but I kicked the driver, and they weren't able to get me in the bus. I guess my mother took me home. The third thing I remember about kindergarten was one morning taking off my school clothes and running naked under my bed. I refused to come out. That's when my mother called in a social worker to come to our house to deal with me.

After the first two schools, I started to settle in at the Field Elementary School in Sierra Madre outside of Pasadena. I don't know why I went to this school, since it was outside the mostly Hispanic barrio in east Pasadena where we lived. This was considered to be the bad side of Pasadena. It was mostly Mexicans and blacks who lived there. I started at the Field school in second grade.

I actually liked the Field school, even though I wasn't a very good student. At best, I got Cs and probably some Fs. It's not that I had a short attention span. I liked to deviate from the norm. When someone tells me to do this, I do the opposite. But overall I adjusted to elementary school. I don't remember, but it's possible that my mother got me some counseling. The school itself was mixed. I remember a lot of white students. Maybe about a third of the students were Latinos. All of my teachers were white. Actually, the main reason I liked the school was because some of my cousins also attended and I could hang around with them. I didn't talk to many of the other students, including my own sister, since we didn't get along. One specific thing I do remember about elementary school occurred in the fifth grade. This one incident really embarrassed me. I had to go to the restroom really bad but for some reason was too shy to raise my hand to ask to go. So I peed on myself. Instead of sending me home like I thought they would, they gave me someone else's underpants to wear. It was so embarrassing!

After fifth grade, I attended Washington Middle School, which was right up the street from where we lived. It was a barrio school and was run-down. It was made up mostly of Latinos with a minority of black students. It was an ugly school. This is where my real problems began. I was really calm from third to fifth grade, but when I went to Washington I started hanging out with the wrong crowd. I also started ditching classes. The only class I liked was my home economics one because we made cookies and I liked that. I started smoking weed at about thirteen. The school would call my mom about my absences, but she was busy working so she couldn't go to the school. By this time my mother worked in a garment factory and then started doing housework, which she still does. We were also on welfare for a while. My mother's younger brother, my uncle Lupe, who was single, moved in with us and with his salary from his job helped us out. We never got any money or child support from my father. It was hard for us, and this probably in part explains my behavior.

I hung out with other Latino kids, both boys and girls, who also ditched. A few of my teachers tried to help me, but I didn't want to be helped. I didn't want anyone to tell me what to do. I wanted to be myself. But I kept getting into trouble. My mother yelled at me about not going to school and hit me. But after a while it wouldn't hurt anymore. She got my aunts to talk to me, but this didn't work either. This one time I was ditching, and when I crossed the street to go to the liquor store, my mom was at the stoplight in the car that she now drove. She saw me and gave me hell. Actually, I forget why I was going to the liquor store because I didn't drink— at least not yet. Some of my friends did drink and would get drunk.

By comparison, my sister was a good student and never missed class. I hated her for this. I also hated my mother always comparing me to my sister. This only made me behave worse. I resented my mother because I thought then that she loved my sister more. I know now that this wasn't true. My poor mom really suffered with me.

Somehow I graduated from middle school with a D average, even though I rarely went to classes. They probably just didn't want me there anymore. I wasn't going to go to high school as far as I was concerned, but my mother made me.

I attended Pasadena High School, which was closer to the Field school. It was in a nice area. The students were mostly Armenians, Latinos, and some blacks and whites. Some of my friends were there as well as my sister.

I actually felt good during the first few months of ninth grade. I seemed to be settling down. I was excited that I got accepted into the Graphic Arts Academy, which was part of the school. We took the same basic curriculum as everyone else except that we also had classes in graphic arts. I liked this. I was going to classes and even doing my homework. I also no longer hung out with the bad crowd, and I met new friends.

However, this positive change didn't last long. It all started during the December holiday. At a Christmas party I ended up getting into a fistfight with a girl classmate. It was stupid. It was over a stuffed animal that this girl had and I asked to see it. When she refused, I took it but she snatched it back. I got mad and punched her, and we ended up in a fight. I had a bad attitude that I couldn't seem to suppress. I then fought with other students, including friends, over the next few years of high school. These fights would occur in school, and the police arrested me twice. They wrote me up, and I had to do community service that I didn't actually do. I would go and check in, but then I didn't do anything. So the punishment didn't affect me because there were no punishments by the police in my school.

I fell back into ditching classes. I hated school again. I hung out with some of my new friends, and we would party and drink. This is when I started drinking. I also got into some heavy drugs. I was introduced to these drugs by a neighbor who was a boy about my age. I liked the drugs; they made me feel good.

My mom found out what I was doing. She at first didn't talk to me, but she was pissed. She finally took some action after I did an awful thing. My mother had just bought a new car with her savings. One night I wanted to go to this party, but none of my friends wanted to pick me up. So I waited until my mother fell asleep and took her keys. I took her car without knowing how to drive. I didn't end up crashing, but another car crashed into me. I totaled my mother's car. That's when my mother said I needed professional help. She got a public psychiatrist or counselor to come see me, but I refused to talk to her.

"I don't want to hear it! I don't want to talk to you!" I screamed at her.

So this didn't work. But I was doing things that really hurt my mom. Number one, I wasn't going to school. Two, I was staying out until two or three in the morning. My mom worried. I even missed my sister's graduation night. I was in tenth grade then. That night I was out with my friends until three in the morning. When I got back, I got the beating of my life. But that was OK with me. I knew it was coming and knew I could take it.

By the time I became a senior, I was in a very difficult academic situation with the possibility of not being able to graduate. I had gotten suspended both in tenth grade and eleventh grade and had not been allowed to take my finals. I would have to make them up. I decided I had one last chance, so I started to go back to classes in my senior year and to make up prior classes and take those finals. I was helped in this by the fact that almost all of the friends I ran around with had dropped out of school. Most of the girls had also gotten pregnant. I went back to class, but it was difficult. I couldn't understand most things, and I was still alienated. Somehow I got through and graduated with a 1.3 GPA in 1995.

Because of all my ditching and bad behavior in high school, I didn't participate in any school activities. I wanted to go to my senior prom, but my mom refused to pay for my dress because of my behavior. I also wanted my class ring, but she wouldn't pay for that either. I wound up getting a job at McDonald's for a month to pay for my ring. But I didn't attend my graduation.

Even though I graduated, I wasn't proud of it. On the other hand, I didn't regret and still don't what I did those years, even though I got into trouble. I had fun in high school, and I don't feel bad about this. What I did and the trouble I got into, I honestly blame on my dad. I picked up his attitude. Although I look more like my mom, I turned out more like my dad.

My sister, of course, had graduated on time two years earlier, and she had been a good student. But she didn't go on to college. She worked in different jobs and finally settled in as an accountant for the Fuller seminary. Only recently has she gone back to college at Pasadena City College.

Although there were gangs in my neighborhood and related to the schools, I never associated with gangs. I never hung around cholas. Actually, in middle school there were gangs like the CWAs and the CFKs. There wasn't much if any gang activity in my high school, since it was mainly Armenian and less Hispanic. The gang activity was related to Latinos and blacks, and there were tensions between both groups. In my neighborhood, there was a lot of black gang activity with the selling of drugs and police raids. It was scary, but somehow life went on. Although there was a lot of Latino gang activity as well, I don't remember gang members or anyone else using the term "Chicano." I didn't hear that term until I came to UCSB. My friends and I in high school identified as Mexican.

After high school, I worked at a few part-time jobs while continuing to live at home. No one encouraged me to go to college. My mom didn't know about college. I have over sixty-five cousins, and none of them have graduated from college (yet). After about three or four years, I decided to enroll at Pasadena City College. I don't know why. I picked easy classes like screen-printing, although I did take a criminal justice class that I liked. But all of this proved to be another disaster. I reconnected with some of the bad crowd from high school who were also at the college as well as with mostly new, questionable friends there. I started taking drugs again and drinking. We would show up to classes "happy." I also was hanging out more with the guy neighbor who was really heavily into drugs. He later had to go to a mental hospital because of all the drugs.

Even though I was taking classes, I still continued to work. I liked having money, especially to shop with. I liked buying clothes and shoes. But now that I was working, my mom insisted that I help with the rent. At one point I was giving her three hundred dollars a month, but I was pissed off that I had to give her money. I just didn't understand at the time that my mom needed money. It was also at this time that my mom helped me get a credit card. That was a mistake. To this day I owe thousands of dollars on that card.

With my card, I also started partying even more. I now liked Mexican and Latino music and would go to clubs to dance to this music with my friends. I would party sometimes five nights a week. My mom didn't like this or my getting into drugs, so she kicked me out of the house. I bounced around, staying with friends. When my mom kicked me out, I became even more rebellious. I didn't care. I was going out with guys, doing drugs, drinking. It was bad, but at the time I felt I was having fun.

My mother asked me to come back home when she decided to rent a regular house to help accommodate a sick brother from Mexico who needed treatment in Los Angeles. She wanted me to help out with the rent, and I could have my own room. I agreed.

It's about this time that I started to think that I needed to change my lifestyle. "I need to get serious about school," I told myself. I reenrolled at the city college. I stopped experimenting with drugs. A lot of the change had to do with my current boyfriend, who wasn't into all of this. Because of him, I became a different person. I also got a big break when a Mrs. Rosas at the college invited me to become part of the PUENTE program, which aimed to get Latinos into four-year colleges. After thinking about it, I agreed to become part of the program. It was the best thing I could have done.

The program, in addition to other classes I was taking, involved an English class and a guidance class. In that guidance class, I began to see everything differently. We mostly talked about transferring to a four-year college, what choices were available, and how to apply. We had guest speakers from different universities, field trips to nearby colleges, and visits by former PUENTE students. I remember this one young woman who talked to us about her experience in the program and how she got into USC. She even passed around her acceptance letter, and when I read it I thought, "This could be me; my name could be in this letter." From that point on, I was like, "This is what I'm going to do." It was just an excellent class, and everyone got to know each other.

The English class was also great. Everyone got to know each other as well, and we had a great and supportive teacher. We were all together for two semesters. I had never written so much, including twelve-page research papers.

From the PUENTE program, I was asked to be a speaker for other prospective students. When I talked about my life, it gave me even more motivation to go to a four-year college. I benefited a lot from this program.

But my boyfriend, who had already graduated from Cal Poly Pomona, was also motivating me. He kept pushing me to apply to other schools, even though I knew I wasn't really ready because I still needed to take certain classes. He wanted me to go away to college, to get away from my difficult home situation and my past problems. He pissed me off sometimes with his pressure, but at his urging I applied to Loyola Marymount. I don't know why that school. Of course, I got rejected. Still, I benefited from his encouragement and support. My counselor at the city college was also very supportive.

At home, my mom was just glad that I was calming down and that I was going to school and taking it easy. She also liked my boyfriend and appreciated his positive influence on me. On the other hand, my sister was not supportive. She kept saying that I was too stupid to go to college and that no school would accept me. I proved her wrong. After I completed other classes at Pasadena City College, I applied to a number of four-year colleges, including UCLA. I didn't get accepted into UCLA, and I knew that was a long shot, but to my pleasant surprise I got into UC Irvine, UCSB, UC Riverside, and Cal State Northridge. When I got my first acceptance letter, I was so happy. You can't understand what it feels like to receive that letter.

I had to then decide what school I would accept. I had really wanted to go to UCLA for the prestige, and I cried when I wasn't accepted. I didn't want to go to a Cal State school, and so Northridge was out. I didn't like the Riverside area and so turned down UC Riverside. I had visited UC Irvine and liked it, but on a second visit I changed my mind. And so that left UCSB. I hadn't visited the campus and had never been to Santa Barbara. But I knew that the school was by the beach and ocean and I have this thing about the sun and water, so I decided on UCSB.

I entered as a junior in the fall of 2002. I came up with my cousin and a friend and found an apartment in Isla Vista that I would share with three other female students. This proved to be a real problem for me. I had to share my bedroom with a student of mixed Latino and white background, but it wasn't her ethnicity that was a problem—it was her mental state. She proved to be anorexic, bulimic, and bipolar. She also stopped taking her medication, and she was a big freak show. Part two of my adjustment with her was our age difference. She was eighteen, while I was already twenty-four. I hated my living arrangement and went home every weekend just to escape. I lasted the year, but it was long. With the help of my boyfriend, I got my own studio apartment for my senior year. It's a great experience to live by yourself. My other living problem was my debts. I still had huge credit card bills, plus my financial aid paid only half of my costs, so I had to take out loans. I was in the red every month, especially due to my credit card bills since I was forced to still pay my expenses using the cards. Fortunately, my boyfriend, who had a good-paying job, helped me a lot, especially with my rent.

Like most other incoming students to UCSB, I was first struck by the amount of reading required in my classes. I couldn't believe it. I didn't read anywhere as much at my community college. "How do they expect me to read this much? I won't have a life." I also had to adjust to the quarter system. I knew that it was going to go fast. I was a little nervous about not being able to do the work. I transferred in as a sociology major because I had taken some sociology classes at Pasadena City College and liked them. That first year at UCSB I took all sociology courses. I struggled my first quarter and got all Cs and one B. I would have liked to have done better, but at least I didn't get any Ds or worse. But to my surprise I got all Bs in the second quarter and then in my spring quarter got all As and actually made the dean's list! I think I improved because I was influenced by the way my two other roommates—not the one I shared a room with—were very studious and by the way they sat down and read by locking themselves into their rooms. That summer I still had to fulfill some general education classes. But other than that, all of my classes have been in sociology with the exception of two Chicano studies classes.

Into my second year, I had some difficulties again, primarily because I had to be hospitalized when my appendix ruptured and I had to be out of school for a couple of weeks. I wound up dropping two classes that quarter. I salvaged two Bs in my other two classes. The other difficulty I had into the rest of the second year was that I was working two campus jobs, and this took a lot of my time. But I needed to work because of my financial problems.

My biggest challenge at UCSB has not been my academic work. I adjusted to the amount of reading by making sure I read a certain amount each week. If you're serious about your education, you adjust. The biggest challenge for me has been money. It's been hard to concentrate academically because of my financial pressures. I always worry how I'm going to pay my bills. Still, I'm more excited about learning and my education than I've ever been. I even plan to go to graduate school. I want to get an M.A. in counseling and be an academic counselor at a community college, just like my counselor in the PUENTE program.

I've not gotten into any social clubs or campus organizations. I didn't do this in high school, and this has carried over to college. I went to a MEChA meeting once here, but I didn't like it. The members were too political for me. They spent most of the time fighting over stupid things instead of actually doing what they're meant to do. The only involvement I'm in is ENLACE [Engaging Latino Communities for Education], which I learned about in one of my sociology classes. I tutor a Latino kid in Isla Vista and get paid for it. He's in the eighth grade and lives with his mother and assorted relatives and boarders. Besides helping him with his homework, I also serve as a translator and intermediary between the family and the school. I translate into Spanish school notices for the mother. I think my work has helped make a difference in that the boy went from being a bad student to being able to stay in school. He also doesn't get into fights anymore. He reminds me of me.

Because I go home every weekend in the car I bought with my financial aid while at Pasadena City College, I don't have much of a social life here. I go back to be with my family, even though we've had problems in the past. Of course, I go to be with my boyfriend. Actually, what I miss more are my two dogs. They really make me so happy.

I'm very excited about my upcoming graduation. I'll be the first in my immediate family to get a college degree, although one cousin graduated from San Diego State and another will graduate from Cal State LA. It's unbelievable that I'm graduating. I'm thankful more than anything. I don't fully understand what happened to turn my life around. At the same time, I'm proving that those who had given up on me were wrong. It's more "In your face." For me, graduating isn't the proof that I could do it. Transferring to UCSB was the proof. That was all the proof I needed to know that I could do it. It means everything to me. I'd better do something with it now. My mother, who probably had her doubts, is so proud of me. I'm looking forward for the first time to wearing my graduation regalia, especially since I didn't attend my high school ceremony. I'm such a crybaby. I cry when I get mad, when I'm sad, and when I'm happy. So I know I'm going to cry at my graduation for sure.

Growing up and becoming an adult has meant various cultural changes for me. I grew up in a Spanish-speaking family. I spoke just Spanish until I went to school. After I started school, I became more of an English speaker. I speak English with my sister, my cousins, and my friends. But with my mother it's still in Spanish, although once in a while I'll throw in a few English words. She knows how to speak English but with a very thick accent. She's embarrassed to speak it. But she knows how to write it and read it and understand it. So with the older crowd in my family, I speak more Spanish, but not with my generation, although I do have a friend with whom I speak mostly Spanish. I tend to express myself better in English. In Spanish, sometimes I can't find the proper words. Most of the time, I don't pronounce anything correctly. My Spanish is really bad. I've lost a lot of it, although I use it, like with the mother of the student I tutor.

In my family we eat only Mexican food. My mother is the best cook. All of my extended family acknowledges this. At family gatherings she makes the big Mexican dishes. It was just Mexican food until my parents divorced, and when my mom had to go to work she had less time to cook. She would then take us to McDonald's or Taco Bell. Finally, as my mom's schedule stabilized, she went back to cooking mostly Mexican food. I came out of my McDonald's diet and began to eat once again my mom's delicious Mexican food. My favorite is chile rellenos. More recently, my mom has started to watch her weight and diet, and so she also cooks pasta and other more healthy things. I don't cook and hate to cook. So at UCSB in my apartment, I survive on macaroni and cheese with hot dog wieners. The only thing I can make is chicken and white rice. That's why I look forward to going home on weekends, to have my mom's home-cooked Mexican food. I want to keep her recipes and for her to show me how to cook some of them so we can keep the family tradition.

My mother is very religious, very Catholic. Both my sister and I were baptized and made our First Communion at St. Elizabeth's Church in Pasadena, which has always been our family church. I was also confirmed but in Mexico. On one of our visits to Tepetongo, there was a mass confirmation, and so my mother had me put on a dress and get confirmed with about a hundred other kids. My mom always insisted that we go to Mass every Sunday, even during my wild years. I often disobeyed my mom but not on weekly Mass. I knew that it was mandatory, even though I hated it and never paid attention. As I got older, I stopped going, and my mom didn't force me, although she always tried to make me feel guilty about it. The last time I went was a few years ago for one of my cousin's funerals. My mom is just the opposite. She's very involved in the church and is a reader in Spanish at masses. She also organizes First Communion, weddings, *quinceañeras*, and fund-raisers. At home she also prays at night and has a picture of Our Lady of Guadalupe in the living room and a crucifix given to her by a Latino priest, Padre Nelson, at the church. She would have more icons at home except that my sister and I won't let her. We don't want to have too many religious figures at home.

I also didn't have a *quinceañera* and didn't want one. Besides, my mom didn't have the money for one, and even if she had she wouldn't have given me one due to my bad behavior. Instead, we had a barbecue at the park for my fifteenth birthday. My sister also didn't have a *quinceañera* because she didn't want one. I think they're a waste of money. One of my cousins had a *quinceañera* but instead of an elaborate party, the money was put into a savings account for her. If I have a daughter, I'll ask her if she wants one, but I hope she won't.

My tastes in music have also evolved. In middle school and high school I was into heavy rap. But after high school I rediscovered Mexican music such as *rancheras*. I don't know where that came from except that it had become quite popular at that time. This is when my friends and I started to go to Mexican and *ranchero* clubs. Pasadena didn't have such clubs, but we went to one in particular in La Puente. They knew us by name there, and we made friends with some of the guys who went to dance there. Some were braceros or immigrant workers, but others were not. Many of the guys wore cowboy attire with hats and boots. I and other women wore dresses. It was a very dark nightclub with live *ranchero* music. At first I didn't knew how to dance to this music, but I have rhythm and quickly learned. I became a very good *ranchero* dancer. We danced with the guys who went there, although not all of them. They would come up to me and ask, "¿Podemos bailar?" [Would you like to dance?] And depending how they looked, I would accept or not. They would have to be good-looking. My interest in Mexican music went on for about two or three years. Then I started to listen to Spanish rock that I had picked up on a visit to Tepetongo. I listened to Spanish rock for a while until I came to UCSB. I now prefer alternative music in English such as Dave Matthews and Incubus. I can't stand *ranchero* music anymore.

As a kid I watched exclusively English-language television. I loved cartoons and couldn't get enough of them. I would wake up early Saturday mornings to watch cartoons all day. That was my passion. I never watched Spanish-language TV. My mother did, especially the *novelas*. Today, occasionally I'll watch a program like *El Gordo y La Flaca* in Spanish because I like gossip programs. But while I watch TV, I don't go to movies. I've never been a movie person, and I also think watching DVDs at home is boring.

Since my parents were divorced, it was only my mother who had to deal with my sister and me about dating. She didn't want us to date or have a boyfriend until we were sixteen. I didn't really listen to this and had a boyfriend in middle school. In high school I dated a lot but also had steady boyfriends. My mother never knew I had a boyfriend because I would always go out with a group of friends, mostly guys, or have them over to my house. My mother preferred that I have friends over because at least she would know where I was, but she had no idea that one of these guys was my boyfriend. My mom and I never had that mother-daughter talk. We never have talked about relationships.

At first I didn't date Latino guys. I wasn't attracted to them. Through high school, I dated mostly blacks and a few whites. I never told my mother I dated black guys, but once I asked her, "So what would you think if I dated someone who was not Mexican?"

I was surprised by her answer: "As long as he treats you nice, it doesn't matter to me."

It was only after high school that I started dating Latinos, including my current Latino boyfriend, whom my mother loves. His family is from Costa Rica. I think if she had a chance, she would marry him. She thinks that he's a perfect fit for me and that he will take care of me. Because of this and my age, she and my sister have been pushing marriage for me and for my female cousins who are my age. They think if we wait much longer, we won't be able to have kids.

If and when I get married, ideally I would like to have a family. I want three children. I think I also would have a career. I get bored at home. But then again, I'll have children, so I don't know. Hopefully, my husband will be making good money. I see my aunts being at home all day, and I don't know how they do it.

I didn't use to think about just marrying a Latino, but now I do. I want to pass on to my kids some Mexican/Latino traditions, even though I've lost many of these myself. But I do want them to know Spanish and to like Mexican food, and I want to take them to Mexico. If I marry my boyfriend, who is from Costa Rica, I don't see any culture clash. He's been in this country for a long time, and he's also lost a lot of his Costa Rican traditions. But between the two of us, we can pass on some Latino culture to our kids.

Until I came to UCSB, I didn't think much about ethnic identity. I didn't consider myself anything. I was never asked, "What are you?" I guess everyone just assumed I was Mexican. However, when I came to UCSB, everyone, or at least many of the Latinos, were identifying as Chicanos. I didn't relate to the term and, in fact, don't recall hearing it very much if at all before UCSB. I didn't like the term "Chicano," and I still don't. Slowly, I started learning that it's OK for those who want to use the term to use it. But it's not for me. Forced to state my ethnic identity, I'll say Mexican and of course Latina. I also don't like the term "Mexican American." Why add the American?

I'm a U.S. citizen. When I'm in Mexico people ask me if I'm from El Norte, and I say, "Yeah." When they ask me where I was born, I say Los Angeles. I'm a Mexican from here. I feel part of the United States.

I can honestly say that I've never personally felt discrimination, even though I know it exists. This country has never done anything bad to me or to my family. I vote and try to encourage others to vote.

After graduating from the University of California, Santa Barbara, in 2004, Adriana Valdez received an M.A. in social work from the University of Southern California in 2008 and is working as a clinical social worker for an outpatient children's counseling center in South Gate, California. She married her Costa Rican boyfriend.

AMÍLCAR RAMÍREZ

My father was born in Honduras in Central America in a very poor family. He never really knew his father, who left when my dad was very young. Besides his mother, he was raised by a stepfather. He was the second of eight children. He was also the only black child. The rest were mixed, including his mother, but on the lighter side. Because he was the sole black child, his mother was especially protective of him, and they developed a very special bond.

Life was hard for my father and his family. They barely survived. They would buy cheese and try to sell it to others. The need to help provide for his family meant that my father obtained very little education, probably no more than an elementary one. Yet he always wanted more education and wanted to learn new things. He's a very intelligent person.

It was because of his sense of responsibility toward his mother and his family that my father decided to leave Honduras around 1970, when he was about eighteen, to come to the United States and find work.

My father left Honduras with another man, and they crossed first into Guatemala and then into Mexico. My dad didn't have any documents. It was a hard experience for him, and he faced much discrimination as a black man. In Mexico, the police jailed him because my father claimed he was a U.S. citizen and, of course, he wasn't. They didn't keep him very long, and eventually he came all the way to Tijuana, where he crossed into the U.S., again without papers.

He worked in San Diego for a while and then went to LA. All his jobs involved manual labor, including janitorial work. From LA he traveled all over the country in search of work. It didn't help that he knew no English. He's since learned the language but still has an interesting accent. Much of whatever he earned he sent to his mother. In time, not only his siblings but his mother also came to the U.S. His stepfather did not. By this time, my dad had returned to the LA area, and the whole family settled in Pasadena.

My father wanted to be more than a manual laborer, and so he started attending night school not only to learn English but to enter a profession. His hard work paid off, and he became a real estate agent after he got his license. He's been selling houses for over twenty years and now has his own small business in Pasadena.

My mother grew up on a farm outside of Tegucigalpa, the capital of Honduras. Her father raised pigs, and I visited the farm when I was younger. She was the oldest of five children and played a strong leadership role with her siblings. Her background is quite different from my father's in that he was always hustling to earn money to help his family, while my mom had a more traditional upbringing where, even though life was also a struggle for her family, the farm provided enough food for them. Her father was the patriarch of the family. She left her family in her early teens to find work in the capital. She, like my dad, didn't have more than an elementary education. But unlike my father, my mother was more white.

But I don't really know that much more about my mother—or my father, for that matter. They have never really told us much about their past. I've always tried to find a way to get it out of them so I can learn about my family and about myself, because I don't have that connection to Honduras. But it's been hard to get this information. My parents keep a lot of this to themselves.

My parents met in Honduras on one of my dad's return visits. He would return a few times, primarily to arrange for the rest of his family to come to the U.S. When he would return, he would find work for a while. He was working in a hospital when he met my mother, who was also working there as a nurse's assistant. It was love at first sight, or so they say. My dad then returned to Pasadena, and my mom prepared to also come. Although she was pregnant with my older sister, she made the trip—without documents—with one of my dad's sisters. It was hard for them, but not as hard as my dad's experience.

I was born March 18, 1984, in Los Angeles. I have two older sisters. I later had a younger sister. So I'm the only boy. All of us look black, even though we're mixed.

My earliest memories are of my parents getting up early and going to work. I remember one of our neighbors, Doña María, coming over to take care of us. We lived in northwest Pasadena in a house that my father was able to buy. That was my dad's goal, to buy a home. As I grew up, my friends and I referred to our neighborhood as the ghetto area. There was crime and a lot of stuff going on. Most of the people were poor. It's just the way we grew up.

Our neighborhood was predominantly Latino and black, and it still is today. Our neighbors to our left were either Jamaican or African. Our neighbor to our right was an African American elderly lady, but she always had her extended family around. I loved this grandmother and her family. She was a great person, and she and her family always looked out for us and cared for us. In fact, the whole block was like this. The other side of the street was mostly Latino, and our side was mixed. But the whole chemistry of our block was just beautiful, even though there were a couple of troublemakers here and there. But who doesn't have that?

I grew up speaking only Spanish. That was my first language. However, my dad put me in a Head Start program when I was three, and I started to pick up English. I also picked it up from my two older sisters and from watching TV. So I became bilingual. At home we spoke mostly Spanish. This wasn't because my parents insisted on this but because they were more comfortable in Spanish. When my aunts and uncles came over, they all spoke in Spanish. However, to my sisters I spoke English.

I've been in public schools all my life. From the very beginning I loved school. I loved learning. I remember always asking questions and getting in trouble because of this. The teacher sent me to the corner. That became my signature, being sent to the corner. Yet my teachers liked me. Whenever they talked to my dad, they'd say, "You have a smart boy, sometimes a little too smart."

But my dad always told me as I grew up, "Whatever people tell you is not necessarily the truth. You have to ask questions." My mom was the same way. So that's why even today, people tell me stuff and I'm like, "OK, but I don't have to believe it. I'll question it and find out for myself."

I was in the Field Elementary School until fifth grade, when I was then transferred to the new Washington Accelerated Learning Center during my fifth grade year. This was a school for "gifted" students, although I think many who remained at the Field school were also "gifted."

I had many good teachers and some not so good. School was always an experience. When I was in third grade, they put me in an ESL class, even though I already knew English. In fact, most of the other Latino students in that class knew English. To make matters worse, there were even some African American students in the class, and they knew only English! My dad was pissed when he learned I was in an ESL class. He knew these classes didn't help the students. He went to see the principal, and they put me in a regular class.

But I also had some great learning experiences with some fantastic teachers. Some really inspired me and made me work harder. One elementary teacher really loved educating and teaching. I loved being in her class. In fact, I had perfect attendance that year because going to her class was so much fun and I learned so much. She always gave us extra textbooks to advance us.

All of my teachers were white in elementary school with one exception, a Dr. Jones, who was black. He was a great teacher. He connected with us. He always wanted his students to do the best. He would tell us, "You guys are so intelligent. Just prove it to everyone. Don't back down. If you know you can succeed, go for it. There's nothing holding you back."

In both the Field school and Washington, the students were mostly Latino and black but with enough white students to make it pretty diverse. I loved this diversity. I learned so much about different peoples that I don't think I would have learned just by reading a book. My parents would always say, "Don't judge people by the color of their skin but by who they are."

My parents were very vigilant about our education. They made sure we did our homework. My dad would ask me questions and made sure I learned my times tables. He basically gave me a day to learn all the times tables, zero to twelve. They also regularly attended PTA meetings and other conferences with teachers and the principal. By this time, they both knew enough English to talk to my teachers. My father had no hesitation in raising questions with teachers or the principal. My dad has always been the outspoken one. He has no shame. He will talk to anyone and has a way with words, and he's not afraid to confront people.

Growing up, I surrounded myself with friends who always wanted to make themselves better and who were hungry to learn. I never really looked at a person's race or culture with respect to friendship. If you and I have a common interest, then we're going to be friends. A lot of my friends were Asian, white, black, and Latino. We didn't care about our skin color. We just cared about trading X-Men cards or pogs and going to each other's homes.

Still, I have to admit that sometimes I felt sandwiched between Latino kids and black kids. This was kind of hard. I'd approach blacks and they were like, "What? Amílcar, what is that?"

"It's Hispanic," I'd say.

"You're black-skinned and you say you're Hispanic? You can't be black and Hispanic."

"Well, I'm black. What is black? My parents are from Honduras."

All this caught the black kids off guard because I guess they had never seen a person like me before. Some were cool about it, while others would not accept me as black. I didn't care for the latter and thought they were ignorant.

Now, among the Latino kids I got the opposite reaction.

"You're not Latino," some would say.

The majority of Latinos at school were Mexican. So they were awed by me because they had no experience with black Latinos. Some even straight-out rejected me.

"No, you're not Latino; you're black."

When people said this, I didn't really think much of it. It didn't matter. I was just going to be myself. And I was, even though I was always faced with choosing sides. This even pertained to sports. My favorite sport is soccer, which my dad had taught me. He had a passion for the game. My love of soccer coincided with that of other Latinos. However, for African Americans, their sports were football and basketball. They couldn't understand why I, who looked black, played soccer.

"What are you doing over there?" they'd say. "Why are you playing that?"

I remember talking to my dad about all this. He'd say, "People who are like that are ignorant. You don't want to associate with them."

My sisters experienced similar reactions, since they're black-looking. One, however, tended to associate more with Latinos, while the other had more black friends. It was kind of strange. Their personalities were just different.

While going to elementary school and then middle school, we did have the problem of gangs in our neighborhood. I remember sometimes not being able to go outside a lot. My parents wanted us to stay indoors because of the gangs. At one point there was a drug house across the street. I remember the police always being over there, breaking in and arresting whomever. Sometimes they'd raid every night. All we could hear were the police sirens and the police helicopters flying over. Gang members would yell and scream in the streets, cursing each other out. I remember hearing shootings once in a while. We could hear the gunshots. It was just a period when things were out of control. There were both Latino and black gangs, and they often fought each other.

My father took the gangs on to try to get them off our streets in order to protect us. He was very confrontational with them. He was not afraid of them. He'd go up to the gang members and talk to them. A couple of the gang members wanted to beat the shit out of my dad. But I knew that my father was not scared of them. Back in Honduras, he wasn't a gang member, but he had to fight every day to protect himself. He had to prove himself and stand up for who he was. My uncles and aunts tell me that my dad was a hell of a fighter. Although he was skinny, he packed a punch and won the majority of the fights.

I then went to Pasadena High School, which was one of about five other high schools in Pasadena, both public and private. Pasadena High was the most diverse, similar to my middle school. While blacks and Latinos represented about 55 percent of the students, there were also many whites and Asians. My experience there was unlike any other. This was one of the most educational experiences of my life, not only academically but culturally. I learned about many ethnic cultures and how the world works. It was just a great experience. The majority of the students were open, and that's what made my high school years so meaningful. As for me, I still often found myself in between ethnic groups, and some couldn't really understand who I was. At first, everybody thought I was African American. When I tried out my freshman year for the soccer team, all of the other players were Latinos, and they couldn't understand why a black played soccer. The coach wasn't Latino but he had a degree in Spanish, and so he spoke Spanish to the players—except when I came along, he shifted to English, thinking I was not Latino.

"No, coach," I told him, "go ahead in Spanish. I speak Spanish."

He was awestruck, but they all accepted me. They had heard about black Latinos but had never seen one until me. I didn't actively play that year because I got injured, but I did play the next three years.

Some of the black students at first had difficulty accepting me, but fortunately some of my black friends from middle school stood up for me. Also, my sisters went to the same school, and so they were already accepted and that helped me also. Here and there, I'd still hear people saying that I wasn't really Latino or that I wasn't really black, but I just shook that off. I continued to associate only with those who were not biased. I had a very mixed group of friends. In fact, we called ourselves the "ethnic group" because we literally represented a variety of cultures: Latino, black, Asian, white, Armenian, Arab, et cetera. It was beautiful.

Our group was different because most of the other students self-segregated themselves, especially at lunchtime. The black students met around the cafeteria, the whites and Asians around the library, the Armenians around a certain bench area, and the Latinos in a certain corner of campus. My friends and I thought this was ridiculous. Our group had a spot near the cafeteria, but every day at lunch we also walked around the campus. We didn't want it to seem like we were just all in one place like the other students. There were ethnic tensions and fights here and there but, as in middle school, no major outbreaks.

Academically, my high school was a mixed picture. A lot of students didn't really take academics seriously. I noticed that many just cared about the way they looked and how popular they were. I knew a lot of students who wouldn't go to class and ditched. There was a pretty good number of dropouts. Some girls got pregnant. A couple of guys ended up in jail. But there were no gangs to speak of. Some guys walked around hard, but others just looked at them like they were stupid. On the other hand, my school had some very intelligent people. But what was interesting also was that these very smart people were respected by the other students rather than made fun of. And these top students were not just white and Asian; they were also Latino and black. This was beautiful to see.

I did well in my schoolwork, although I could have done better, especially in my first two years. But when I got injured playing soccer and very badly broke my leg and missed a lot of school, I began to lose motivation to do well in my classes. I also had problems with a couple of my teachers whose teaching strategies I didn't care for and said so. One also showed favoritism to some students, and I was not one of those students. I never tried to kiss up to her.

But into my sophomore year, my dad started getting on me as he realized that I was slipping in my grades. This had an effect on me, and in my junior year I began to concentrate on doing better. It wasn't that I couldn't do the work; it was that I didn't want to do it. But this changed, and as I took a number of AP classes, I did very well. Still, as I look back now, I could have done even better. I had a lot of Bs that with a bit more effort could have been As. When I graduated, my GPA was about 3.4.

What I enjoyed the most in school was playing soccer. Although the doctor told me that I probably would never play again due to the severity of my injury, I bounced back and played the next three years. I just told myself that nothing was going to stop me from playing and playing well. Our team was almost all Latino, but in our league we played teams that were mostly white except for our main rival, which was Latino. We had good teams my sophomore and junior years, but I knew we could do better. As a senior, I vowed to myself that we were going to win our league and advance to the CIF [California Interscholastic Federation] playoffs. I also wanted to accomplish certain personal goals in soccer. I got most of this. We won our league, pretty much blowing everyone away, including our chief rivals. We went undefeated. We had a great team. I was named player of the year for the whole league and first team in my district. I led the team in scoring. I was all over the field. The one disappointment was that we lost focus after our league play and some of the guys started goofing off and got suspended from the team. As a result, we were not the same team in the playoffs and lost our first game. This hurt because I wanted to win CIF. I wanted to put Pasadena High on the map.

But on the bright side, prior to the playoffs, our team was written up in the *Los Angeles Times*, which included a color picture of me. My dad was so proud that he went around collecting copies of the paper and passed them out to family members and friends.

I received a couple of college soccer offers, but I didn't pursue them. I've thought of trying out for the UCSB team but haven't done it. I might, but I'd have to get back in shape.

In high school, I went to parties and had a lot of friends. But I always went to the parties just to show my face. During my first two years I didn't have a girlfriend, but there were sure many beautiful women in my school. Wow, I was just blown away. But I also didn't like the way women were treated and how some of the women acted. So I just did my thing. I was mostly into soccer and school. However, in junior year I did have a girlfriend. It was a great relationship. She taught me a lot. She taught me about myself and everything. She was a wakeup call. But then we broke up.

In my senior year I met another girl who also really impacted me. She made me open up and talk to people. I could tell her anything. We're not together now, but she was a really great friend and was Armenian. The fact that she was Armenian proved to be a problem. It wasn't her but her family culture. She told me that Armenian families expect the daughter to only date Armenian guys and marry one of them. She was too afraid to tell her parents about us. I could understand this to a point, and then I realized we couldn't go on. We're cool now and just friends.

As my two girlfriends indicate, there was a good deal of interethnic dating. Some people didn't like this, but others and I just did our own thing.

I didn't really belong to many clubs. I joined the soccer club because I played that myself. But I didn't join other social clubs. There was a MEChA group, composed mostly of Mexicans. Most of the Latinos at school were of Mexican background, although there were, like me, some Central Americans and a few South Americans. You could tell what their ethnic background was by the way they spoke Spanish. At school, I never heard the word "Chicano." Students called themselves Mexican or Honduran in my case or just Latino.

At home, Honduran culture was practiced as much as possible. My parents always stressed that we shouldn't lose our Spanish, but the Spanish as spoken in Honduras. It's different from the Spanish spoken by Mexicans. Hondurans speak it with a faster tone. You can always tell who is Mexican or Central American by the accent and by certain words used. So my parents would say to me and my sisters, "We know you don't go to Honduras, but never lose the Spanish and don't forget where you're from." We also love the Honduran music called *punta*. We listen to that at home. It's very fast. It's called *punta* because you dance on the tip (*punta*) of your toes. It involves a lot of hip movement. I love it to death. If I ever hear it at a party, I'm going be the first one on the dance floor. But my taste in music has changed. Because of the area we lived in, rap and hip-hop was big. I love that music but prefer the more serious lyrics in rap.

At home my parents don't watch too much Spanish-language television. My dad likes to listen and watch the news but prefers the English-language news. He doesn't like the way the Spanish-language stations give the news. He thinks they don't tell everything and that it is one-sided. My mother watches a couple of Spanish-language *novelas* or soap operas but also likes the news.

We also eat mostly Honduran food at home, especially *arroz con frijoles* [rice and beans] and chicken and corn tortillas. My mother has never gotten into "American" cooking. As for me, I love McDonald's. I always tell people you can never go wrong with burgers, fries, and a Coke.

We were raised Catholic, although my mother at first was more religious than my dad. She would take us to Mass when we were little, but then when she started working on Sundays, this wasn't possible. My father wasn't religious until he won a prize to go to Israel and came back a changed man. From then on he'd go to Mass every Sunday, and he'd take us with him. At home, my mom had one prominent icon, which was the Virgen de Suyapa, the patron saint of Honduras. She's the equivalent of the Virgin of Guadalupe in Mexico, and like Guadalupe she is a mestiza virgin. My mother always made a big deal about Suyapa's feast day on February 3. She puts her picture on the dining table and lights candles to her. My mom loves Suyapa. When we go to Mass, it's always the Spanish-language ones.

We also have a lot of friends from Honduras whom we socialize with. Some we met at the soccer fields. My godparents, who live here, are from Honduras. My parents stay in contact with their families in Honduras. They call usually once a week and send money to them. My dad goes to Honduras twice a year and my mom once a year. The first time I went with my parents, I was just a baby, and the last time I was about six or seven. My mother usually goes in August, and that's when I've been in summer school, and my dad goes during the school year, and so I can't go then. But I'd like to return someday.

By junior year, I had started to think of going to college. I took the SATs both years and did fairly well in both the math and verbal. At first my thought was to go to a school where I could play soccer. My top preferences were Berkeley and UCLA, but I didn't get admitted to either. I looked at other schools where I could play soccer, but nothing came of this. I then focused on other UC campuses and Cal State ones. My academic counselors weren't too helpful because they were always so busy with so many students. One of my sisters, who was attending UC Riverside, helped me in filling out my application forms. I got accepted at Riverside, Irvine, and Santa Barbara. I didn't care for the first two, and although I had never really thought about UCSB, I was more impressed with it. I liked that it was a good distance from home but yet not so far that I couldn't frequently visit my family. My parents strongly supported my going to college.

Some of my friends also went on to college, but others didn't. Some stayed home and worked but later regretted this, and so now some are in community college and trying to transfer to a four-year school. A few friends joined the military because they really wanted to. I myself even considered this and was heavily recruited by the military, which came to our school once a week. For a while recruiters were calling me several times a week. But I lost interest in it, especially as I disliked how the U.S. was responding to worldwide situations.

I preferred to go to college. I always wanted to leave home and be on my own. My dad always emphasized my becoming a man and growing up. I really felt that my going away to college was a step toward being a man and into manhood, where I could start making my own decisions, take care of my responsibilities, and not be dependent on others.

At first I wasn't too excited about participating in high school graduation. It didn't matter to me. I knew that I had done the work and was going to graduate. I'd rather be at home watching the World Cup. But I did it for my family. They wanted to see their children graduate and go on to better their lives. So I did it. And I'm glad I did because graduation day turned out to be one of the happiest days of my life. I was so pumped up that when they called my name I did a little jump dance, to everyone's surprise. Most had always seen me as a quiet type, so my little display of emotion shocked them, but they positively responded. What was interesting about my graduation, as I look back upon it, was that when I entered as a freshman, there were about 600 students, but when I graduated, there were only 250. I guess many dropped out or transferred. Needless to say, my family was very proud of me and thankful I was not one of those who left school.

That summer after graduation, I was fortunate enough to go to Europe for a couple of weeks to play soccer. Some on my soccer team and a few others from nearby schools fund-raised in order to pay our way to go to England and Sweden to play against other teams there. It was a fantastic experience. This literally was one of the greatest experiences in my life. I got to see the world differently from what I was used to in the U.S. When I came back, I was depressed because I wanted to be back in Europe. That rest of the summer I worked a bit with my dad but mostly just relaxed at home and got ready to go to UCSB.

I was assigned to the Santa Cruz dorm. I picked that dorm because it's the multicultural dorm, although a good number of white students live there. What blew my mind initially was how white the campus was as a whole. This was a different experience for me. But I adjusted to this and felt that if this is the way it is, then that's OK with me.

My roommate was white and was from Culver City, but he also lived in a very diverse community. We hit it off right away. He's a real cool guy. Dorm life was a transition. It was fun and hectic at the same time. My roommate and I ran for dorm co-presidents, and we won. We were in charge of the hall council and allocated our budget for various dorm activities, such as dances. We did whatever we could to build a sense of community.

The biggest drawback in the dorm was how dependent people are on alcohol. They would drink in the dorms, even though it was prohibited. Many would also go to parties in adjacent Isla Vista and get drunk. I never could understand getting drunk. I don't drink and never have. What's the point of it? You can have fun without drinking. As in high school, I started hanging around with friends who thought like me.

Most students don't continue in the dorms after their freshman year, but my roommate and I did because we got selected as resident assistants in two different dorms. As an RA, I assist the new students in their transition. I counsel them about available student programs and how they should meet their professors. I love the experience. I get a room to myself, and it's free.

I definitely also went through an academic transition at UCSB. It was hard. The hardest thing was the freedom. I now had (or had what I thought was) free time between classes. I didn't know how to manage my time. So my first quarter was very hard. I didn't do very well. But in the second quarter, I just stepped it up and realized I needed to stop playing around. I did much better. However, in the spring quarter I took some very difficult classes and didn't understand much of what the professor was talking about. I did OK but could have done better. So my first year was a real learning experience for me, and now into my second year, I'm motivated to do much better.

Now in my sophomore year and after having taken Introduction to Chicano Studies and a class on the black civil rights movement, I've decided to major in either law and society or global studies. I'm very much interested in world issues and want to eventually do something in international relations. I really don't like seeing how the U.S. is depicted around the world.

Here at UCSB I haven't joined any ethnic organizations, whether black or Latino. I think that these groups are too separated from the rest of campus and exclude themselves from other groups. I don't care for this. I've been asked, as I was in high school, why I don't fit in with either blacks or Latinos. My response is, "What is your organization going to do to make my life here at UCSB better?" I do my own thing. It really bothers me when people question who I am or what I am. I see the world as a whole, and it's very diverse. If you try to exclude yourself from others, you're missing out on everything else that this beautiful planet has to give us. If anything, I would join a multicultural organization, but there's none on campus that I feel comfortable with. Some of my friends and I have talked about organizing a multicultural group. My friends are of all different ethnic backgrounds, and I like this.

It's interesting because I still get the same reaction at UCSB that I got in high school. People see me as black and then get blown away when they hear me speaking Spanish or when in a class I respond to the name Ramírez. This doesn't bother me. I love that. I always expect the unexpected.

My biggest dream is to play professional soccer. I want to play in Europe. That's always been my number one dream. Another dream I've had is that I really want to spend the rest of my life outside the U.S. I want to learn other cultures and languages. I definitely want to go back to Honduras and settle there for a year or so. I want to do something for the people there who struggle so much. Perhaps I can build homes for them or something like that. But whatever I do to help them, I want to do it quietly. I basically want to help people but not get the credit for it. Back in Pasadena, I want to do whatever I can to promote education so that other young people can also have goals and not just think negatively. These are things that have been instilled in me by my parents. I've been taught to never turn people down. When you help others, it's more rewarding than anything else.

Professionally, I want to go to law school and maybe go into politics. I don't care a lot about politics, but I've realized that in order to have a significant impact on people, you have to have some status, like celebrities and politicians do. Running for elected office may be a way for me to shake things up and help open people's minds.

At the same time, I want to be well off. I want the best car on the road. I also want to have a family, but not until I'm professionally and economically secure so I can provide adequately for my wife and children. As for me marrying in the future, I think I would prefer to marry a Latina, but a *morenita*, a black Latina like me.

Amílcar Ramírez graduated from the University of California, Santa Barbara, in 2006, majoring in Latin American and Iberian studies with a minor in global studies. He received his law degree from the University of La Verne in 2012, is preparing for the bar exam, and is working at an immigration and bankruptcy law firm in Pasadena as a legal assistant.

ALEJANDRA VARGAS

My dad is from Michoacán, where his family is from. His father was killed when my dad was very young. I think he was killed over a land dispute. They say they know who killed him, but it's Mexico and so the police didn't do anything. My grandmother remarried. In fact, she's been married four times! And all of her husbands have died on her except for the latest. The grandfather I know has been married to my grandma for twenty-five years, but he's not really my grandfather. My grandmother had seven children. The three oldest are from my real grandfather, then two are from another person whose name I don't even know, then another one from another person, and the youngest is from my grandfather now. My youngest uncle is about twenty-two or twenty-three, which is the same age as my older brother. My grandmother actually has grandchildren older than her sons.

My dad's family is from a small village in Michoacán where there are a lot of little *ranchitos*. I'm not sure what my real grandfather did, but he probably farmed like most in that area. My dad, Fermín, was born in 1957. He's the second oldest and the oldest son. He doesn't talk much about his early history. He had only a sixth grade education because he had to go to work to help his poor family. He worked on farms milking cows and things like that. He picked fruit and even shined shoes for extra cash.

My mother's family is also from Michoacán, although after my mom, Hortencia, was born, the family moved to the state of Colima and settled in the capital of Colima. The state is along the west coast of Mexico, about two and a half hours from Guadalajara. My mom was born in a rural town called Trojes. She was born in 1956. She was one of the oldest of twelve children, although two died. My mother's parents worked, but they were better off than my dad's. My mother actually attended and graduated from college in Mexico. Later, when she came to the U.S., she got her GED and learned English. Sometime in the early 1960s, her father came to the U.S. as a bracero worker, and my grandmother later joined him. They left the younger children in the care of the older ones, including my mother. Later in the 1970s, her father would come to the U.S. with the three oldest children to work in the fields picking grapes for a couple of months at a time, then return to Mexico for the rest of the year.

When my father first came to the U.S., he was in his late teens or early twenties. He was the first of his siblings to come, and he crossed without documents. He later took advantage of the amnesty in the 1986 immigration law and got his papers. He went all the way up to Washington State because of the harvest season there. He did field work, and in between picking seasons, he worked in packing factories and in a meat market. In about a year, my paternal grandmother, who was in between husbands, also came to the U.S. with the rest of her family. She settled in Carpinteria, California, where she still lives. My own parents met in Washington.

My maternal grandfather was able to get his green card, and he arranged for papers for my grandmother and the oldest kids, including my mother. My mother first worked in the fields and then in the same meat market as my dad. She worked selling the food while my dad was a butcher. My parents first dated in secret because my mother's father was very protective of her and didn't allow her to date. He didn't know that my mother was dating my dad until my dad went to ask for her hand in marriage. My grandfather agreed, and my parents returned to Mexico and got married in Colima in 1980.

After my parents got married, they moved to Southern California and eventually to Carpinteria, where my paternal grandmother and her family lived. My older brother was born in Santa Barbara, but I was born in Mexico. My mother, after she got pregnant with me, went to have me in Mexico because the hospital stay wouldn't cost as much. I was born in Michoacán, but my birth was registered in Colima. I was born on July 12, 1984. We returned to Carpinteria when I was three weeks old. My mother had her papers, so she was able to return with no problem, and she was able to arrange for my papers at the border. My paternal grandmother, who had gone down with my mother to help her, didn't have papers, so she crossed without documents with the help of a coyote. My father hadn't gone down with my mother because he didn't have his papers yet.

My father first worked in a factory in Carpinteria and then as a housepainter. For a number of years, he worked on his own; recently he started working for a large apartment managing firm, painting apartments.

In Carpinteria we first lived with my paternal grandmother, who rented an apartment in the downtown area in a two-story building. Her place was above a movie theater and a barbershop, both of which are still there. After a while we rented our own apartment in the same building. I started kindergarten at Canalino School and went there through second grade. It only went through the second grade, and I was then going to attend elementary school at Aliso School, but I had tested into the GATE [Gifted and Talented Education] program and Aliso didn't have it for that grade. So I was assigned to go to Main School for third grade but then went to Aliso for fourth and fifth grade because it had the GATE program for those grades. We still lived above the theater.

I remember that in second grade I was really good in math. They gave us one hundred multiplication problems, and I was the first to finish so I got the highest grade. I was doing division problems when the other kids were still doing multiplication. My mom, my brother, and I are all good at math.

At Main School, I remember my teacher telling me that she was going to have a special meeting with Spanish-speaking parents and to ask my parents to attend. My dad couldn't go because of work, and my mom hesitated because she couldn't speak English well. My mom finally went, but only one other parent showed up. I remember my mom saying that Hispanic parents didn't pay much attention to their kids' education because they worked too much and were too tired to go to a meeting. I had to translate for my mother at these meetings.

My mom in time understood more English but still has problems with pronunciation. My dad actually learned to speak English pretty well because he had to deal with his white customers. But my mom can write English better than my dad.

When I started school, I don't remember being able to speak English. Even though my older brother had already learned it, I don't remember picking it up from him. But I learned English right away in school. I didn't have any traumatic experiences. I do remember later on thinking it wasn't fair in spelling tests that we got words that only the white students were more familiar with.

My elementary schools were mixed with white and Mexican American students. But since I was in GATE classes, most of the students were white. By the fourth grade, my mother must have thought I was losing my Spanish, so she had me attend a class primarily for white students to learn to speak, write, and read Spanish. I felt embarrassed doing this because I was the only Latino in that class and because I thought it was a dumb class. I only did this for a year. I was never in a bilingual class. All of my teachers were white except for Ms. Rodríguez in second grade.

I got along well with the white students in my GATE classes. In fact, most of my friends then were white. Later in middle school I had a couple of Hispanic friends. The white kids would invite me to their homes for sleepovers, but my mom wouldn't let me go. She wouldn't even let me do this with my cousins. In middle school, my Hispanic friend invited me for a sleepover, and again my mom wouldn't let me go. But when a white friend did the same, my mom considered it, even though she still didn't let me go. She was more inclined to let me sleep over at a white friend's home than at a Hispanic's. I thought this was very strange, but she said she trusted the white family more, even though she didn't know them but did know the Hispanic family.

In elementary school, I was a good student but shy, even though I was kind of a teacher's pet. I always cleaned up after myself and helped the teacher clean. I did this at home also. I really liked art and always drew pictures of fish for my fourth grade teacher, whose name was Ms. Fisher.

By the time I started middle school, my family had moved to Ventura, where we bought a house. I shared a bedroom with my little sister. Our street didn't have any Hispanics but had all white neighbors. But a couple of blocks away was the infamous Ramona Street. It was famous in Ventura for being a pretty bad area. There, mostly Hispanics lived.

Although we now lived in Ventura, my mother felt that the schools there were not as good as the ones in Carpinteria. She made an agreement with the school district that allowed my siblings and me to stay in the Carpinteria schools. My mom now drove, and so she'd drive us every morning to four different schools: I went to the middle school; my older brother went to the high school; my younger brother went to the elementary school; and my younger sister was at Canalino School. She then picked each of us up in the afternoon.

Carpinteria Middle School was sixth, seventh, and eighth grades. I was in the honors classes with most of the white kids who had been in the elementary GATE classes, although this time there were a few other Latinos. I did well and passed all of my honors classes. I didn't participate in extracurricular activities or sports because we lived in Ventura and I couldn't stay after school. Besides, I didn't care for sports, including soccer, which my brothers played and even my dad did in an adult league. I didn't like the competitive part of it.

At school I only spoke English, but at home I spoke Spanish with my parents. With my siblings I spoke English. My mom wanted us to learn to speak proper Spanish and frowned on us mixing English and Spanish. At school my teachers and classmates called me by my proper name, Alejandra, although some teachers, especially substitute teachers, could really mangle it. They would pronounce it funny. Some white friends started calling me Ale, and later in high school it became Alex.

From middle school I attended Carpinteria High School. My mom did not want me to go to Ventura High, which had a bad reputation academically and for gang-related fights. Besides, my older brother was already going to Carp High. In fact, he already had a car, and so he drove me to school, which relieved my mom from driving so much, even though at that time she was working in Carpinteria taking care of the elderly.

Carp High was a small high school compared to others. It had about eight hundred to nine hundred students on a very nice and large campus. Most of the freshmen I knew, since we all came from the same middle school. Because there were more elective classes in addition to honors classes, I met more Hispanic students in these other classes. At first I was nervous going to high school because I had heard it was much harder. But I didn't find that to be the case. I think our middle school classes, some of which were pretty hard, prepared us well for high school.

One major difference in high school was that I became more aware of the number of Mexican students, even though they had all gone to the same schools as I had. I enjoyed this because we had things in common. If we talked about what we had for dinner the previous evening and some said tamales, or if someone mentioned going to a *quinceañera*, we all could relate to this without an explanation. At the same time, getting to know more Mexican students was a sad reality check because it made me realize that most had not been in honors classes. At that time, I unfortunately held the stereotype that if they weren't in the honors classes, this meant that they were dumb and lazy. Some, of course, were, and I couldn't understand why they didn't just do their homework. Now, looking back, I realize that many other white students could be just as bad and that not all the Mexican students were like this.

At this time, I didn't call myself Latino or Hispanic. I always called myself Mexican. I also never said that I was white, even though some whites thought I was white. I remember thinking that this was a compliment, but I never went along with it. I've always been Mexican, and I said I was Mexican. At the same time, I didn't care for the Mexican students who dressed up and tried to act like cholos. This meant shaving their eyebrows and applying lines to them as well as to their lips, or the shaved head with Dickies pants and bandannas on their head. The cholo style didn't attract me or the other Mexican girls whom I became friends with. I wore T-shirts, jeans, and sandals, the casual look. The so-called cholo students weren't really hardcore cholos in that they weren't in gangs or into violence.

I did pretty well in my high school classes. I never really had to struggle. Looking back, I should have put more effort into my classes because I didn't really study much. The only exception was my calculus class in my senior year. I didn't like calculus, and I didn't really need it since I already had the required three years of math. So I wasn't motivated and as a result struggled, although I got a passing grade. I was mostly again in honors classes and as a senior was in AP history and AP English. I didn't take Spanish for my language requirement because I already knew it and wanted to do something new. Most of the kids took Spanish because they could get an easy A. I took French and really liked it. All of my teachers in my classes were white, although there were a few Hispanic teachers at the school. I graduated with a 3.8 GPA and in the top 10 percent.

Dropouts at my school were not many. The kids who did drop out or were in danger of failing were sent to Rincon High right next door. It was mostly for them to get their diploma. I knew someone who went there, and the classes are not hard. At the end they take a test to get their diploma. Mostly Mexicans attended or white girls who were pregnant.

I knew since I was in middle school that I wanted to go to college. This was also part of being in the honors programs. We were expected to go to college. My mother also very early on supported the idea of her children going to college. My older brother went to Santa Barbara City College. He played soccer there but still has to graduate. In high school we had academic counselors but not really college counselors, or at least I never received college counseling. What helped me and others was being in the honors program, which was structured to meet UC requirements. I didn't know it at the time but did later when I applied to the UC schools. From the beginning, I favored UCSB because it was close to home and yet far enough away to give me some independence from my parents. But I also applied to UCLA, UC Santa Cruz, and UC San Diego. I didn't get accepted to UCLA or UCSD but did to UCSC and UCSB. I had visited UCSB once when my brother played a soccer game there. I also had heard from a friend a year older than me who went to UCSB that it was a good school. I was excited when I got accepted. My mother was also excited and supportive. My dad never really promoted college, but he didn't discourage it. He was like, "You're old enough to know what you're doing." He also didn't discourage me from living away from home.

In high school when I was sixteen and after I got my driver's license, I started driving to school. My mother bought me a car because this would help her. She wouldn't need to drive me to school, plus my older brother had now graduated. So I drove myself and my little brother to school. Having a car also carried other responsibilities. I used it to go buy groceries for the family and to go and pay bills like the gas bill. I didn't drive around with my friends. I didn't want to get into any trouble, like getting a ticket. But having a car did give me some sense of independence.

I also started working when I was fifteen. My aunt was a supervisor at the Boys and Girls Club in Carpinteria, and she got me a job there working after school. I watched over the kids and did some office work. I used my salary to pay for my gas and to buy my clothes and food for lunch.

In high school I was still limited in extracurricular activities because of commuting to Ventura. I didn't play any sports, although I did some kickboxing. I only rarely attended the football games because they were on Friday nights and it was hard for me to drive back from Ventura for the games. Also, my church club met on those days at the same time as the games, and I preferred to go to these meetings. I did belong to a few school clubs. One was the Interact Club, which was a community service club. It was also a way of fulfilling our sixty hours of community service required at school. We visited some elderly ladies with Alzheimer's who didn't have any families. At Christmastime we sold candy to raise money to help out a poor family. With the money, we helped them pay their rent and bought them groceries and toys for the kids. In my senior year I was president of the club. It was mostly Mexicans who belonged to this club.

I was also in the student council and a member of the French Club. In my sophomore year, I and other members of the French club raised money so we could go with our French teacher to Paris for a week. We went during spring break in 2000. This was a lot of fun. Despite the short amount of time in Paris, we visited a lot of museums and tourist spots. My teacher knew Paris very well, and so this helped. Before the trip, she cautioned me not to take my usual sandals because she said it would still be cold in Paris, and she was right. My mom was really excited about me going. She's always wanted to travel to Europe, and so she was happy for me. My dad was also supportive. The trip gave us the opportunity to practice our French when we went to restaurants or to the market. I would love to return there as well as to travel to Spain and Italy. I already knew Mexico well because we would go there every year.

At home, we eat mostly Mexican food. We eat tortillas, beans, and meat almost every day. At the same time, we celebrate holidays like Thanksgiving, even though my parents and their older relatives didn't even know what this is all about. I don't even know myself. Why are we celebrating white people killing a whole bunch of Indians? We don't actually celebrate Thanksgiving at home. We go to my grandmother's in Carpinteria, and the whole extended family shows up. Everyone brings different kinds of food, including a turkey that one of my aunts cooks. But we also have tamales. It's more of a buffet. Growing up, in middle school and into high school I really got addicted to McDonald's, but later on I got more food conscious and learned about how fattening McDonald's is. I stopped going and started bringing my own lunch. Mexican food is definitely still my favorite, but I also like Chinese food and pizza but not sushi or tofu.

At home, my siblings and I speak mostly Spanish with my parents, but among us we speak English. But all of us can speak Spanish well, although I sometimes see my little sister struggling with some words. We're all bilingual.

My father is a musician and has always played the guitar. He loves *ranchero* music and mariachi. Maybe because I grew up hearing this music, I didn't really care for it. In middle school I'd listen mostly to hip-hop and R&B. I didn't really like rap. But by my senior year in high school, I started listening to some Latino music like Shakira and Ricky Martin. Today, perhaps because of the Chicano studies classes I've taken, I have more of an appreciation of Mexican culture, including music. I actually now enjoy some of my father's singing, like the songs of Vicente Fernández, and I sing along with him. I also like mariachi, but still I don't like *banda* because of its monotonous beat.

At home, my mother watches Spanish-language television, especially the *novelas* or soap operas. My father also watches the same channel but prefers sports, although he will watch some English-language action movies. I used to watch some of the *novelas*, but they took too much of my time. You had to watch every day to keep up with the story. I watch English-language shows in my bedroom, where I have my own TV.

I used to go to see movies, but I don't much anymore because it's so expensive, and sometimes I don't even like the film.

I was raised Catholic. My maternal grandmother in Mexico is very Catholic. She goes to church and prays the rosary every day. She passed this religious devotion to her children, including my mother. My mother made sure we received all of the sacraments: baptism, First Communion, and confirmation. We went to Mass every Sunday when we were young but stopped going because my mom sometimes had to work on Sundays or, having worked hard all week, she needed Sundays to rest up. My dad never goes to Mass. When my mom stopped going, I also didn't attend, but then I started going again when I joined a church group in high school. It's called Grupo Apostolíco de Cristo, and we meet every Friday at Mission Buenaventura in Ventura, which is where I also attend Mass. It's a mostly Mexican group, and we meet each Friday evening and talk about religion and being a teenager and play games. Our discussion leader is a young woman in her early thirties. The membership ranges from age sixteen to early twenties. I've been a member since I was a sophomore in high school, and I'm still a member now that I'm at UCSB.

When I turned fifteen, I had my *quinceañera*. My birthday is in July and so we had it then but in Colima, Mexico. I actually didn't want to have it. I don't like dancing, and I would have to dance the traditional waltz with every guy, and I didn't look forward to this. I also thought it could be a waste of money, because my mother estimated it would cost $10,000 if we had it on this side of the border. "Just buy me a car," I told my mother. But she really wanted me to have it, and so I finally agreed. We had it in Colima because it would be less expensive. My uncles and aunts there pitched in and paid for the band and the reception hall and other things as well. In the end, I'm glad I had my *quinceañera*, and I got the car, too! My sister will have her *quinceañera* next summer, also in Mexico.

We have some religious figures at home. Most prominently, in our dining room we have an image of La Última Cena [The Last Supper]. We also have a crucifix and an image of Our Lady of Guadalupe.

Although I think my family used to be more patriarchal, this has changed. My dad thinks he still rules, but on a lot of issues my mom does. My dad used to express a great deal more machismo, but he's changed. He used to say that he could smoke inside of the house because it's his house. But now for health reasons—our health—he smokes outside. I would say that my parents have a more equal relationship today. They both have to agree on most things. In fact, it's my mother who saves money for the family, not my dad, who tends to be more of a spender. It was my mother's money that first bought my older brother's car, then mine, and more recently my younger brother's car.

But I also see that patriarchy sometimes still creeps into our family culture. For example, my older brother has always gotten more liberties than I did growing up. He also was never required to help around the house, including cooking, cleaning up, or going to pay the bills. But I've had to do all of these things. I still do, even though I'm in college. Because I live at home on the days I don't drive to UCSB, it falls on me to clean the house and cook dinner since everyone is out working, including my mother, or at school. I don't like cleaning up, but I don't mind cooking. I cook Mexican food such as carne asada, enchiladas, and chile rellenos. I also like to sew. By contrast, my mother doesn't like to cook or sew.

Ever since I was young, my family goes to Mexico at least once and sometimes twice a year. We go in the summer and in December for the holidays. We usually would go for about two weeks, but as I got older I would stay longer, sometimes the whole summer with my mother's family in Colima. None of my dad's relatives are there anymore. I have cousins my age, and so I hang out with them. They speak almost no English, and so we speak Spanish. Sometimes we take side trips, like to Manzanillo or Guanajuato. This summer I'll go back for the entire three months, and I can hardly wait to do so. I love it there.

After I graduated from high school, I prepared to go to UCSB. I didn't do the orientation program because I didn't know about it. The only orientation that I had was learning how to go online to register for classes. I had expected to live in the dorms that fall, but I also didn't know that my dorm application needed to be submitted earlier that spring, and so when I inquired about what dorm I had been assigned to, I was surprised to learn that I had no dorm. This meant that I continued living at home that fall and commuted to campus about forty minutes each way. I was told I could live in the dorms starting winter quarter.

I received financial aid but still had to take out loans, especially to pay for the dorm that year. I figure that I've taken out about $10,000 in loans, and by the time I graduate, it could be as high as $24,000.

I didn't experience a big change or shock my first quarter at UCSB. Maybe it was because I still lived at home and pretty much had a similar kind of schedule as in high school. I went to classes in the morning and returned home in the afternoon. Also, I was expecting college to be more difficult anyway, and so I was prepared for it. One change was the larger classes, like ones with over five hundred students. There definitely was more reading, but in my English classes in high school we had to read a lot, and so this wasn't something new for me. I liked that in college we didn't have tests every week or so, although in my discussion sections we had weekly quizzes. This was true of Introduction to Chicano Studies, which I took that fall. Some disadvantages of commuting that fall were that I wasn't able to meet new friends (although I had a good friend from high school who was a year ahead of me) and I couldn't stay on for later afternoon or evening events.

I didn't work that fall or in my freshman year. I thought it was best to just focus on my classes. My mom supported me in this. After that year I got a work-study job tutoring kids at the Boys and Girls Club in Carpinteria and at Carpinteria High School.

That winter quarter, I moved into the Santa Rosa dorms, which had mostly white students. My roommate, who was white, was very nice, and we got along really well. We liked to see the same TV shows in our room. But I didn't get to know many other students in the dorm because by the time I moved in, everyone already had their groups of friends. I didn't experience any homesickness because I talked on the phone a lot with my mom and, because I had a car, went home mostly every weekend. Still, during the week, because I wasn't working and still didn't have many friends on campus, I got lonely and bored. I didn't know what to do with my time.

Other freshmen and I were told that our grades in our freshman year would probably fall and not be as high as in high school. So I wasn't too surprised that I didn't get all As that first year. I got mostly Bs and got a 3.00 GPA. It's funny because I actually did worse that year when I lived in the dorms and had all that free time. Later when I started working, I did much better. My grades didn't bother me as much as my financial situation. I was worried about accumulating so much debt. UCSB charged us for everything. In the dorm, we had to buy a set meal ticket whether we used it or not. Since I spent most weekends at home, I didn't use it all of the time, but I was still charged for those meals. I could have asked my parents to help me, but I didn't because I knew they couldn't afford it anyway. I wanted to be responsible for all of my college costs. But my concern about having too many loans convinced me to move back home my sophomore year and commute.

Commuting again limited my time on campus, although I did a few more social things, like parties, because I had gotten to know more people through my classes. I also did better in my classes. I had started out as an art studio major, but I changed to Chicano studies. I didn't care for all of the art history prerequisites in the major. It's a lot of Western art, so it's Picasso and impressionism that's interesting. But a lot of other stuff isn't. It's like a white board with a black dot in the middle, and that's supposed to be art. I don't like that kind of art. I also didn't like the art history teacher. I had thought of majoring in art studio because I love to paint and draw. I've done this since I was a kid. I've painted a lot of things but just keep them in my closet at home. I did do some paintings for my younger sister to hang on her bedroom wall. One painting that I've been working on for a couple of years is my version of the Last Supper: all of the faces are brown faces—Chicano faces—and I've included some different food items, such as tamales.

I changed to Chicano studies because I liked the classes better. I didn't know much about my Mexican background or about Mexicans in the U.S., and this interested me. I took all of the introductory classes plus this year one upper-division class in Chicano/Latino art history. I just enjoyed these classes more, and after I had taken several, it seemed to make sense to major in it.

Although I am a Chicano studies major, I don't call myself a Chicana. I still call myself Mexican. I have always associated the term "Chicano" or "Chicana" as being more political and connected to the Chicano Movement. Since I'm not part of this background, I don't think it's fair for me to call myself Chicana. It just doesn't seem to really fit me, and so I find it uncomfortable to use it. At the same time, I identify with the content of the classes and know that it's part of my experience. It's refreshing and good to know that other Mexicans and Latinos have had similar experiences. I tell my little sister a lot of what I'm learning in these classes so she'll have already a better understanding of our background. I even talk to my parents about this.

Actually, I plan to double major with a degree in Spanish. I think it complements Chicano studies. It's also practical for me. Although I speak Spanish well, I don't write it well. I need to learn about accent marks and other aspects of using it. This will make me more fluent in Spanish.

This academic year I also decided to not live at home but in Isla Vista next to UCSB. I decided this for a few reasons. The most important was that my class schedule changed, and instead of having classes only twice a week, which made it easier to commute, I now have classes five days a week, which would make my commute harder. So I decided it would be easier to move up and live in Isla Vista. The other important reason is that I felt I was losing out on a major college experience of being on my own and living with other roommates. My parents supported my decision. I found a place online, and it's worked out pretty well. I share a two-bedroom apartment with three other girls, and I get along with my roommates. The girl I share my room with is white; one of the other girls is Korean, and the other is half Asian and half white. I do things with them, but I also have many other new friends, both Mexican and white. Many, especially the Mexicans, also are Chicano studies majors.

I have changed a lot in college. I still have my basic values given to me by my parents, but I also have a more critical way of looking at things. For example, I've stopped going to church. I definitely still believe in God, but I'm disappointed about certain things in the Church. I consider myself Catholic, but I don't agree with the Church on a lot of things. At first I felt guilty about not going to Mass, but I don't now. Even when I go home on Sundays, I don't go to church.

I'm excited and, at the same time, scared about graduating next year. I remember thinking last year that I just wanted to graduate and that's it and just work and take a few months off and travel around Mexico. I still want to do that except that I want to get my master's in education right after I graduate. I'm thinking that if I stop for a little bit, it's going to be harder to get back into it. I then want to be a teacher. I'm not sure yet at what level I'd like to teach. I love working with elementary kids, but then I think that in high school I have a lot more potential to reach kids and teach them something that's going to stick with them. For example, I'd like to teach about Chicano studies in the high school. I could do Spanish classes that would incorporate Chicano culture. I never learned about Chicano studies in high school, and I'd like to change that, especially in schools that are more than 50 percent Mexican. I'd like to stay in this area to teach because I like it. I would not mind teaching at my old school, Carpinteria High, because I think many of the teachers there were not as good as they could have been, especially in teaching Mexican kids. I think I could be a good teacher because I'm patient with kids and understand that their lack of progress in comparison to other kids is not because the Mexican kids are dumb but because they don't comprehend English as well and are not exposed to the middle-class experiences that influence educational curriculum. I'm really motivated to help kids to learn. I've been hearing this ever since I was young because my mother always said I could be a good teacher. I taught my little sister how to read.

I plan to get married and have kids but not until I finish my education, including my master's. After that, marriage and children are a real possibility. My grandma had twelve kids and said that whatever God wants to give you, you should accept it. I'm all for what God wants to give me, but twelve kids is a bit too much for me. I know I don't want to have just one child because that would be a really lonely childhood, and a lot of only children are spoiled brats. I think three, maybe four, kids would be fine. I was one of four children and that was OK except that I never had my own room. I still don't, even at home or here, where I have a roommate. I wouldn't want that for my kids. I also think that I can combine my career with a family. As a teacher, I would have summers off and could even take a year or more to take care of my babies. With my education and teaching credential, I can always return to the classroom. I want to be with my kids when they're younger.

Although I've dated both white guys and Mexican guys, I think I would prefer to marry a Mexican. When I've dated white guys, I've noticed that I always find something wrong. I've also noticed that the most serious relationships I've had have been with Mexican guys. I think it would be ideal to marry someone of Mexican background because I just love my culture so much that I wouldn't want to lose any part of it. I just feel that I can relate better to Mexican guys or at least to someone who's aware of the culture. I don't discriminate—like, if you're not Mexican I won't date you—but I kind of foresee myself marrying someone of Mexican background. I believe that my ethnic background plays and will continue to play a strong role in my life.

Alejandra Vargas graduated from the University of California, Santa Barbara, in 2006 and received an M.A. and teaching credential from UCSB in 2007. Since then she has been teaching first grade in the Goleta Unified School District in California.

SUSANA GALLEGOS

When I was a little girl, my parents took me and my siblings to live closer to my parents' families in Mexico. They lived in the small rural town of La Angostura in Michoacán, close to Zamora, Michoacán. I got to meet my Grandma Rita, who has since died. My grandfather still lives there and has remarried. My father, Enrique Gallegos, was born there on November 15, 1941. He is the oldest of eleven living siblings. His father, like his grandfather, was a small farmer. My grandfather owns a couple of plots of land that he has now distributed to his sons but not to his daughters. My father owns one of these plots, which he rents out to other farmers. When my dad was growing up, he and his siblings had to go out and work on the land. My grandfather grew corn, tomatoes, and beans and had a field of papaya trees. In fact, later on when we lived there, my mother did not allow us girls to go work in the fields to do farm labor like they did when they were young. We did do it a few times when my father needed more hands to pick tomatoes or corn. On those occasions, I had to go out early in the morning and work the fields.

My mother, Theresa Navarro, was also born in the small town. Her father was a farmer. However, my mother's family was smaller. I don't know how my parents met or about the courtship. They were engaged for a couple of months and then got married in La Angostura. My mother was twenty-two and my father about twenty-four.

Neither of my parents graduated from elementary school. My father attended up to the fifth grade, and my mother didn't finish the fourth grade because every year during the crop season, they were pulled out of school to work the family land. They can both read and write. My father likes to read the Bible. Because my mother's family was smaller—only eight children—they had to work in the fields at an early age because my grandfather couldn't afford to have other workers. My mom and her siblings worked a lot. "Nos trabajó como burros"—my mom would tell us

216

how they had to work like burros. It was like a hunter-gatherer society. The larger the family, the more kids had to work the land.

My parents started their family in La Angostura. My oldest sister, Lourdes, was born in 1967. Then after my parents came to the U.S., my brother Enrique was born. After returning to Mexico, Alex was born. On returning to California, I was born, and then on returning once again to Mexico, my youngest sister Lili was born. We're a real transnational family.

Migrating to the U.S. to work was a common pattern in my parents' town. My paternal grandfather had come as a bracero in 1942. The first time my father came was as a bracero in 1961. Both worked in Arizona and California. So my dad was already familiar with others from his town who lived in California and knew where to go and find work. It wasn't unusual for young men like my dad to come to the U.S. and work some growing seasons here and then return and work their lands in Mexico. It's different today. The young men in La Angostura don't want to stay there and work their family lands. They prefer to go to the U.S. and stay permanently and just send money home.

After my parents had their first child, they went to the U.S., and both crossed the border without documents. I don't know the details. They came to LA where, on an earlier crossing, my father along with one of his brothers were renting an apartment and where my father started working in a furniture company making furniture. When my parents first came to the U.S. together, they left my sister Lourdes with my maternal grandmother for almost one year. They then returned and brought her over. It wasn't until some years later, after I was born, that my parents legalized their status and got their green cards. By then my mother, who was a homemaker, began to work as a seamstress with different companies in downtown LA. She sewed denim pants, dresses, and stylish clothes. She worked only after my father injured his back at work and couldn't continue. He sued the company and got a small settlement. By this time, my mother was already working, but she now had to work more since she was the main breadwinner.

I was born November 27, 1972, in LA County General Hospital in Boyle Heights. My early years were in LA until we returned to Mexico in 1984, when I was about twelve. Before we moved to Mexico, when we lived in LA my father would take my younger siblings and me to a recreational hall in Echo Park, in the area that we lived, and we'd spend the day there. It was a long walk to the hall, but they served free lunches during the summer. By the time we walked back we were so tired we fell asleep. On weekends my parents would take us to the same park where there was a swimming pool, and we'd spend the day swimming and playing in the pool.

We lived in a basement apartment in an eight-story building right on the edge of downtown LA. It was a one-room apartment. The sleeping arrangements were interesting. My older sister Lourdes slept in a sofa bed. Then in a bunk bed, Lili and I slept in one bed, each facing the opposite direction. Enrique slept in the upper berth, and Alex slept on a mattress on the floor. My parents had their own bed. Then there was a very small kitchen and a dining area plus a full bathroom. It was tight, but I don't remember any of us complaining, and I remember being comfortable there. It's funny because now that I have to share a room with a roommate, I complain about this.

I started my education in an elementary school in Echo Park. I went to kindergarten. I think I already knew some English because of my older siblings, who spoke English. At home we spoke only Spanish. I don't remember being traumatized about a language barrier when entering school. Although we lived in a mostly Latino neighborhood, the school was more mixed with Latinos, Asians, and whites and a very small number of blacks. The teachers were mostly white, although I did have a Miss Brito for fifth grade and a Miss Cano for sixth grade. The one teacher I really remember was my fourth grade teacher, whose name I don't remember. She would punish students who did not do their homework. I've never liked doing homework, and so this affected me. She would have us go to her classroom during lunch where we would finish our homework. The point was that we had to do it.

I didn't finish sixth grade in the U.S. because that's when my parents decided to return to Mexico and build a house there. They actually played a trick on us. They first told us that we were only going for a short vacation to La Angostura. I was thrilled to be getting out of school and returning to Mexico and playing with my grandfather's farm animals and going to the *tortilleria* with my grandma. But I should have realized that something else was going on when we took all of this furniture with us. Our house there was already being built by one of my mother's brothers, and so we soon moved in. My father installed a stove and bought a refrigerator and a television. After a while, we started asking our parents, "When are we going back to LA?"

"Why? You have a home here."

"But we want McDonald's and pizza."

"I'll make you hamburgers," my mother would say.

But they were never like McDonald's.

Then we knew we weren't returning.

Alex, Lili, and I were placed in the only elementary school La Angostura had, and we were all backtracked a few school years. I don't know the reason for this, but it worked out OK. I was backtracked from the sixth grade to the fourth grade, but the curriculum seemed to be the same as in my sixth grade from the U.S. school. I then later graduated from the sixth grade in Mexico and started *secundaria*, that is, middle school. Lourdes and Enrique were enrolled in the *secundaria*; they had to take *el camión* [the bus] to get there because the closest *secundarias* were in the neighboring town of Ixtlan or Vista Hermosa.

My siblings and I adjusted well in our new schools, primarily because we knew Spanish. Actually, I lost a good deal of my English since we didn't use it very much. Sometimes my siblings and I spoke it with some cousins and friends who, like us, had started school in California, but their parents had also returned to La Angostura. We would play some games in English like tic-tac-toe. We did have English classes only until we attended the *secundaria*, but they were very easy and I then recognized that I had lost some of my facility in it. By the time I started my *secundaria* education, La Angostura had built its own *secundaria*, which meant that my brother Alex and I didn't have to take the bus to Ixtlan or Vista Hermosa.

While school was not a big adjustment, other things were. This included getting used to all of the fiestas in each of the towns that celebrated their annual saints' days. The saint for La Angostura was San José or St. Joseph, and we celebrated it each March 19. These fiestas were wonderful events with not just religious ceremonies but many community events as well. Everyone in the town participated to make the fiesta a success.

One other major adjustment was realizing that most homes did not have indoor plumbing. People used outhouses. Fortunately for us, our new home had a built-in bathroom, although it was not connected to the main house.

Our family in the three years we lived in La Angostura went through other changes. My brother Enrique didn't like it there, and so he ran away from home and went back to LA. I don't know how he did this. My mother went and brought him back, but some time later, he saved money and ran away again. This time he lived with some of our relatives in LA. He found a job and earned his keep. He did not go back to school and didn't graduate from high school.

The other change was that my older sister eloped in La Angostura. She met her boyfriend there, and without telling their parents they eloped. She was nineteen. After they eloped, to save face and out of respect to their families, my sister moved in with one of her boyfriend's aunts for a couple of months until they got married. If she had moved into her boyfriend's house or anywhere with him, that meant they were having sex prior to getting married, and that would have been disrespectful to my sister's family. Whether they had sex or not was not the point. It was to show that her boyfriend's family respected my sister's family. They then got married in both a civil and Catholic church wedding. So when my sister returned to LA, she was married and attempted to complete her high school diploma by attending Roosevelt Adult School and taking evening classes. It was difficult to get this accomplished because she now had a husband and children, and to this date she has not graduated from high school.

After over three years in Mexico, my parents decided to return to Los Angeles. They realized that their children preferred to return and that we missed being in LA. So they rented out our home and we all recrossed the border again. Years later, I would return to La Angostura for visits during La Fiesta on March 19 but never again permanently.

When we returned in 1987 to LA, my dad felt good enough to work again in making furniture. However, he got injured again when some heavy material fell and hit him in the chest. He never has worked again. He does handy work for relatives, on occasion. He never received disability for his injury. This meant that the burden of maintaining the family fell again on my mother. She started working again as a seamstress at a garment factory until it burned down during the LA riots in 1992. Since then, for a long time she has worked for the XOXO factory in Commerce.

When we returned to LA, we first moved in with my *tío* Jaime, my dad's brother, in Boyle Heights. We lived there for three or four months until we found a place to rent, also in Boyle Heights. My sister Lili and I then enrolled in Belvedere Junior High. I was fourteen and was placed in the eighth grade. I should have been in ninth, but I was also backtracked here. I had lost some of my English, and so I was placed in the ESL track. It only took me a while to regain my facility in English, but they still kept me in ESL not only that year but through ninth grade as well. I don't understand why they did this since I could speak well in English. I should have been placed in a regular English class, which is what I requested, but my counselor didn't make the change. I had and still have a problem with my counselor's action.

At the same time, I enjoyed and appreciated Ms. Anchondo, our ESL teacher. She really encouraged us to study and to practice our writing and speaking in English. She was a short, chubby lady but cute. I think she was Mexican. She told us if we studied hard, we could get into the regular classes. Although I didn't get into those classes, I did learn a lot from her. Although I have a slight accent in English, it's not as pronounced as others'.

All of my friends at Belvedere were also Mexican, and they were all in the ESL program. We were all transferred together from one level to another. Because we were grouped together, that's how we made our friendships.

After junior high, we all took off to different high schools. These included Roosevelt, Garfield, and Wilson. My sister and I were transferred to Roosevelt, but most others from my group went either to Garfield or Wilson.

Unfortunately, when I started at Roosevelt I was kept in the ESL program. I couldn't believe it! They said I had to finish the program through the tenth grade before I could be in regular English classes. I resented this, but what could I do? I asked to be given a placement test in English, but my high school counselor also refused to do this. I did very well in my classes. I particularly remember my speech class where, on the spur of the movement, I had to improvise a speech during which I showed others how to do something new. I just happened to have some gift-wrapping paper in my backpack and gave a lesson—all in English—on how to wrap a present. I got a good grade for this. In my last semester in ESL, I actually became the teacher's assistant since my English was so good. I helped manage the class, including explaining to the other students what their assignments were and helping them in their compositions. I never saw being in ESL as a stigma, even though all the ESL students hung around together and usually at lunchtime stayed on the edges of the campus. I enjoyed the other ESL students, but I wanted to be part of the rest of the school. I wanted to be in regular English classes, and that's what I resented, especially since there was no reason that they should have kept me in ESL.

I did well initially in high school. I was an A student. I also was on the student council. In my junior and senior year, I joined the drill team and really loved it. It became my passion. It was also a lot of work and responsibility. I had to get to school early for 7 A.M. practice and then had to stay after school for more practice. Every Friday was Spirit Day, and we had to perform. My uniform had to be nicely pressed; my gloves, socks, and shoes had to be perfectly white; and my hair, with a ribbon, had to be nicely combed. But I accepted this responsibility. It made me feel good about myself.

But I didn't feel the same responsibility about my classes into my junior and senior year. I became more alienated from them. Outside of the drill team and my homeroom, I didn't care for my other classes. I didn't like doing my homework at home, so I would do it in my classes. But I didn't like history or any science or math classes. I was never in AP classes. I did OK in my grades, but I wasn't self-motivated.

At the same time, I knew I wanted to go to college. Some of my girlfriends were applying to UC campuses and other schools. This meant that they would be going away to school and leaving home. I wanted to do this also. It was perhaps more the idea of being on my own that interested me. I filled out a number of school applications for colleges outside of LA. But I had this overprotective mother who said, "No. You can't leave home to go to school." She supported the idea of my getting a college education as long as I lived at home. She possessed this very Mexican and Catholic mentality: a young woman stays at home until she gets married in the Church. Because I was still my mother's dependent, I needed her signature for the application, especially for financial aid, but she refused to sign it. She told me I could go to Cal State LA or even to UCLA or USC, but I had to live at home. I didn't want to do this. Taking the bus to these schools would have taken hours. I couldn't believe this was happening to me. Here I was, a good girl who never got into trouble at the same time my younger sister and older brother would ditch school and my brother would go to ditching parties, and yet my mother didn't trust me to go away to college to get an education.

"Go to Cal State LA; it's close to home," she kept telling me.

But I didn't want to go to Cal State LA. I had nothing against the school except that my mother wanted me to go there.

My father had no say in this matter. He said nothing.

I graduated in 1991 from Roosevelt High but didn't go on to a traditional college. Instead, I enrolled in a vocational college and became a certified legal secretary. I found it hard to get a job as a legal secretary because I didn't have any clerical experience. I wound up working for a broadcasting school in Hollywood. I worked there for about a year and a half and then worked for a vocational training school for another year and a half. In the meantime, I took evening classes at East LA College, about two classes per semester. My dream was still to complete my AA degree and transfer to a four-year university. Unfortunately, I got very ill in 1995 and had to be bedridden for a year and a half.

After some recovery from my illness, I went back to East LA College. I took more classes and became quite involved in school activities since I was now a full-time day student. I was elected president of the Economics Student Association Club and also was appointed as commissioner of the Educational Center in South Gate, south of downtown LA. The Educational Center is an extension campus of East LA College. My responsibility was to work with the student population at the center in any way I could to tie student activities together to the main campus. I went once a week and focused on encouraging students to apply to a four-year college, which, of course, was also my dream. At this time, I further became involved in community affairs, primarily the first campaign by Antonio Villaraigosa for mayor of LA. I enjoyed these activities and felt good about my leadership skills.

I think I first showed leadership ability when in the tenth grade I represented my homeroom class in the student council. I also became a leader with our drill team. I would also speak out in my classes to help the teacher quiet down other students. This leadership and activism seemed to come out more often after my illness and when I returned to East LA College. I wanted to be heard and to help others.

Although I had not been very interested in my high school classes, I became a better student at the community college. I knew I had one last chance to get a college education and to transfer to a four-year college, so I became more serious about my classes and doing well. This is something I had to do for myself.

By this time, I not only was still living with my parents but was the only one still at home. All of my other siblings were gone and married. This meant that I now had my own room and more space for myself.

Being at home for all these years also meant being influenced by my family's cultural traditions. A lot of this was enhanced over the three years that we lived in Mexico. My favorite tradition was Las Posadas during Christmas. These were nine days—El Novenario—depicting the search by Mary and Joseph for shelter (*posada*). These were beautiful ceremonies. Each night the ordinary people selected to play Mary and Joseph went to various designated homes seeking *posada*, only to be turned away. Many followed in procession, praying the rosary as we walked from one of the homes to the next. Finally, at the end—also a designated home—they would find shelter. This was accompanied by everyone sharing food and other treats and later by wonderful Mexican Christmas carols. A big treat for me was when I was selected to play the role of Mary. I was the Virgin Mary a few times. In Mexico, we didn't get Christmas gifts until January 6, El Día de Los Reyes or All King's Day, commemorating the visit by the three kings to the manger where the baby Jesus was born. For Christmas, my mother would cook tamales and pozole (hominy soup).

Other major celebrations mostly linked to religion in Mexico included the feast day of Our Lady of Guadalupe on December 12 and the feast of St. Joseph as the patron saint of La Angostura on March 19. One of the biggest days that is celebrated everywhere in Mexico is September 16, Mexico's Independence Day. We had a parade, music, and food.

When we returned from Mexico, we adjusted to the U.S. Christmas traditions again. We celebrated on Christmas Eve. We didn't participate in Las Posadas because we didn't know many of the other people living in our neighborhood, unlike in our small Mexican town where everyone knew each other. Still, my mother cooked her delicious tamales and pozole. We put up a Christmas tree and everyone exchanged gifts. We put the figurine of *el niño dios* under the tree. My father and my brother Alex and his wife, Erica, go to Christmas midnight Mass, but the rest of us usually stay home.

Part of this cultural adjustment in the U.S. is that we celebrate Thanksgiving. My mother started cooking a turkey only because at work the company gave out turkeys to the employees.

"How am I supposed to cook a turkey?" I remember my mother asking the first time.

I took it upon myself to watch Martha Stewart on television, and when she showed how she cooked her turkey, I wrote down notes and translated them to Spanish. This way, my mother had an idea of how to cook the Thanksgiving turkey. We added a Mexican twist to Martha Stewart's dinner by also including pozole and rice and beans.

Of course, when we returned from Mexico, my siblings and I gorged ourselves on McDonald's and pizza.

In Mexico, I really got into watching TV in the classic black and white and watched Mexican films, but when we returned to the U.S., there were few if any channels that showed these films. Back in California, I liked watching English-language TV but also Spanish-language TV. I would get home after school and watch English-language TV shows. But then my mother would get home from work and make dinner, and then she and my dad sat down to watch the *novelas*, the Mexican soap operas, from 7 to 10 P.M. I got into watching them as well.

My musical tastes also reflected this variety. I didn't care for popular U.S. music such as the Beastie Boys, Michael Jackson, and Madonna. But then I really got into Paula Abdul and Whitney Houston. When I visited my cousins here in LA, we'd dance to this music in the living room. After returning from Mexico, I didn't listen to Mexican music. I liked it, but as a teenager, I was now kind of embarrassed to listen to it. Everybody my age and my Mexican friends listened to American music. It wasn't until after high school that I got back into Mexican music. I started going out with my friends to listen to *banda* music that just took off among the Latino population. I loved La Banda Mexicano, La Banda Machos, Arkangel R-15, and other such groups. I went with the flow and enjoyed it. Now I also love to listen to great Mexican singers such as José Alfredo Jiménez, Antonio Aguilar, and the late Jorge Negrete. They have such beautiful songs. Some of the more modern songs, in my opinion, are ridiculous and degrading to women.

We also have maintained, as we have grown up, various Mexican religious traditions. This is especially the case with my dad. Since he can't work, he devotes a lot of time to religion. He belongs to a group called La Adoración Nocturna at a small church in East LA called El Santuario de Nuestra Señora de Guadalupe. The Adoración Nocturna group is a confraternity devoted to Our Lady of Guadalupe. He also has a special devotion to San José since he's the patron saint of my dad's hometown. My mother isn't as religiously engaged since she has to work and doesn't have as much time. But when we were kids, the whole family went to Mass; it was a big thing to do on Sundays.

My dad still goes regularly and encourages us to do the same. However, as we got older, my siblings and I didn't go as often. My dad still tells us that it's a sin if we don't go to Sunday Mass and that God knows who's there and who isn't.

We didn't pray as a family at home, but we did individually. We do have religious images throughout the house; my mother bought a painting of

La Última Cena [The Last Supper], and it hangs prominently in our living room. When my dad goes to Palm Sunday Mass, he gets the palms and makes them into crosses that he hangs at home. We also have images of Our Lady of Guadalupe. I have one a best friend gave me; I have it in my bedroom at home. In my parent's room, my dad constructed an *altarcito* where he has various religious images, his rosary, the Bible, and candles.

My parents give me a blessing all of the time. When I go on a trip they bless me. My mother blesses me by hugging me and by doing the sign of the cross on my forehead. My father does the sign of the cross in my direction as I drive away.

I really wanted a *quinceañera*, but I didn't get it. We had returned from Mexico earlier that year, and my parents didn't have the money. So my dream of my big fifteenth birthday celebration never happened.

My parents were not especially strict with my siblings and me because they were busy working. We were expected to behave in a certain way. They didn't have to tell us; it was just expected that we were not to bring dishonor to our family. Still, within this, there were gender differences. My brothers were allowed to come and go whenever they pleased and at whatever time. But if my younger sister, Lili, or I were to tell my mom, "Bye, Mom, I'll be back later," she would respond: "Where are you going? No one is allowing you to leave. Who are you going with?" So we could never leave our home if Mom didn't say it was OK.

For high school dances, I had to ask my mother for permission to go. I would tell her days in advance, but she would always wait until the final day to give her approval. She would make sure that she gave me the exact amount of money to pay the entrance fee and a little bit more for me to buy a refreshment, but not a dime more. My older brother would have to drive me and pick me up after the dance. The only exception to this was if one of my girlfriend's fathers drove us to the dance and picked us up. Then I had to be back at a certain time, usually by 12:15 after the dance finished at midnight. But sometimes my friends and I just wanted to hang out a bit longer, so I would stretch the time to get back home first to 12:30, then 12:35, and then 12:40.

"Are you coming home a bit later tonight?" she would ask me as she waited up for me.

Even today she still waits up for me. That's OK if it makes her feel better that I'm home safe.

In high school, I was not allowed to date. I did have a boyfriend who was not in my high school. He was a marine stationed at Camp Pendleton.

My mother allowed me to go out with him but only because I would see him infrequently when he had a pass to come to LA. Other than that, I couldn't go out on a date with guys, and I would never be allowed to bring a guy to my home to visit me. It was just something a girl didn't do. It was viewed as disrespectful to your parents. I did go to my senior prom but with a guy who was only a friend. But at first my mom told me I could go only if I returned by 10:30 P.M. She was worried because the prom was at the Disneyland Hotel, and she didn't want me out late at a hotel! I had to explain to her that I would not be in a room at the hotel but in the hotel ballroom. She finally agreed and I could come back later. Even then, I couldn't be driven by this guy. We had to carpool.

As I'm getting older, my parents have become more relaxed about my social life. This was especially true after my severe illness and during the long months of recuperation at home. During this time, a number of my guy friends would come to visit me, and my mom got to see that they were nice young men who were concerned about me and my well-being. Since then, she's not been as vigilant about my social life and dating, although she still wants to know whom I'm going out with.

My dad has never been directly involved like my mom in my social life. If he was concerned, he talked with my mother about it, but he let my mother deal with me. He felt this was an issue between women. But now that I'm in college, I have a more open relationship with my dad. We sit down and talk like adults. He gives me his opinion about certain aspects of my life, and I give him my opinion.

Throughout all of this time, I've been able to maintain my facility in Spanish. I'm very bilingual. I still speak Spanish at home. With my siblings, we speak in both languages, although sometimes we revert to Spanglish, where we mix the language. But if I start in one language, I try to finish with it. All of my siblings have also married other Mexicans, and they try to speak Spanish at home with their children. My brother Alex's wife, Erica, can't speak Spanish as well, but after she got married to my brother, she enrolled in Spanish classes at East LA College to perfect it. Their son, Steven, also has some problem with Spanish, but we encourage him without ever making him feel bad about it.

I graduated from East LA College in the spring of 2001. I always knew I wanted to transfer to a four-year university. In fact, the summer before graduating, I participated in a program that assisted community college students in successfully transferring to a university. It was a program sponsored by UCLA called SITE (Summer Intensive Transfer Experience), held at UCLA. It was a great program. It was for an entire week, and we lived in the dorms. They helped us to make sure we were taking courses that were transferable to a UC campus. There were workshops on how to study and how to organize our time, and it exposed us to lectures of the kind we would experience in a university. They also gave us information on making applications and the deadline. One thing in particular I learned was that if I transferred to a UC campus, I didn't want to live in the dorms. I couldn't handle the noise.

In my last year of community college, I applied to all the UC campuses. I didn't know which one I would like to attend, and so I applied to all of them. I didn't apply to a Cal State campus because I was determined to go to a UC one. Besides, if I applied to the Cal State system, I would probably wind up at Cal State LA, only a couple of miles from my home, and this would mean that I would continue to live at home. I didn't do this. It was time for me to be on my own. It had been my mother who had refused to let me go away to college after high school, and I didn't want to repeat this. I was now much older and a returning student, and I had had a significant recovery from my serious illness that kept me out of school for two years. And so I believed I had a right to be on my own and get a BA degree.

I got accepted at about four or five UC campuses. I narrowed it down to UCSB and UC Santa Cruz. However, when I visited UCSB on a trip sponsored by East LA College, I knew that this was the campus for me. I can't explain it. It was just a feeling, and I tend to follow my instincts. It was a good choice.

I knew that my parents, especially my mother, wouldn't be too keen on my going away to school. They were very used to my being at home and helping out. I decided to let them know gradually, even after I received my acceptance notice from UCSB. I had already mentioned to my parents that even if I were accepted at UCLA, I would not continue to live at home. I just couldn't stay home and concentrate on my studies. I knew it would be intense at a UC campus. If I stayed living at home, I would have to pick up my mother at work when my dad couldn't and would still be responsible for housework. I would be distracted by the phone and even by my friends. All of this would be detrimental to my studying.

I finally made my formal announcement of my decision to go to UCSB on my graduation day from East LA College. My mother after the ceremony treated my family and me and my best friend, Martha, to dinner.

At the restaurant, my brother Alex asked me: "So, Susana, where are you going to school now?"

I leaned over to Martha and whispered: "Here it goes; let's see how everyone reacts."

"Okay," I said, "I've decided to go to UC Santa Barbara."

My parents didn't say anything, but I could tell that they were happy for me. Everyone clapped and congratulated me. They all were happy that I had graduated from community college and that I was going on. My mother accepted this but still in time let it be known that she would like me to come home every weekend. I would have liked to, but I knew that I couldn't because I had new responsibilities.

I received a fairly good financial package, including grants, loans, and work-study. I will be in debt but perhaps not as much as other students. My boyfriend, who is also a transfer student, will graduate with much more debt than me.

I had no idea what I would major in when I filled out my application to UCSB. I was just so excited about the idea of going to a UC school. I was very open to any possibilities of what I would study. The last thing I filled out was my intended major. I finally decided to put down cultural anthropology. I liked different cultures and people and felt this would be a field that would complement my interests. I wasn't wrong.

Perhaps the most difficult part of my transition was that I knew I would not have as many friends at UCSB. At East LA College, I knew so many other students and had a lot of friends. But I deliberately decided that at UCSB I didn't want to have many friends because they would distract me from my studies. And that's the way it's worked out. My friends are my roommates plus my boyfriend, and that's fine with me.

At first I didn't know where I would live. I knew I didn't want to live in the dorms, but I didn't have any information on off-campus housing. I thought I might have to initially live in my car. The rents for a single room in Santa Barbara and Goleta were astronomically more than what my mother paid for an entire house in East LA. Fortunately, one day at East LA College when I was in the computer room looking for possible housing, a friend came by and told me he had a friend who was attending UCSB, and she lived in a rented house. He thought she might help me out and let me stay there until I found my own place. So I called her up, and initially she said I could sleep in the living room. However, good luck followed when one of the roommates decided to leave, and this gave me the opportunity to permanently move in and share a room with another girl. Into my second and final year at UCSB, that's where I'm still living. It's a three-bedroom house, and six of us share the bedrooms: four girls and two guys. It's worked out fine, and everyone does chores.

I first thought that my transition to my classes at UCSB went fine. But this was because my initial classes were not very demanding. One class only required a midterm essay and final term paper. So my grades were fine, but then the second quarter wasn't as good. There was much more reading required, and one class had a discussion section where the TA brought in his own material entirely different from that of the professor's, and so I didn't know what to concentrate on for the exams. My grades went down, including in a computer class, where I received the worst grade I've ever gotten. I began to realize that I didn't know how to study. Fortunately, one of my roommates knew about some of the campus programs that helped students how to study. I went to them and received useful counseling, and so I'm doing better now. The other big transition was just getting used to a ten-week quarter system, where everything is so confined, as opposed to the eighteen-week semester I was used to at the community college.

Taking exams also posed a problem for me. Due to my earlier illness, I have mental loss and mental disability. I learned that I could apply for a program for disabled students that provides them with more time and even a quieter space to take exams. I tried to get into the program but have not been successful because I need written verification from the Social Security Administration. The problem is that because of my mental disability, my mother is listed as my legal guardian. Only she can request and sign any verification for me. So I couldn't sign the paperwork to be classified as a disabled student, and my mom has tried multiple times to call the Social Security office and get the paperwork but hasn't been successful. So what I've resorted to is just personally explaining to my professors what my problem is and asking if they could agree to give me more time on my exams and to let me take the exams in a quiet space outside the classroom. They've been very understanding and helpful.

My first year and a half, I found myself going home about every weekend. As I was moving in with my roommates, I had to make several trips to LA to get my things. But I also found it convenient to go home and do my laundry and buy my food. I also missed my friends, and so this gave me an opportunity to see them. I think too it made me feel good to go home and be with my parents, who enjoyed seeing me. But more recently I haven't gone back that much due to the pressure of my classwork.

Although I still have to take a few courses in the fall, I went through the Chicano graduation ceremony. In fact, I was a member of the planning committee, the only campus group that I joined while at UCSB. The event was particularly special for me because my maternal grandmother from La Angostura was there. My mother and father both became U.S. citizens about five years ago, and so they were able to legally bring my grandmother to Los Angeles. They did this just a couple of months prior to my graduation, and so I insisted that she had to come along with the rest of the family to the ceremony. Only my older sister, Lourdes, who lives in Las Vegas, couldn't attend. When I went up to get my diploma, I especially thanked my grandmother for being there, and of course I thanked my friends and my whole family for the support. Just as I was in line to be recognized, I picked up my cell phone and called Lourdes and kept her on the line so she could hear my little speech. I'm the first in both my immediate and extended family to receive a college degree. I felt good about accomplishing this, but I know I have much more to accomplish in my life.

As for my future, I know I don't necessarily want to live in LA anymore. I feel like I've moved on and that I don't fit there anymore. I feel like a visitor there. I hope to find a place for myself and look for a career. I want to go to graduate school but not right away. I want to work and settle a little before doing that. I'm leaning toward doing social work or some kind of community work. I want to work with people and especially help students go on to college. So perhaps I could be a college counselor in a community college. Whatever I do, I want to give back to my community.

As for marriage and a family, I'm not sure. When I was younger, at age nineteen or twenty, I dreamed of the classic traditional wedding, but a few years later I developed a negative outlook on marriage. I saw my cousins' marriages dissolve and in general see that women are treated badly. I saw my friends, both men and women, getting divorced or separated and becoming single parents. I don't want to go through this, and I certainly don't want to be part of a bad marriage. I would rather just stay on my own.

This doesn't mean that I've completely given up on marriage; it's just not for me right now. If I were to get married, it would have to be to someone who is very career oriented, who is family oriented, who is also Catholic (because it always works best to stay within the same religion), and, of course, who is handsome and with a nice personality. But even if

I got married, I would still maintain my career. As for children, I couldn't see myself with too many. It wouldn't be practical anyway. In six years I'll be thirty-six, and my health would be a factor for me as well as for the baby, so I have to think about these things. And, finally, I'm not certain I want to bring a child into this world. But it's something I think about.

My mother has never said anything to me about getting married. However, my *tías* and cousins often do. "¿Cuándo te vas a casar?" they ask. I don't really respond as I shrug them off. It's my business and nobody else's. But we'll see what life brings. Love could strike me right now.

Susana Gallegos graduated from the University of California, Santa Barbara, in 2004 and was an admissions officer at Charter College, a career training school in Ventura, California. She married her college sweetheart, Juan López, and spends much time with their six-year-old daughter, Nehli Paulina.

RAFAELA ESPINOZA

I don't know much about my biological mother because my parents got divorced when I was still young and I was raised by my father.

My dad's name is Hector Espinoza, and he was born in 1957 in Sinaloa on the Pacific coast of Mexico. The town was Higuera de las Vega. It's very tropical with lots of agriculture. My paternal grandmother died when my father was really small, and so he grew up without a mother. My father basically raised himself. He had to steal, beg, and do whatever it took to survive. He and his two sisters were badly treated and neglected by their aunt. They were treated like stray dogs. Nevertheless, my dad was able to go to school up to the sixth grade.

My grandfather worked in the fields. He'd get up at five in the morning and work all day and then go home, eat, sleep, and do it all over again. As far as he knew, his children were being taken care of by his sister, but my grandfather also physically abused my dad. I don't think in Mexico that they think it's physical abuse, but it is. My father used to stutter sometimes and still does, but it used to be really bad as a child. He couldn't make sentences sometimes. But my grandfather thought my father was only joking, and so he tried to scorn him into not stuttering by hanging him from a tree. My grandfather thought this was discipline, but I think it's child abuse. There were other forms of abuse, not just by my grandfather but by my dad's uncle.

My father had to quit school in order to work in the fields. He also did other odd jobs until he got married when he was eighteen. He decided he didn't want to toil and toil in the fields like his father and have nothing to show for it. So he decided to go to the United States with his first wife.

My dad first crossed in 1975. He and his wife didn't have documents. But there already was a family history of going to the United States. My grandfather in the 1940s often crossed to work and also without documents. He was caught and deported multiple times. Later in the 1950s and early 1960s, he came as part of the Bracero Program.

My dad and his wife crossed at Mexicali. But they were caught and were deported.

Soon after they returned to my dad's hometown, he divorced his wife because she couldn't have children. It was a mutual divorce because she knew that my dad wanted kids and she couldn't give them to him.

My father crossed again at Mexicali when he was twenty, and that time he succeeded. He hid in a dry canal for three days. He then paid a truck driver to hide him in the back of his truck and drive him to Los Angeles.

My mother was María del Carmen Reyes Soto. She was born in Mexicali, but I don't know where my maternal grandparents are from. My mother had a rough life and grew up poor. Her father was an alcoholic. In fact, so too was my father's dad. My mother didn't come to the U.S. until after she met my father. She attended school up to the ninth grade. They met in Mexicali at a party that my mother's sister was having. My dad was thirty-one and my mom was only eighteen. My mom was always a wild child, even at eighteen. My father already was living in the U.S. and had his papers. However, he often traveled back to Mexico to visit his family.

At that party that my aunt Josefina hosted, my parents gravitated toward one another. At the end of the party, my dad told my mom: "Well, I have to go; I'm driving down to Sinaloa."

"Oh, really?" my mom said. "I want to go."

"But I'm leaving now."

"That's OK. I'll go with you."

That's what I mean when I say my mother was a wild child.

So they drove down to Sinaloa to visit my father's family. That's about a twenty-hour drive from Mexicali. They decided to stay together, and my mom got pregnant with me. But my dad wanted me to be born in the U.S. He had his papers, but my mother didn't. He helped her cross without documents, and they went to LA, where they got married.

In LA, my dad had first started working at a swap meet. That's when he got married to a white woman specifically to get his papers. The woman did that for money; my dad paid her and he got his papers. He also started to learn English and got his GED. He knows English pretty well. He then became an auto parts salesman and much later, after taking some technical classes, a smog technician. He lived in South Central LA on 120th Street. It's close to where we live now. He didn't really have a home; he lived in a mobile home that he parked wherever.

When my parents came to LA together and got married, they lived in South Central and stayed in the mobile home. Growing up, I never had a real home for a few years except for the mobile home that was on top of a truck. I first thought that this was cool. We also lived in areas that were both Latino and black.

I was born December 1, 1988. Within a year my biological sister, Clarisa, was born. I say biological because I also have four half-sisters, one half-brother, and one stepsister. This is a result of my parents' later divorcing and getting remarried.

Even though I was very young, I do remember my mother getting angry and leaving for a couple of months to Mexicali. She left us with my father. When she ran out of money, she would return, and my dad would take her back. I think he felt he had no choice since she was our mother. But after a while that didn't work, and my father wanted a divorce. We then went to live with my mother for a while in Mexicali. My dad had official custody of us, but he agreed to let us live with my mother. But he then changed his mind when he realized that as U.S. citizens, my sister and I should get educated in the U.S. and take advantage of other opportunities here.

So we returned to live with my dad. Because we were still so young—preschool age—he hired a couple whom he knew to be our babysitters. He would take us each day to their home where the wife would take care of us along with her own young daughter. However, this situation led to a lot of abuse, verbal, physical, and sexual. My father had told this couple to discipline us just like they would their own child, including physical punishment. But this couple, especially the husband, went beyond the normal spanking. He was very physically abusive and not just to us but to his own daughter. He was a very angry man. He also hit his wife. I remember a lot of beatings.

The sexual abuse was not done by this couple but by a couple from Honduras who lived next door to our babysitter. We used to play with their daughter in their apartment, and this is where the sexual abuse took place by the father.

Our babysitter didn't know this was happening until one day we told our father. He and the babysitter called the police, and eventually the neighbors were deported.

A few years later, when I was about seven, my dad remarried. He met his new wife through my aunt Josefina in Mexicali on one of our trips there. My aunt seemed to be quite a matchmaker. This woman's name is María Josefina Valenzuela. At first it was like a business transaction. My dad could offer her legal entry to the U.S. She could offer my dad a new mother to take care of his children. Their understanding led to their marriage.

It was hard for my sister and me to accept this woman. First of all, my dad didn't tell us right away he was marrying her. On a subsequent trip to Mexicali, we gave her and her daughter a ride to LA. But when we got to our apartment, my dad told us that she was staying, that he had married her.

"You can call her Josefina," he said, "or Mom, or whatever you like. But she's going to take care of you now."

I was stunned. No one had bothered to tell us that my father had re-married. At first it was really hard, especially for me because I was the closest to my dad. I felt that Josefina was trying to steal him away from me. I didn't like that at all.

That first year was bad. There was a lot of fighting. I fought with Jose-fina all of the time. I didn't want her there. But in 1997 she got pregnant with my half-sister, and there was no going back from that. She was there to stay. My dad even sat me down after he got tired of my being a brat. He just told me to stop it and that Josefina was staying and I had to get used to it. I was like, "OK."

At the time that my dad remarried, we lived in a one-bedroom apart-ment. My dad and Josefina slept in the living room, and my biological sister, Clarisa, and my stepsister and I all slept in the bedroom. However, when Josefina got pregnant, we moved to a two-bedroom place so that she could have a room to care for the baby.

But I got used to all this. In time, I accepted Josefina and called her Mom. She was Mom, and my biological mom was "real mom."

During this time, Clarisa and I were still seeing our real mother. We visited her every two weeks as my father had promised her and spent Christmas and summer with her in Mexicali. This went on until I was either in the third or fourth grade. It ended when my real mother started doing drugs. This was all very strange for me and my sister. My mother in the evening would get all dressed up with lots of makeup and go out. She would spend the entire night out. She would return in the morning and sleep all day. She was doing this even though she had a new hus-band with two other daughters. I don't think I knew then what a prosti-tute was, but looking back, I think that's what she was. But she also was taking drugs and apparently selling drugs.

After one visit with her, I told my dad: "Dad, I think Mother's taking drugs."

He looked at me and said, "OK, you're not going to visit her anymore."

We stopped visiting her completely. We lost track of her. She lost everything. She even left her husband and two other daughters. We then heard that she was in jail for drug trafficking. She was also pregnant when they put her in jail. All that was pretty devastating for my sister and me. After she was released, we saw her once or twice. The last time I saw her was in 2003, and I haven't seen her since.

I began school at West Athens Elementary School. It's on 120th and Vermont. This is where I started preschool. I only knew Spanish and was put in a bilingual program in my early grades. I was taught only in Spanish through second grade. I officially started learning English in third grade. I already knew some English by watching TV in English, but I didn't know how to spell it or write it. I learned to read and write in Spanish before I did in English.

West Athens, like my other earlier schools, was attended mostly by Latino and black students. However, because I was in bilingual classes, I had all Latinos in my classes. For short periods of time, I attended a couple of other elementary schools, such as Wilmington Elementary in Wilmington, but I always returned to West Athens. These changes had to do with the family moving to different neighborhoods, but because my parents liked West Athens, they would always return us there, even though it meant driving us quite a bit. I graduated from West Athens.

At West Athens, I did very well and liked all my teachers. But Mr. Stanley in fifth grade inspired me the most. He was the only teacher who was mixing academics with the arts, such as music and art. I got the best of both worlds. Mr. Stanley pushed us to different places that weren't usually explored. Later, after I graduated, he had me work with him helping the other students. He was always very encouraging of me.

When I graduated from West Athens, because I was one of the best students in my class, I got the honor of giving a mini-speech. It was about what I wanted to do when I grew up. It was pretty cool. I remember saying that I wanted to be a gynecologist. People were surprised because they wondered if I knew what a gynecologist did. But I knew because my mother was pregnant when I was in the third grade, and I learned that she had to see a gynecologist. So I knew that they took care of pregnant women and women in general. But somehow I realized that gynecologists all seemed to be men, and I thought this was weird. They should be women. I wanted to fix this, and so this is why I said I wanted to be a gynecologist. Later in middle school, I wanted to be a plastic surgeon. I always wanted to be a doctor.

I think my siblings and I did very well in school because my parents, especially my mother, disciplined us to do our homework. Because my mom was a housewife and always at home, she always made sure we did our homework. Both my mom and dad helped us with our homework when, in the early grades, it was in Spanish. But when we started to have homework in English, they couldn't help us. My dad knows English pretty well, but he's still insecure in using it. He did not like us speaking English to him. He always insisted in Spanish at home. My mom always made sure that we weren't out in the streets when we should be doing our homework. My dad also always told me that I had to be better than him. That's why he had come to this country, so that his children could become better than him. I never forgot that.

But it was my mom who was the real stickler about our homework. She would look over our work, and if it was not neat, she made us do it all over again. Later in middle school, she separated us into different rooms and locked us in until we finished our homework. She would tell us, "You're fed; you're good to go. Get in your places and start working until you're done."

We were allowed to watch some television but not until our work was done. The TV was in the living room, so we had no choice but to watch television with our mother. When we moved into the two-bedroom apartment, we were allowed a TV in our room. We got our dad to extend our bedtime because we wanted to watch *María la del Barrio*, the *novela*.

We were also allowed to play with other kids in our apartment complex, but only after we finished our homework. We spoke English with the other kids but only Spanish at home. I did speak English with my sisters.

From elementary school, I attended Henry Clay Middle School for sixth, seventh, and eighth grade. It's on Western and El Segundo in South Central. Here, everything exploded. It was violent. Younger kids couldn't go to the bathroom for fear of getting beaten up. There was a lot of race stuff. There were always fights between blacks and Mexicans against each other. The school was half black and half Latino, mostly Mexican. Kids hopped the fence and left school. The school spent a lot of money on security, and guards were everywhere. We weren't allowed to roam the school during lunch and nutrition time. We were confined to two places: the cafeteria or the PE field. But there were still so many nooks and crannies where people could hang around and do bad things. This was not a pleasant experience. My middle school was not the school you wanted to go to.

When I first entered middle school, I was placed in a regular academic track. In sixth grade, I had really good grades, but I was also developing an attitude. I started thinking that the teachers didn't deserve my respect. But one of my teachers saw through this and knew that this wasn't me, and that's why they kept me in the academic track.

Although in elementary school I was with only other Latino students, this was not the case in middle school. In fact, I distanced myself from most of the Latinos because they didn't seem to be interested in academics and just got into trouble. Instead, all of my friends were black girls who, like me, focused on their academic work. We did our homework and studied together.

I especially liked my seventh grade computer teacher, Mrs. Hickman. In her class, she had us play the role of entrepreneurs so that we would get interested in business and in a career in business. She brought in successful black entrepreneurs to inspire us. We also got to organize our own business. I decided to be the CEO of a doughnut shop, and for this I sold doughnuts in my class and school. She also took us on a field trip to a huge black career expo in downtown LA. All of this was new and exciting to me. Mrs. Hickman especially pushed college for us. I had heard of college but didn't really know what it was all about. I knew that it was education after high school but not more than that. Mrs. Hickman explained what college was about and the importance of a college degree if we were going to be professionals. She convinced me in middle school that I had to go to college.

But Mrs. Hickman's class was more exceptional. Some of my other classes were more difficult. In fact, in some there were actual fights between the students. This was usually in classes conducted by younger teachers who didn't know how to control the students. The bad students quickly sensed this and ate their teachers up. Girls would fight other girls and rip their braids off. And I'm like, "What's happening?" I always felt I had to put up that wall pretending that I was tougher than I really was. I was 5 feet 2 inches and weighed no more than a hundred pounds. I'm not tough, but I had to act as if I was in order not to be attacked. The kids were brutal.

But this picture didn't always work. It didn't help that my mother insisted that my sister and I always wear uniforms to school. The official school policy mandated uniforms but didn't enforce this policy. However, my mother, being from Mexico where students wear uniforms, made us go dressed in them anyway. They consisted of blue skirts, white blouses, and black shoes. Because we wore uniforms, the other kids taunted us and made fun of us. We asked my mother not to dress us in uniforms, but she said that we had to because it was the school policy and also because it saved money for clothes. The only exception she made was that on Fridays we could wear regular clothes.

Middle school was also where I became aware of gangs. These were both black and Latino gangs. There were gangs everywhere, and everything was tagged. There were boy gangs and girl gangs. There were the kids who always broke the rules and tried to do anything they wanted. One such girl whom I knew would smoke weed in the bathroom and have sex on campus. One of my teachers found two students having sex on the PE field. All of this stuff made me streetwise. The school was intense.

For the most part, I had good teachers. But they always had to deal with behavioral problems rather than just teach. Even in the more advanced classes that I was in, the teachers still had to deal with these problems. I had a history teacher whom I really appreciated, but she had to really exert her authority to control the class. I did really well with her, but she didn't seem to get along with anyone else but me. The other kids challenged her authority, but she wasn't having that. She was very strict, and the students hated her for this. Most of my teachers were either white or black. I didn't have Latino teachers in middle school.

As I mentioned, I only had black friends in middle school. One of my best friends was Ahkiema. She would often come to my house. Her parents had divorced, and this made for difficulties for Ahkiema, which is why she enjoyed spending time with us. It was a bit weird because she's black and didn't know Spanish and my mom doesn't know English, but she and my mom got along great. We would have a snack and do our homework. She also lived nearby. Both blacks and Latinos lived in the neighborhood, although there was segregation—not by law but by preference. On my block, some apartments were occupied only by Mexicans and some only by blacks.

There was tension between blacks and Mexicans in the neighborhood. I hate to say this, but if there was any trouble on my block, it was always black people. So my mom really tried to protect us by not allowing us out if she couldn't see us. The street could be dangerous.

In middle school, I could have walked to and from the school or taken a bus, but my mother wouldn't let us. She knew, for example, that all the kids who got on the bus were not good kids. But she wouldn't let us walk, either. Instead, after she learned to drive, she drove us to school in the morning and picked us up in the afternoon.

One highlight of my middle school experience was being enrolled in an after-school art program called Inside Out. Students had to be approved to be in it. It was not just a program for our school but also for other high-needs schools. It was aimed at keeping kids off the streets after school. It met once a week on our campus. We explored different art experiences such as writing, acting, and painting. At the end of the year, we as a class got to write our own play and perform it. We wrote about things in our personal lives, like our neighborhoods and school. We then performed it at USC. It was a great experience.

Through the program, I also got to go camping for the very first time. This opened up a whole new world to me. They took us to a camp in the Santa Monica Mountains in May. We stayed a weekend in cabins. This was with kids not only from our own school but from others as well. We went to the beach, and I ate food I had never had before, such as spaghetti. I also had alfalfa sprouts for the first time. I even went hiking. We also had a talent show. My sister and I danced and sang a Shakira song. It was silly but nice. But we also had to take time to practice our plays because the camp was held just a couple of weeks before we acted in our play.

I was in the arts camp both in seventh and eighth grade. It was a really good experience for me because at the time, I was going through some deep emotional issues. My biological mother was released from jail, and I was old enough to realize that she didn't want to be a part of my life. This made me very angry. I wasn't really lashing out at anyone. It was just inside. I hated myself. I thought it was all my fault. I thought it was me. But what helped was that the teachers in the arts program, who were all painters, actors, or writers, also in a way served as counselors and mentors to us. They really cared about us and talked to us about our personal situations. This helped me deal with the emotions I was experiencing.

Our play also helped us in exploring our own lives during our difficult times as adolescents. One of our plays was about homeless people. In our second year, we did a play about teen pregnancy. At the time, I didn't think about it, but now as I look back on it, this was heavy stuff for thirteen-year-olds, to be talking about teen pregnancy. Thirteen-year-olds should not be talking about this, but this was real to us. We also talked about drugs. We talked about things that normal thirteen-year-olds didn't talk about, but it was part of our reality. I really enjoyed it and benefited from the arts program.

Growing up through middle school, my life didn't go much beyond our neighborhood area. Every Sunday, my dad would take us to a nearby park where he liked to play volleyball. He would leave us in the care of some of the Mexican women who were there with their own children. They loved us. I was aware of other places in LA, but my knowledge was limited. I don't remember ever going to the beach. We once went to Disneyland, and it was a shock to me because I had never seen so many white people in my life. It was also not until middle school that I even went to a mall. I was always just around Mexican and black people.

As we progressed in school, my mom attended parent-teacher conferences, but not my dad. He was too busy working, and besides, as part of the agreement in marrying my stepmother, she was responsible for us at school. My mom never had to go to our school because we were bad or because we weren't doing well in classes. Still, she went whenever a regular conference was scheduled. She didn't know any English, and so my sister and I translated for her. I didn't feel any pressure in doing this. I was really good at both languages. Switching back and forth wasn't a problem. It's just what I had to do. I also didn't feel embarrassed, because every other Latino parent also didn't know English, and so their students translated for them. We were all in the same boat. I didn't feel different. I translated for my mother on other occasions as well. If someone called at home in English, I took the phone from my mom and dealt with it. If we went to a restaurant with an English-language menu, I translated here too. I've always had to translate, but I've never felt strange about it.

Originally I was supposed to attend Washington Prep High School, but we moved the summer after I graduated from middle school. We left South Central LA and went to Gardena. My dad bought a house there. After many years of working at an auto parts store and after taking classes, he qualified to become a smog check technician. He opened up a smog check station in Gardena, and that's why we moved there. He had saved enough money for this. Gardena was a couple of miles from South Central. We moved in 2002, and that's why that fall I started at Gardena High School.

The school was mostly black and Mexican. There were a few whites and some Asians. It was a little more diverse than middle school but not much. It had around three thousand students. I felt scared going there because I didn't know anyone. All of my friends from middle school stayed and went to Washington. On top of this, I didn't look at first like everybody else because my mother still insisted that I wear a uniform. Fortunately, this only lasted about a month; then I couldn't take it anymore.

"You're going to ruin my social life if you keep making me wear a uniform," I told my mother. I guess she finally understood. Plus, with my dad's new business, we were doing much better financially, so we could afford to buy my sisters and me new school clothes. Still, I was terrified at first at high school.

What really helped me in this transition was enrolling in *folklórico* that fall of my freshman year. When I was arranging for my classes, my counselor asked me if I wanted to take regular PE, aerobics, or *folklórico*. All of these qualified for PE credit. I didn't care for PE or aerobics because I didn't like undressing in front of others.

"I'll take *folklórico*," I told the counselor.

I had no idea of what I was getting into. It ended up being a very wonderful experience. I danced *folklórico* my first three years and then danced for a semi-professional dance group, the Pacifico Dance Company. But when I started, I had no previous experience. It was hard work. It was also a class of two hundred kids, almost all Mexican girls. In fact, the few boys were also all Mexican, as was our teacher, Mr. Ruiz.

Learning initially the basic step was very hard. I cried at home because I couldn't get it. But I worked hard and was a fast learner. After about a month I picked up the steps, and after that it snowballed. By the end of my freshman year I was dancing six *cuadros* or styles of Mexican *folklórico* from six different regions: Veracruz, Aguascalientes, Sinaloa, Baja California, Jalisco, and Colima. They all have similar steps but stylistically are different. My favorite style was Veracruz because it's very classy. You don't hop up and down as much as in the other *folklóricos*. It's performed closer to the ground and takes a lot of skill. It also has beautiful costumes.

Although we performed for school assemblies, we actually performed more in the community. My real first community dance that I participated in was at Disney's California Adventure. I performed with fifteen other girls for about two minutes. I was scared, but it worked out OK. A girl who was a sophomore took me under her wing and helped with the dances and with putting on the costumes that the class provided. She helped me with putting on makeup I had never worn before because my parents didn't allow it, but they accepted it for my dancing. *Folklórico* also helped me in meeting new friends, especially that first semester. I don't know what I would have done that first year without *folklórico*. It also turned out to be a shelter from the rest of the more difficult school environment.

Initially my classes were more difficult than I had expected. Some classes were particularly challenging, such as English. I had a hard time. My writing was not that good, nor was my vocabulary. But my English improved over time. Science classes, especially chemistry, proved also to be difficult for me. Chemistry was the only class that I didn't initially pass. I was also just overwhelmed by the sight of the school with about three thousand students. I was lost at the beginning because it was a totally new system that I wasn't used to. In addition, I was scared because there were so many other students who were much older than me. I was a year ahead in my classes, and so when I started high school I was thirteen. But now I was in school with kids who were seventeen, eighteen, and even nineteen. On the other hand, the ethnic composition was familiar in that most students were Mexican or black.

What helped me in my adjustment besides the *folklórico* class was that I was placed in the honors track. There were several tracks: AP, honors, regular, and ESL. Those in the honors track took AP classes as well. I also took some regular ones that I needed to take to graduate, such as health. Honors classes were typically composed of Mexicans and Asians. My teachers especially in the honors classes were very nice and helpful. If I had a problem, they were always willing to help.

In my freshman year, I wanted to study French instead of Spanish since I already knew Spanish. However, my parents wouldn't hear of it. They were afraid that I was stepping away from my Mexican roots and going into something they didn't understand. My mother even went to speak to my counselor, and I had to awkwardly translate for her.

"My daughter just doesn't like Spanish; that's the problem," she told the counselor.

But this wasn't true. I tried to convince my parents of this, but they wouldn't listen.

While I was there translating for my mother, another Mexican girl was in the office doing the same for her mother. She overheard my mother and later said to me: "You don't like Spanish? You don't like being Mexican?"

"That's not true," I replied. "It's not that I don't like Spanish. I just want to learn French."

I never got to learn French and was instead put into Spanish classes.

My middle school had a lot of race conflict, but it was even worse in high school. It was very intense. There were major divisions between blacks and Mexicans. At lunch and recreational time when kids congregated with their friends, the school was literally racially divided. On one side of the school were the Mexicans, and on the other side were the blacks. That was it. There was no middle ground.

These racial splits led to racial conflict. The year before I started at Gardena, a kid was shot on campus as a result of these tensions. I don't remember if he was Mexican or black. The whole school had to be shut down that day. After I was in the school, I remember either in my sophomore or junior year the SWAT team coming on campus because of a rumor of a big gang fight involving weapons. Fortunately, nothing happened, but the whole school got shut down. We weren't allowed to go anywhere. There was one Cinco de Mayo when no black students showed up to school. None. Literally half the student body was missing because the black students had heard that the Mexican kids were going to riot against the black kids on that day. I had never seen the school like that. Each year the race wars intensified.

By race wars, I mean that black gang members and Mexican gang members fought each other on campus. I never felt personally threatened because I didn't associate with either of these kinds of students. But I was certainly aware of them. They were very visible with their gang attire that for some reason the school administrators allowed. There was a dress code, but they didn't enforce it. Or they enforced it selectively. We couldn't wear shorts or flip-flops, but as long as gang members, for example, had a shirt, pants, and shoes on, even though it was gang attire, it was OK. The main Mexican gang at school was part of the largest Mexican gang in Gardena. They called themselves the G-13 or *trece*. G stood for Gardena and 13 for the thirteenth letter of the alphabet, *m*. *M* stood for marijuana.

Gang fights on campus occurred maybe once a month and a really big race riot once a year. The school administrators, as far as I knew, did nothing to bring blacks and Mexicans together. For example, during Black History Month in February when the school would have a large assembly, the *folklórico* group was asked by the administration to perform, but we were not allowed to do so by the black students because we were Mexican.

Part of the gang problem on campus also had to do with drugs. Students could easily get drugs on campus. Guys walked around selling drugs, primarily marijuana. I got offered drugs, and this had never happened to me before.

"Hey, you wanna buy weed?" the guy asked me.

"No, thank you," I replied.

He just walked away and approached someone else.

The kids didn't smoke openly but in the bathroom. That's where they hung out. You'd walk into the bathrooms and you were like, "Yeah, OK. I'm leaving."

To deal with the drug problem as well as with the gangs, security increased every year I was at Gardena. In my freshman year we had a Mexican American principal. He was very nice, but I don't think he knew how to control the growing violence and drugs on campus. So he was removed, and we got a white principal who was very strict. He just started cracking down. We now could not go into certain areas of the school during lunch or nutrition periods because no one could watch us there. They packed us all into one area so they could keep an eye on us. The principal walked the campus with his radio and broke up fights or separated kids who looked like they were going to fight. He stayed late to make sure everyone was going home safely and that there was no loitering. I appreciated what he was doing because he took a genuine interest in making sure we could study in safety.

The segregation between blacks and Mexicans extended to the athletic teams. Football, for example, was mostly black. There were just a few Mexicans. I went to a lot of the games because I liked one of the football players. He was one of the few Mexicans. I went with one of my Mexican girlfriends, and we sat in the stands surrounded by black families. I never saw a Mexican family at a football game. But the black parents there were all nice to us and joked with us. We sat there because most of the other students sat in cliques in other parts of the stands or around the field. Maybe because not too many Mexican students went to the games, I never saw a fight at one of the games. These were all evening games.

But the racial segregation extended to the cheerleading squads. There were the Pantherettes, and they were all black. Then there was the drill team, and this was composed of all Mexican girls. The flag team was mostly Mexican.

Other sports were also racially separated, such as basketball and track, which were all black. By contrast, soccer was all Mexican. I didn't know about baseball since I didn't attend those games.

There was a MEChA club on campus. I didn't really participate, although I went to a few meetings. All I knew about the club was that it focused on ethnic pride. But the club was disorganized, although members attended MEChA conferences in other parts of LA. That was the only Chicano or Latino club on campus. There was also a Black Student Union club and a Chinese club, but both were very small, as was MEChA.

There were no Chicano studies classes, and in my history classes I don't remember the teacher in U.S. history mentioning Chicanos. In fact, my honors history classes were pretty bad. Once I had a teacher who had had a stroke, and he would fall asleep in class. My other history class consisted of just note taking, and I don't remember any of that work. Fortunately, because these were honors classes, the kids were pretty well behaved. There were some, though, who were not in honors classes but somehow were in this history class who behaved pretty badly, especially with the teacher who fell asleep.

Cinco de Mayo was celebrated every year that I was at Gardena, although I had no clue what it meant. No one told us. I knew it wasn't Mexican Independence Day, but I had no clue what it celebrated until I got to UCSB. Cinco de Mayo at my high school consisted of an extended assembly period where those of us in *folklórico* performed. One year I got to play master of ceremonies, and I introduced each song and dance. It was cool. But unlike the Black History Month assembly where *folklórico* or anything Mexican was excluded, we invited the Pantherettes to perform, and they did. We felt like they were part of the school as were the other black students, and we wanted to include them.

There were many students who dropped out of school. I had a few friends who dropped out. They just had no motivation for school. They just went to school to do all of the wrong things. Many girls dropped out because they got pregnant. My own sister got pregnant when she was sixteen. As these girls started to show their pregnancies, they left school, and some went to alternative schools until they had their babies. However, once they had their babies, they could return to Gardena. My school now actually has a child care facility for returning mothers and their kids. My sister did finish high school despite having a baby. At age twenty, she is a single mother and works at a bank.

When these girls got pregnant, the guys responsible, as far as I knew, didn't marry them. And if they did, it didn't last long. These were usually boyfriends who got their girlfriends pregnant. Some guys and their families were supportive of the baby, but others were not. In my sister's case, her boyfriend's parents at first refused to accept that the baby was their son's. My sister had to get a paternity test to prove it. Then the boyfriend's parents accepted the baby as their grandchild and have remained supportive. My sister's boyfriend recognizes the baby as his and does spend some time with the child, but he and my sister are no longer together.

But there were other teenage pregnancies in my family. Some of my cousins also got pregnant. This didn't make it any easier when my sister got pregnant. My sister didn't tell my parents; it was my aunt who found out about it. My dad was furious. It was one thing for a niece to get pregnant; it was another for his own daughter! He thought he had raised her better. He had actually talked to us about not having sex. He wanted nothing to do with my sister.

"Pack her stuff," he yelled at my mother. "Get her out of my house because I'm afraid of what I might do to her."

My sister had to move out and live with my aunt for a couple of weeks.

My mom's reaction was to feel that my sister had betrayed her. My mom knew that my sister had a boyfriend and she was OK with it, but she thought my sister was being honest with her by assuring my mother that she was being careful. This dishonesty hurt my mother the most. At the same time, she felt protective of my sister. All this made for a lot of intensity in my family.

On top of this, this news came within a month after my sister had tried to commit suicide. I don't know if this had to do with her pregnancy, but I knew she was going through a lot of emotional pressure. I couldn't understand it. I really didn't. I'd visit her in the hospital after her attempted suicide, and I just didn't understand. I couldn't picture in my mind how bad things had gotten for her. Then she got pregnant! I didn't know what to do. The first thing I did do was to tell her she should have an abortion. That wasn't very popular in my family when I said this.

"I can't believe you're saying this," my mother responded.

"Mother, she's sixteen! Her boyfriend is a bum. We're broke. How does it make sense for her to have a child right now?"

I also told my sister that if she didn't have an abortion, she didn't have to keep the baby.

"You don't. This is the freaking twenty-first century, for God's sake! We have choices!"

My sister didn't listen to me. I think being pregnant was like a glimpse of something for her. I think the baby gave her new hope. So she had the baby.

The fact was that it was common knowledge at school that many kids were sexually active. A lot of girls, both black and Mexican, were getting pregnant. This was not hidden. We even had a medical clinic on campus that dispensed birth control pills. It also did pregnancy tests and dispensed other forms of contraception. This was sponsored by the UCLA Medical Center. Everyone knew when someone came out of the clinic with a little brown bag what was in it. So it wasn't that my sister didn't know about birth control and where to get it.

This widespread sexual activity involved kids from freshmen to seniors. My sister was only a sophomore. One of my friend's sisters was like fourteen when she started having sex and got pregnant later.

Even though we had the medical clinic, we didn't really have much counseling about sex or pregnancy. In the health class, we got the sexual intercourse talk. The teacher taught us how to put condoms on the boy. But other than that, no one ever talked about it. Teachers, counselors, and administrators seemed to just accept it. And it happened very often. A lot of girls got pregnant and still do. All of this just increased the dropout rate.

As in the case of middle school, my parents were not involved in my high school. My dad worked all day, and my mother didn't speak English. At the same time, my sister and I always gave our parents our report cards, and so they were aware of our grades.

Also as in middle school, we did our homework at home. In my case, my mother would pick me up after *folklórico* class and take me home to start my homework. I never did my homework in the school library because the library was a joke. It wasn't even a real library. There was nothing there. I don't think there were more than six computers for three thousand students! And there certainly were not three thousand books, either!

At home we had a desktop for my sisters and me to do our homework. My parents were not computer literate, although my dad has learned to do some things with computers for his work. My sisters and I also shared one cell phone. We usually did things together, so having one phone was not a problem. When we overdid text messaging, we were then permitted by our parents to text only on weekends. I didn't get my own cell phone until I went to college. At school, very few students had laptops. The school itself was not very technologically savvy. Only a few teachers, for example, used PowerPoint. And the books were old and outdated. The school was a hundred years old, and the books looked a hundred years old! We also only had two computer labs for the entire three thousand students!

Although I didn't take vocational classes, there were such classes. Some students took wood shop, which I thought was ridiculous. They didn't make anything in that class, and even if they did, how was this going to help them in the future, especially in finding jobs? The school also had horticulture. Students went into a barn on campus where the teacher had his own horses as well as other animals.

Fortunately for me, I developed a special relationship with Scott Olson, my academic counselor. I met him through my sister, who, of course, was having a lot of problems, including her pregnancy. Mr. Olson noticed that even though I was a good student, I seemed to be troubled from within. Just growing up, I didn't really understand where I was going. I didn't know who I was. So he took me under his wing and was always there to talk to me. He helped me a lot. In my senior year, I served as his TA, which gave me credit. I helped in arranging for other students to set up appointments with him. Getting to see an academic counselor aside from setting up your class schedule wasn't easy. We only had maybe five or six academic counselors for three thousand students. Even arranging for kids' classes wasn't easy because most wanted to get into classes with teachers who had a reputation for being easy graders and lax in discipline. These classes were always filled immediately. During my TA time, my counselor talked to me extensively about what I was feeling and setting goals. He helped me work through a lot of emotional issues that I was dealing with.

I was never allowed to date in high school. My dad said I wasn't allowed to date until I was married. So I really didn't date until I left for college. What could he say then? I was two hours away. None of my sisters were allowed to date. That's why when my sister got pregnant it almost killed my dad. We couldn't date and we couldn't have boyfriends, which obviously didn't affect my sister.

I didn't go to high school dances because my parents wouldn't allow it but also because no one went to our high school dances. They were lame. The gym where the dances were held was lame. It was old and gross.

I also didn't go to parties at friends' homes because most of my friends didn't have parties since their parents were as strict as mine. We started going to social events when my friends started to have their *quinceañeras*.

I went to friends' houses, but my mother had to have met and talked with at least one of their parents.

But my dad did let me go to my senior prom. It was held at a ballroom in downtown LA. My mother and I went shopping for my prom dress. Selecting my dress didn't take very long.

"Which one is the cheapest? That one? All right, I'll take it."

My escort was a very sweet Mexican boy whom I had known for some time. I never considered him a boyfriend, just a friend. He sometimes came over to my home, and my parents knew him and didn't see him as a threat. We sometimes would go out and have something to eat, but I came home right away. My parents even let me go to the prom in his mom's car. I had a great time. They had a DJ who played the music. It was mostly hip-hop, but he also played some *reggaetón* that had just become very popular with the Latinos. But the ethnic separation that affected our school also affected our prom. The black kids congregated on one side and the Mexicans on the other. We all danced to hip-hop, but when the DJ played *reggaetón*, the black kids refused to dance to it. I couldn't understand this because both sounds are very similar. I danced to both and with whomever asked me to dance. I had a great time.

I also was not allowed to go to the movies until I was about a junior or senior. I had to go with my sisters or my friends. We went to the South Bay Galleria to see the movies. This was the closest mall, and mostly Mexicans and blacks shopped there. I mainly watched horror movies, which seemed to be the only ones playing. It was a lot of blood.

By high school, English was my dominant language. I spoke it with my sister and my friends. However, at home I spoke Spanish with my parents. To this day, my father insists that I only speak Spanish to him. The only time I speak English to him is when I get so frustrated with him that I can only say what I need to say in English. I also speak Spanish with people I can tell are Spanish-dominant.

I also used Spanish when we traveled to Mexico during the summer. We'd go to Mexicali to visit my mother's family, my stepmother's family. When I was a freshman and sophomore, we'd spend the entire summer, but I got to hate this. It was unbearably hot, and I wanted to see my friends back home as well as dance my *folklórico*. So by my junior and senior year, we started only going for two weeks at the start of summer and two weeks at the end of summer. There just wasn't much to do there but go to the movies with my cousins. Besides visiting Mexicali, we would sometimes go to Sinaloa where my dad would return periodically on his own because he had started working his family farm again. He would go down to supervise the planting and harvesting.

I think the highlight of my coming-of-age years was when I had my own *quinceañera*. I turned fifteen in December but didn't have my *quince* until April. I did it not for religious reasons but because I wanted to have a party. My dad isn't religious and never went to church. He never spoke to me about God. Only when my stepmother came into the picture did I start getting into Catholicism, although we still never attended church. I finally made my First Communion when I was fourteen, and I couldn't have a *quinceañera* until I made my First Communion. But I have not been confirmed.

Because we were doing OK financially, my dad agreed to give me my *quince*. It wasn't as expensive as many other *quinceañeras*, but for us it was still expensive. My dress alone cost about eight hundred dollars. My dad also had to rent the hall for the reception and for the use of the church for the Mass. He also rented a limo for me and my escorts. It wasn't a stretch one but seated about ten. What saved money was that my mother cooked most of the food and my aunt did the decorations for the hall.

My *damas* consisted of my two sisters and two of my best girlfriends and one of my cousins. Then all of them had partners, or *chambelanes*. For my partner, I wanted the guy I liked who played football. I asked him, but he turned me down. It broke my heart, but I got over it eventually. So I just got some random boy who agreed to be my partner. He was a friend of one of the other partners, and he showed up at one of our rehearsals. I recruited him on the spot.

I sent out about a hundred invitations, and about two hundred people attended the party. No one outside of my family went to the Mass at a church in South Central. The reception was held at a hall in Gardena because I wanted my party to be close to my neighborhood so my friends could easily attend. It was a wonderful party. I danced the first dance with my father. I was in my pretty white dress. My dad can't dance, so he just kind of hugged me as we moved from side to side, which was really funny. But it meant a lot to him. He really took pride in giving me my *quince*. He told me how pretty I looked and how proud of me he was. My dad was also drinking a bit. He usually does not like parties, but at this one he relaxed and had a great time. In fact, he wanted to continue partying even after we had to leave the hall.

I think, as I look back on my *quince*, that what it meant to me was having a party where everyone looked at me and thought, "She's pretty." I hadn't thought of myself as pretty, and so I thought a *quince* would make me look pretty. How could I not look pretty with my dress and hair and makeup? I just wanted one day where everyone would look at me and be like, "OK, you're OK."

But if I ever have my own daughter, I have mixed feelings about giving her a *quince*. It's just too expensive, and the money can be used for better things, like college. My little sister wants a *quince* when she turns fifteen, and I keep encouraging her to just have a nice party at home. A *quince* is too extravagant. I like keeping the tradition of the *quinceañera* but on a much more modest level. My little sister is very, very smart and I want to make sure she goes to college, and the *quince* money would be better put in a college fund for her.

While my *quinceañera* was a highlight of my teenage years, the next year unfortunately brought a major tension into my life. My sister Clarisa and I found out that my father was having an affair with another woman. He actually admitted this to us. He said that he had never loved my mother and that all along this was almost like a business relationship where he married her in return for her taking care of his children. He reminded us that it was he who had remained faithful to us and not our real mother. He was the one who had raised us and provided a home. He put a guilt trip on us and told us that in return we basically should shut up about his affair. I couldn't believe all this. All these years he had been holding us to high moral standards, and then he drops the bomb on us about his own infidelity. What were we supposed to do? We were young teenagers. We didn't know about these things. So we said nothing to our mother. She finally found out a few years later, actually, when I was already in college. She was very resentful and bitter toward me for not telling her. But what was I to do? She finally got over that. She did, however, divorce my father, who then married his girlfriend.

My father and I have grown closer over the years. As I get older, my father's actions are less reprehensible, and I understand him more and more each day.

My sister especially took it very hard. It was within a year of us know-ing of my father's affair that she tried to commit suicide and then got pregnant. I know really what a hypocrite my father was when he found out about Clarisa being pregnant by her boyfriend at the same time that he was having his own affair.

I took my father's affair very hard also, but I didn't let it destroy me like my sister. I talked to my counselor about all this, and he helped me. "You're going to get through this," he would tell me. And I did. What also helped was that I had a plan for myself. I knew that I wanted in time to leave my home and my neighborhood and get out of all of these prob-lems and go to college. And I did. But if it wasn't for my counselor and my plan, I might have fallen just as hard as my sister.

As I mentioned, Spanish was very much a part of my life growing up. However, being in an English-language school environment in time made me English-dominant. Although I consider myself bilingual, it's not an equal balance. Here at UCSB I don't have many Latino friends, and so I don't have the opportunity to speak Spanish. But when I go home, I'm immersed again in a Spanish-speaking world, and not just at home but everywhere in my neighborhood. Still, English is my main language. I guess it's sort of me running away from that side of my life. I know that a lot of people on campus can't relate to where I'm from or to my fam-ily background. So I guess I've felt that I had to be more American than anything else.

Spanish at first did influence my television watching. When I was younger, all I watched was Spanish-language television. I watched tele-novelas with my mother all the way through high school. When I go home now, I will sit and watch a telenovela with my mom. My favorite telenovela was *Rebelde*. It was intense.

However, as I grew up and after my sister and I were allowed a television in our room, I started to watch more English-language shows. I watched a lot of MTV and reality shows. I'm still very much into reality shows just for the simple fact that I like to watch other people's dramas. I don't like to have any drama of my own. I have better things to do than fight over petty things. But other people fighting over petty things, that I watch.

My mom is also a big telenovela fan. She watches them religiously. She says they make her relax. My dad didn't like telenovelas and actu-ally liked English-language programs such as science and history ones. His English was good enough that he understood them. I never had to translate for him.

My musical tastes also reflected my growing bilingual and bicultural characteristics. Up to middle school, I mostly listened to Mexican music. In middle school, I listened to a lot of rap because all of my friends were black and I also really liked it. But I still listened to some Mexican music, like Selena, which I really liked. Of course, when I got into *folklórico* in high school, I danced to Mexican music. In fact, my tastes in Latino music even expanded in high school because one of my best friends was Nicaragüense, or her parents were from Nicaragua. She introduced me to salsa, *cumbia*, merengue, and *reggaetón*. I was listening to *reggaetón* even before it became popular in LA. Since being in college, I have tended to listen more to music in English, such as indie rock. But I had never been to a live concert until I came to UCSB.

We never had books in our home, even encyclopedias. But I did spend a lot of time in the public library. In fact, when we lived alone with my dad, he would check books out from the library, both in Spanish and English, and read to us at home. This was when we were not yet five years old. As I grew up, I also on my own spent time at the library.

My ethnic consciousness growing up was that I knew I was Mexicana, but I also had an affinity with other minorities such as blacks since I had grown up with them. I didn't have any particular feelings toward white people because I had little to do with white people. The most white people I ever saw in one place was at Disneyland. So I had nothing positive or negative to say about whites. At the same time, I was affected by the idealization of white beauty that I saw on television and in the movies. This particularly affected me because I was put on a pedestal as white. I'm very light-skinned, along with my younger sister. Understanding that I looked white, in my sophomore year in high school I even colored my hair blond, which had been my actual color as a young kid until it darkened. Because of my whiteness and blond hair, the other Mexican kids called me the "white girl." But they actually called me that even before I colored my hair. Outside of my closest friends, the use of this term was negative criticism of me. They would say: "Oh, no. You're not Mexican. You're the white girl."

Their criticism also was from this sense that I acted white because I got good grades, was in honors, and didn't get into trouble or do some of the things they were doing. On the other hand, the black kids also didn't see me as a minority but as white. So I always felt that I didn't really belong with any group and felt I was more by myself.

All this extended to dating or at least being asked to date, which I couldn't anyway because of my parents. But the fact is that no boys—Mexican boys—even asked me out. Maybe they wanted to but didn't want to be criticized for dating a "white girl."

When I came to college, I stopped being a blond, figuring I couldn't compete anyway with real blond. I started coloring my hair instead brown or black, and now I'm back to my natural brown color.

At home, we ate Mexican food because that's all my mom cooked. I especially liked her chicken soup as well as her other soups. The way my mom makes soup is just amazing. Now, I try to imitate her recipes, but they never come out as good. But my mother never made tortillas at home. She doesn't like to bake, and she considered making tortillas baking. She cooked our breakfasts and lunches. In high school, while we ate lunch at school, still my mother had a lunch for us when we got home. She didn't make dinner since she gave us late lunches. We on our own could prepare something light for dinner if we wanted to. Of course, as I grew older, my tastes for food expanded, and with my friends I would eat hamburgers and pizza. These are foods that my parents would never think of eating. They don't know what feta cheese is, and they're never going to try it.

My sisters and I were never asked by our mother to cook meals. This was her thing. As a result, I didn't know how to cook until I went to college. I didn't know that if you put a tomato in the microwave, it would get soggy, or if you put an avocado in the microwave, it would turn black.

On the other hand, we were expected to do housework: wash dishes, sweep, mop, clean our rooms, do our beds, and all of that. I did my own laundry since we had the appliances at home. Every Saturday was cleaning day without fail. Everybody except my dad had to turn everything inside and out, and we had to clean it all. If we wanted to go out later on Saturday, we first had to finish our chores.

At school I tended to wear the same type of clothes as the other kids, especially when my parents no longer made us wear uniforms. The only difference in my clothes was that I always went for colors. I liked wearing green, pink, and yellow especially. I was a performer with *folklórico*, and so I liked to dress a little more artsy. I didn't wear skirts to school, just pants. Some girls wore shorts, but my parents didn't allow this. In fact, once my dad made me go back into the house and change when he saw me wearing shorts to school. Actually, this was in summer school in June. It's not like I was wearing shorts in December! But he still made me change.

I never had a tattoo, but a lot of kids in school, both boys and girls, did. And they got away with it. There was no school policy, as far as I knew, that prohibited tattoos. I had a friend who had a Felix the Cat on his arm and his football number on his neck. I knew a lot of people with tattoos. The school wouldn't allow me to wear a shirt with thin straps, but they allowed kids to wear tattoos! I couldn't figure this out. Once in middle school I told my dad: "Oh, I want a tattoo." That was probably one of the scariest conversations I've ever had with him. "You're not in prison," he said. He had this negative stereotype that only prisoners got tattoos, or drug addicts.

As I had mentioned, we were raised Catholic but only because of my mother. She's very religious. But we were never forced to go to church because my dad ruled our home and he's not religious. In fact, he doesn't believe in God. But we were baptized, and I made my First Communion. My mother also taught us how to pray. We prayed at night, but we stopped doing that once we were in high school.

My mother has an *altarcito*—a home altar with various pictures of Our Lady of Guadalupe and one of Jesus.

We celebrate Christmas but not really in a religious way, although around our neighborhood we did participate in *posadas* reenacting Mary and Joseph seeking shelter to give birth to the baby Jesus. But we don't go to Christmas Mass. We have a dinner on Christmas Eve and open presents on Christmas Day.

We also celebrate Thanksgiving, but through high school we usually went to other relatives' homes for this. We later started doing it at home, but the problem is that my mother doesn't like to make turkey. She first started cooking just chicken until we insisted on turkey. Sometimes as we were growing up and no one invited us for Thanksgiving, we just went to Chuck E. Cheese and had pizza there.

I consider myself a Catholic but a recovering Catholic. I was raised Catholic and I understand the concept of Catholicism, but I'm trying to forget about it or distance myself from it. Religion is not important in my life. I feel that it serves a purpose for some and I'm glad, but I've experienced too many things already in my life, especially in my family, to believe that God would want things like this to happen to me. I don't believe in the traditional God. I think that there is something that started all of this, but I don't believe that there is a God that actively takes a role in our lives and sends us challenges. I don't believe in an all-seeing God but maybe a God that says, "Hey, let's see what happens." I also don't believe in an afterlife, as terrible as that sounds. I truly believe that we simply die as human beings and that our brain just shuts off and our bodies turn off, and that's about it. I don't believe that there's an essence or a spirit. But just because I don't believe that there's a heaven, I'm not going to go around stealing from people. I'm still part of this society, and I'm going to live in it. I'm going to live my life being a good person and preparing to go to heaven, even if I don't believe there is a heaven.

I would also not get married in church. But I would baptize my kids and even take them to church because I want them to make their own choice about religion. Deep down, I'm still a Catholic, and I'm still scared that if my children died but were not baptized, they would go to limbo.

I first started to think about college in the eighth grade. This had to do with our computer teacher, Mrs. Hickman, taking us to these business expos and my somehow learning that there were colleges and universities. I didn't really understand what college was all about except that I knew it meant more school.

But my inspiration to go to college also came from my dad, who didn't know about college but always told me that I should aspire to a better life. He didn't want me to just go to high school and then work at McDonald's. He told me I was destined for something better. And I took that to heart. I wanted to succeed for him.

My father inspired me, but it was my academic counselor who specifically guided me to prepare for college. "Let's make it happen," he encouraged me. His guidance was critical because I never got such counseling from the one college counselor we had for three thousand students. He was overwhelmed, and it was almost impossible to see him. So with the help of my academic counselor, I made sure that I took the appropriate classes to meet the UC requirements. Being in honors classes also helped me because I was with other students who also wanted to go to college. I learned from them what classes I should take. I knew they were going to college, and so if I stuck with them I would go. So I took, besides honors classes, AP Spanish, AP biology, and AP history. Of these, I passed AP Spanish and also got an 800 on my Spanish SAT. My overall SAT scores were OK but not great. I also took the ACT. I graduated with a 3.5 average.

As I entered into my senior year, I began to think about what colleges to apply to. I knew I didn't want to go to a community college because I knew that people who go to such colleges never leave there to go to a four-year college. Many of my friends were thinking of going to a community college, and I knew that they weren't the best of students. I didn't want to go to a school with not-very-good students. I knew that college would be hard, and I wanted to be challenged. I didn't think this would happen in a community college.

Actually, I wanted to apply to an Eastern all-girls college, but my dad said absolutely not. "It's too far away and we can't keep an eye on you," he said.

I also didn't necessarily want to go to a Cal State campus. The closest to my home was Dominguez Hills, but it was too close and I knew I didn't want to stay at home or in my neighborhood anymore. I also had a sense that a UC education and degree was much more prestigious than a Cal State one. I did wind up applying to Long Beach State because we had performed *folklórico* there and I thought it was a beautiful campus. But my hope was to get into a UC campus. I applied to San Diego, UCLA, Berkeley, and Santa Barbara. Of these, I only got into UCSB. I had thought of applying to USC, which is very close to my home, but I knew my father couldn't afford it.

So my choices were Long Beach State or UCSB. If I chose Long Beach, I would have to live at home, and I didn't want to do that. I had never visited UCSB or Santa Barbara, for that matter. But I was excited when I saw the catalog and there was a picture of *folklórico* dancers. "This is my place," I said to myself. UCSB also gave me good financial aid, initially only of grants, although I later took out loans after my parents divorced. But the only obstacle to my going to UCSB was my dad. He accepted the idea of my going to college, but the issue for him was where. He wanted me to go to a community college and live at home. I was like, "No. There's no way I'm doing that." He got over that, and then he wanted me to go to Long Beach but still live at home. I rejected this as well. What finally convinced my dad to let me go to UCSB was the intervention of my counselor, Scott Olson. Mr. Olson took it upon himself to talk to my dad. He even went to my dad's auto emission shop on the pretense of getting his truck smog checked. There he introduced himself to my dad and talked to him for three hours, including lunch.

My dad came home and said: "I can see now why you want to go to Santa Barbara."

"Yes, yes, I do," I replied.

So if it had not been for Mr. Olson, I probably would have gone to Long Beach.

But my dad's approval came with some strings. First, I had to agree to come home every other week, depending on my schoolwork. And second, my father would manage my bank account. I agreed and for my first two years faithfully returned home.

Graduation day at my high school was surreal. Many students whom I had entered with as a freshman were not there anymore because they had dropped out. I was in awe that I was still there. "Is this really happening?" I wasn't nervous or scared. I was actually happy to be leaving. Because of the problem with my sister and with some of the other girls, I was pretty much done there. I was ready to leave. I threw my graduation cap up in the air with everyone else, but I didn't want it back. "Let's go; let's keep walking."

My parents attended my graduation, although my father left early with my little sister because it was too hot and long. Afterward, one of my best friends and I went to a late lunch with our two mothers. We then attended Grad Night at Disneyland, which was awful with too many people and was just a waste of time and money.

That summer before I went to UCSB, I got a job at LAX selling candy at one of the terminals. Actually, my dad insisted that I get a job so I could have something to do during the summer. I got the job through a friend's aunt who worked there. I got a half-time job and it paid well, but I got the night shifts, so I had to work from five in the afternoon to three in the morning. Because I didn't have a car and just had my provisional license, my mom dropped me at work and then my dad picked me up later. On the way home, he made me drive his truck with a stick shift so I would learn. At first I didn't want to, but it made me a better driver, and now I can drive any car since I know how to use a stick shift.

The first time I visited UCSB was when I came for freshman orientation before classes began. My cousin and her husband drove me up and walked around the campus a bit with me and then left. I was so nervous because I didn't know anyone, and it was a totally new and different place. It was also the first time that I slept in a room with someone I didn't know and showered with other strangers.

My initial impression of UCSB was that it was big, although I didn't actually see too much of it. I stayed that one week in the Manzanita Village dorms and went from there to the University Center, or UCEN. My roommate was a girl of Asian and Jewish background. I didn't know too many Asians, and I had no idea what it meant to be Jewish. I thought all of this was weird. I also met a Persian student and his family, but I had no idea where these people were from. All of this was a big culture shock.

I attended the different orientation meetings where they discussed requirements and classes and helped us arrange our fall schedule. They also talked about drugs, alcohol, and sex on campus. All of this just disoriented me even more.

Above all, I felt homesick. I called home every day, sometimes even at midnight. I cried to my mom, I was so homesick.

"Mom, take me back, I miss you."

"No, *mija*, you have to stick it out. This is your new life there. You've got to pull through."

I did stick it out and then returned for the fall quarter. I again was assigned to the Manzanita Village dorm. This was OK, but these dorms are very spread out and more private, so you actually don't meet a lot of other students. In the bigger dorms you do, and I know students now who have remained friends with students they met in their freshman dorm. I roomed with two other students. One was a girlfriend of mine from my high school, and we had asked to room together. But it's funny because here at UCSB we grew apart and didn't really relate very much to each other. On the other hand, my other roommate was a white girl from Sacramento who was just wonderful. She was eccentric and loud, but we got along great. She was majoring in engineering, which I knew nothing about. But we became very good friends and did a lot of things together. She introduced me to some of her other friends, and they became my friends. She helped acquaint me to college life and to white people. I was like, "OK, you white people are all right!"

I did OK in my first quarter, but it was a big adjustment. This was the first time I actually had to work a lot. I had to open books and read them. This was all new to me because in high school we were not made to read much. Because of this, I struggled in my writing assignments. My vocabulary was limited, and my general knowledge of things was also limited. My writing teacher even told me that I was schizo because in one paragraph I would write and express myself one way, and then in the next paragraph I was totally different.

I think the biggest challenge was getting used to the workload and recognizing how unprepared I was for college work. I knew that I was a good student because of what I had achieved; however, compared to many other students in my freshman classes, I realized I didn't know much about anything. Almost everything the professor and other students talked about was completely new to me. As I look back on it now, all this had little to do with me but with the limitations of my high school. These limitations made college that much more challenging to me, and I worked to catch up.

One other adjustment had to do with the quarter system. I found it too fast and not enough time to really get into a class. I did OK my first two quarters but went down my third. This mostly had to do with my boyfriend, who lived in LA. He made life complicated for me. It was not a healthy relationship and it soon spiraled down, but so too did my grades that quarter.

Freshman year I also faithfully went every other week to visit my family. This was nice, but it took a toll on me because I couldn't get all of my schoolwork done at home. There were too many distractions. One advantage, though, was my mom's cooking that I missed. I found it at first hard to get used to the meals in my dorm. There were foods, for the most part, that I had never had, like pasta. My mom made a pasta soup, but pasta just with marinara sauce I had never had. And then the things they did to Mexican food here, I just didn't understand.

The other problem in going home was the long train trip from Santa Barbara to LA that took three hours each way. It was so boring! However, into the fall quarter, I decided to invite my white roommate to my home for my birthday. Actually, she was part Salvadoran but didn't relate to that part. I said, "I'm going to show you how to party like a Mexican!" She said, "OK." We had a great time, but the Sunday we went to take the train back, our train was canceled due to a fire earlier in that train. So we didn't know how we would get back to Santa Barbara. My dad, who had driven us to the downtown station, said, "Well, you're just going to have to drive back."

"Drive back?" I replied. "How?"

"Well, you can take my extra truck that I'm not using."

"But that's a stick shift, and I haven't driven a stick shift since the summer!"

"You'll do fine," my dad reassured me.

So we went and got the truck and despite my fear, we made it to UCSB. One good outcome of this was that I didn't have to take the train again because my father let me keep the truck.

When I entered UCSB, I had already decided to major in history. I always loved and related to history. It's the only thing that made sense to me. As part of my general education requirements my first year, I took the European intro classes but later that summer also took the U.S. history lower-division classes at El Camino Community College back home. I did struggle through my science general ed classes. But I also took an Asian American literature class and liked it very much.

When I returned for my sophomore year, I felt more at ease. My freshman year had its rough spots, but I survived it and now was more experienced. It had been a big learning process for me. But I didn't have any anxiety about returning. I still sort of felt like an outsider, but then I met this boy, and he was white. This was a whole new experience for me, dating a white guy, and it was kind of strange. But I didn't feel strange. I only felt strange when other people pointed it out. This made me realize that we really didn't have anything in common. This relationship didn't work out. We liked completely different things. He likes to play video games, and I don't. He likes watching particular types of movies that I don't care for. But he did give me a sort of academic support because he was more prepared than I was. He had read a lot more. He taught me so many things that I would have never gotten from someone else. So in a way, the relationship was a good thing, but it didn't work out.

What did work out was moving into the San Rafael dorm, because I now lived in an apartment unit with several other girls, which expanded my friendships. I didn't move off campus because I knew my dad wouldn't be comfortable with that. But this was OK because I had a great time in the new dorm. My housemates were all nice and all different, and so we all learned from each other. One was from Pakistan, one was from Afghanistan, one was black, one was Salvadoran, and there were two white girls. I even by then got used to the dorm food.

I also still at first was going home every other weekend, this time driving down in my dad's truck. But things began to change with my boyfriend. I found myself not going home as often. I felt guilty about this, and my dad wasn't pleased.

"So you're coming back this weekend, right?" he would call me in the middle of the week.

As I moved into my junior and senior year, I focused on my major. I started taking a number of history classes such as European history, history of the U.S. South, African American history, and Latin American history. I also took three Chicano studies classes. It was also in my junior year that I declared Spanish as my second major. Since I had passed the AP Spanish class, I didn't have to take any lower-division Spanish classes but took upper-division ones. I found in these classes that my reading and writing skills were on a par with other students but that I lagged behind in my speaking ones. It's like I had never transitioned from my home Spanish to academic Spanish.

As an upper-division student, I still didn't have many if any Chicano or Latino friends. I felt like the Latino students were only about being Latino. They were only concerned about Chicano pride. I didn't need that since I knew that I was Mexicana. I didn't have anything in common with them. I didn't go to any Chicano student meetings such as El Congreso or MEChA. In fact, I didn't belong to any campus group, period. I just wanted to graduate. I had never heard the term "Chicano" until I came to UCSB. Chicano to me was a Mexican from East LA. There were no Chicanos in South Central.

In my junior year, I also moved to Isla Vista, or IV. One of my sophomore roommates asked me if I wanted to look for a place in IV with her. I agreed, and we found a place way on the far end of IV. It was a two-story house with six other people already living there. There were four girls and two guys. We would now be two additional girls. This was the first time I lived with guys, and it was a disaster. I got along very well with the other girls, but the guys were awful. They had not been used to girls confronting them, and I did so because they wouldn't help clean up the house. They also expected us to cook for them but then wouldn't clean the dishes. I told them off, and they resented this. They wouldn't change, so I just had nothing to do with them.

The following year my same roommate who had found that house and I moved out, and we found an apartment that we shared with two other girls still in IV. This has worked out better.

By my junior year I didn't go home as often, and then I just stopped for a while. My mother understood. She knew I was busy and had a boyfriend. We started mostly communicating by phone. The one who had a problem with my not going home was my dad, but by then my parents were divorcing, so he couldn't do or say much. The divorce hurt my mom very much. She began to realize that she was alone now and that she would not be financially secure. Of course, the biggest blow was discovering that my dad was cheating on her. As the oldest daughter, I tried to comfort her, and she used my shoulder to cry on. This was hard because I didn't know what to say. What do you say to someone who's going through a divorce when you've only had two boyfriends in your life and don't know what marriage is all about? I just let her cry and talk and tried to give her as much support as I could.

At one point, my dad had the nerve to ask me to consider dropping out so I could move back home and help my mother because of the divorce. I actually thought about it but then told my dad I wouldn't do it because it made no sense. I had only a little over a year left before I would graduate, and I was not going to go back home because of a mess he had created.

Some of my friends in their junior year studied abroad, and that interested me also. But there was no way I could do this. My dad wouldn't let me, and he paid my college bills. When you're financially under someone's thumb, you do what they say. I would have loved to go to Spain, but it wasn't going to happen.

My best years academically were my junior and senior ones. I took classes in my major that interested me and did very well. I also got more confident in my writing, and I learned I have to take time to do things like writing my papers. I'll be graduating with a 3.18 overall GPA, but it's higher in my majors.

I'm very excited about graduating from UCSB. I don't have many regrets about my choices during the past four years. I only wish I had made more personal decisions of my own instead of letting my father dictate for me. But that's probably the only thing I regret. Everything else, I did the best I could. I may not have participated in campus groups, but given my situation with my family, this wasn't an option. Given everything I had to deal with in my life, my graduating is a big deal. I'm done! I'm the first in my family to get a college degree. I'm excited because I get to show my little sister she can do it.

I will be going on to an online teaching credential program at USC where in less than two years I can get my credential. I want to teach Spanish and history in middle school. I want to help people, and teaching is one way to do it. But I may decide to look later at other options, such as entering a social policy program or going on to get a Ph.D. and teach at a university. All I know is that I want to change things.

In the meantime, I will be living back at home. But I see this as a transition until I'm able to get my own place. I still have my job at LAX but hope to get hired as a teacher's aide in one of the schools.

As far as marrying and having children, I don't really know if I want to have children. I don't know if I can adapt to being a mother. I'm too selfish. It's all about me, and when you have children, it's all about them. But I'd like to marry someday. Marriage and family haven't been necessarily stable in my life, and so I'm worried about being married and having a family. However, I hope not to become a cat lady; they're unmarried women who live alone and only have cats. But I don't have an ethnic preference when and if I get married. I've realized that it doesn't really matter.

Rafaela Espinoza graduated from the University of California, Santa Barbara, in 2010. She obtained her teaching credential from the University of Southern California in 2012 and teaches social studies at Animo Locke #1 Preparatory Academy in Watts, where she is changing the world.

EPILOGUE

In putting together these *testimonios* or oral histories of these young men and women whom I had the privilege of working with and in finalizing this book, I can't help but feel some nostalgia about this experience. I have fond memories of first meeting them in my classes and then of asking if they would cooperate in my research. In interviewing them for several hours, sometimes spread over a few weeks for each, I came to know them much better. I learned a great deal from their stories prompted by my questions. Each one had a unique tale to share, even though many of their experiences and those of their families have common intersections. I appreciated their openness with me and recall laughing with them about certain humorous anecdotes but also sympathizing with the sad parts of their narratives. It was an educational process away from the classroom and a form of dialogue where each student and I taught each other. They personalized the history that I was teaching in class, and they reflected on themselves and their experiences through my questions and comments based on their responses. Hearing the taped interviews and looking at the photos that I took of them for this book brings back memories of a wonderful experience. This nostalgia, if that's what it is, also reminds me of my own situation as I reflect on the several years during which I was doing these interviews. I can remember both public and family situations that occurred during this time frame. These stories of the Latino Generation say much not only about the students interviewed but also about me and where I, as the historian, can be positioned with respect to this project. As some correctly suggest, one needs to study the historian as well as the history that he or she writes.

I hope through these oral histories (not full life stories, since the narrators are still quite young) that readers will have their own appreciation and understanding of this generation of Latinos who are coming of age in the new millennium. They share much with earlier Latino generations, but they also are carving out their own paths, both personal and public. They are thankful for what their parents and others have done to create new opportunities for them, but they don't want to be made to feel guilty if they don't follow a prescribed direction that others might want for them. They also don't want to be pigeonholed with respect to what their identity should be. They want to be themselves and to create or invent their own particular Latino identity. By studying their early experiences in life, we can learn not only about certain aspects of the Latino past but also about the present and, more important, the future of Latinos in the United States. They will promote new efforts to assure that multiculturalism from the bottom—the real multiculturalism that comes from the people themselves—will remain and expand as well as oppose new efforts to impose cultural conformity. They will be (and already are) in the forefront at the grassroots level to achieve comprehensive and humanistic immigration reform that will bring immigrants, especially those without documents, out of the shadows to live normal lives. And the Latino Generation, as it expands and gives birth to a succeeding generation, will guarantee that into the rest of this century, Latinos will become a major political and cultural force of unprecedented strength. However, they will use this strength not for their own power but for the making of a more just and democratic America.

The individuals in this study as representatives of the Latino Generation are a window into what the Latino future of this country may become, as Latinos in the twenty-first century will constitute one-third or more of the country's population. I personally will not see the full dimensions of this future, and perhaps this is part of my own nostalgia in completing this book in that I see my own mortality in the stories of these young people who have their own futures ahead of them.

I further hope that we learn not only about how these stories reflect a new Latino generation but, as noted in my introduction, about how their personal lives can counter the lingering and in certain cases destructive misconceptions and stereotypes about Latinos in the United States. In reading about the experiences of these young Latinos, the children of immigrants or themselves immigrants, we can better comprehend the human dimensions of the Latino saga. Beyond abstractions such as "illegal aliens," "undocumented immigrants," "wetbacks," "beaners," "spics," and so on, we instead learn about family life, school experiences, becoming teenagers with all of the anxieties and insecurities that this entails, early romances, family tensions and dislocations, family support, a desire to succeed in school, and the dream and accomplishment of being, in most cases, the first in their families to go to college. These are human lives being recorded, impressing upon us how their stories are not that different from ours or from those of our families and children. They are Latino stories; they are American stories. But in the end, they are human stories.

I further hope that these stories will help inspire other young Latino students, both in college and in high school and junior high school, to see themselves in the narrators. I especially hope that for these readers, the stories in this book will encourage them to overcome their own difficulties, both personal and in school, and to make their own commitments to improving themselves by going on to college. Are these narrators role models? Yes, I believe they are. Their experiences can teach other young Latinos and young people in general that they can achieve their goals if they apply themselves to the task. Is this a form of American individualism? No, because in each of these stories, we can see that none of these students succeeded by themselves or overcame adversities by themselves. They had supportive parents and extended family members who encouraged them, including and especially the young women, to stay in school and to go to college. They had supportive teachers and in many cases one special teacher or counselor in high school or junior high who in particular supported them. In college, they found other like-minded students who banded together to inspire each other, as well as counselors and professors who did likewise. As they took Chicano studies classes, including mine, they learned that what opportunities and civil rights Chicanos and other Latinos have gained have come largely through community struggles such as the Chicano Movement of the 1960s and 1970s, which created new openings in higher education, for example, that have benefited the Latino Generation. Through this process, I believe that in their own way this new generation will respond to this history and give back to others what others have given to them. They also will be historical agents of progressive change. I have much hope for the members of this new Latino Generation, that they will do the right thing not only for their community but for their country. They are the voices of the new America.

Finally, I want to say again that it has been my privilege to tell these inspiring stories of young Latinos, introducing to readers what it has meant and still means to be Latinos. I am very proud of my students who are the narrators of this volume, and I expect that I will be even prouder of them as they make their way in life. I have spent some ten years on this project and am sad to leave it now, but I am also excited that it can be shared with others. I look forward to this.